SHARING THE GOSPEL

THE DOCTRINE OF EVANGELISM

A BIBLICAL FRAMEWORK

DONALD E. JONES, PHD

J & A Book Publishers
www.jabookpublishers.com

(C) 2014 Donald E. Jones, PhD

Printed in the United States of America

All rights reserved. No part of this book may be reproduced in any form without permission in writing from the author, except in the case of brief quotations embodied in critical articles or reviews.

All Scripture quotations are from the World English Bible. This version was selected because it is in the public domain and can be quoted without limit. A personal translation of a verse or passage will be designated with (DEJ).

ISBN-13: 978-0615858494
ISBN-10: 061585849X

DEDICATION

I dedicate this book to my Savior and Lord Jesus Christ. He has been with me every step of my journey upon the Earth, and I so look forward to being in His presence forever and ever.

CONTENTS

Introduction	1
Chapter - 1. The Divine Plan	13
Chapter - 2. The Proper Proclamation	19
Chapter - 3. The Proper Motivation	35
Chapter - 4. The Role of God	63
Chapter - 5. The Role of Man	79
Chapter - 6. The Role of Prayer	89
Chapter - 7. The Schemes of Satan	97
Chapter - 8. The Proper Message	111
Chapter - 9. The Proper Methods	133
Chapter - 10. The Positive Reactions	161
Chapter - 11. The Negative Reactions	213
Chapter - 12. The Proper Response	249
Chapter - 13. The Proper Presentation	277
Chapter - 14. The Proper Utilization of Rights	291
Chapter - 15. The Personal Attitudes	303
Conclusion	317

ACKNOWLEDGMENTS

I want to thank my wonderful and gracious wife Carol who has supported me in this ministry with sacrifice, enthusiasm, encouragement, and accountability. Most of all, she has been a constant blessing because of her willingness to listen. I was always sharing with her the truths God had been teaching me as I studied His word and wrote this book. It consumed many hours. Thank you, Carol and I deeply love you.

I want to thank my son Gregory R. Jones for volunteering to be the primary editor of this important book. Without his time and effort in painstakingly and meticulously going over every word and every sentence checking and rechecking the sentence structure and grammar, I would not have been able to complete it. Thank you for your ministry to me. I love you my son.

I want to thank my other children, Krista, Matt, and Kara for their love for Christ and His Word and their willingness to live for Him. I love you all.

Introduction

In A Tale of Two Cities, Charles Dickens wrote, "It was the best of times, it was the worst of times, it was the age of wisdom, it was the age of foolishness, it was the epoch of belief, it was the epoch of incredulity, it was the season of Light, it was the season of Darkness, it was the spring of hope, it was the winter of despair, we had everything before us, we had nothing before us, we were all going direct to heaven, we were all going direct the other way-in short, the period was so far like the present period, that some of its noisiest authorities insisted on its being received, for good or for evil, in the superlative degree of comparison only. The world is in chaos." Indeed, the world is in chaos but not as the author imagines. The world is in the chaos of unbelief.

This chaos has caused numerous problems for man both within and outside of himself. For some, the chaos affords opportunities for wisdom, belief, light, and hope in the good news of Jesus Christ; unfortunately, for most it becomes a time of foolishness, incredulity, darkness, and despair in this life and the life to come. For the problems of this life, man turns often to counselors, therapists, friends, physicians, and others for help, solace, and guidance. These professionals and others may give some comfort and some solutions for this life, but only Christians utilizing the Word of God can provide real supernatural solutions with comfort for this life and the life to come.

One part of Dickens' statement was not true, "We were all going direct to heaven, we were all going direct the other way." Few are going direct to heaven, and many are going the other way. In Matthew 7:13-14, Jesus said that men were to enter in by the narrow gate. The gate to destruction is wide and broad; but to life, it is narrow and restricted. Few enter by it. This verse demands that the gospel must be the foundation upon which all other aspects of the relationships of believers with unbelievers must build.

In Matthew 16:26, Jesus indicates that a man will profit nothing even if he gains everything the world can offer in this life but loses his life in eternity.

> For what will it profit a man, if he gains the whole world, and forfeits his life [soul]? Or what will a man give in exchange for his life?
> Matthew 16:26

Christians cannot love someone into the kingdom of God; they must present the gospel. Christians may help, even give advice and ultimately money to the unsaved, but what have those unbelievers gained when they have lost their soul to hell for all eternity?

Churches definitely bless their city and its citizens by cleaning up trash, rebuilding homes, finding shelter for the homeless, and providing food to the needy which are all good deeds. Yet, without the gospel presented and accepted, all unbelievers in the city will perish in their sins into an eternity of despair and darkness. Therefore, the first and most important blessing and aid churches can offer as they view the needy world is the gospel of Jesus Christ. This would be a truly compassionate response.

The Need for a Saved Evangelist

True Christian evangelism begins with an evangelist who is saved. Initially, this may appear confusing. Why would someone who is not saved, share the gospel? Yet, there are those in the church that appear saved, may even have shared the gospel with many people, yet they themselves have not made a full commitment to Christ. Christian evangelism or sharing the gospel presupposes a Christian evangelist. The term Christian means follower of Christ (Acts 11:26). Jesus commanded His followers to make disciples in the name of the Father, Son, and Holy Spirit (Matthew 28:19). Sharing the gospel or evangelism is the first step in fulfilling the true mandate of making disciples. If one who shares the gospel is not a Christian, he cannot fulfill this important commission in the name of the Triune God. Yes, someone might come to Christ but in spite of the person, not because of them.

True Christian evangelism involves the specific work of the Spirit. Those used of God in ministry were full of the Holy Spirit and wisdom (Acts 6:3, 10; 9:17). These are the foundational elements of true Christian evangelism, whether one is a professional evangelist sharing the good news with thousands, or someone is simply sharing with an unsaved friend. Though someone may present himself as a Christian sharing a true gospel, even bringing some to Christ, does not mean that he is saved. Service does not determine salvation.

In Matthew 7:22-23, Jesus declared that some will come to Him on the day of judgment and tell Him that they had cast out demons, prophesied, and even did mighty miracles in His name but will be turned away. These people served Him but did not know Jesus. Their deeds, although they looked authentic, were false, fake, or from the Devil.

> Many will tell me in that day, "Lord, Lord, didn't we prophesy in your name, in your name cast out demons, and in your name do many mighty works?" Then I will tell them, "I never knew you. Depart from me, you who work iniquity."
>
> Matthew 7:22-23

Jesus will declare that He never knew them. They were not one of His. This book will provide all who witness the tools needed to determine their own true salvation. The question, "Am I saved?" can and will be answered in this book. If they do not have this true saving relationship, this book will fully explain how to receive Christ as Savior and Lord and enter into the kingdom of God through Him. They will need to receive Christ in the same way as those to whom they share.

> *Key Concept: Those who share the gospel must be saved.*

The Need for a Clear Gospel

Some in the church who appear to be Christians may not be saved. They think they are saved but have not entered into a real relationship with God through Jesus Christ alone. Some may rely upon their church membership, their birth into a Christian family, or their involvement in a particular sect of Christianity. Perhaps, others may count on a specific experience or encounter that they may think they have had with God. Still others may rely upon good feelings about God, a life lived by the golden rule, or even attendance at a particular church. These different feelings, notions, actions, and experiences do not save.

These seemingly important things would only save man if he were in charge of deciding how he ought to get to heaven. Yet, heaven is God's domain and only God can choose how the humans that He created will enter it. As we will see, humans were created for a very specific purpose which was not to live anyway they wanted. People were created to be a kingdom for God's Son. Therefore, God has outlined in His Word the very specific beliefs one must have and particular enter into His Kingdom and find salvation.

In 1 Corinthians 5:11, the apostle Paul spoke of "so-called" Christians, who claim Christ but do not behave like them.

> But as it is, I wrote to you not to associate with anyone who is called [so-called] a brother who is a sexual sinner, or covetous, or an idolater, or a slanderer, or a drunkard, or an extortioner. Don't even eat with such a person.
> 1 Corinthians 5:11

This book will give these "so-called" Christians the necessary tools to determine if they have a genuine relationship with Christ (1 Corinthians 5:11). If they do not, it will show how to receive Him as Savior and Lord. Would it not be a tragedy for one to believe he is saved but be damned for eternity?

Key Concept: There is only one divinely chosen way to become a Christian in order to be saved.

The Need for a Doctrine on Evangelism

Virtually all of the books and the literature on evangelism present some aspects concerning the doctrine of evangelism. Unfortunately, they spend the majority of their content on a particular method or methods of evangelism. The majority of the courses in any given seminary that train leaders for careers in the pastoral ministry, deal with many courses on Christian doctrine, a few courses on Christian ministry, and generally one or no courses specifically on evangelism. This is due mostly to the lack of materials specifically addressing this important subject. Some pastors have written books, but these do not handle all aspects since they are taken various passages on the subject rather than a broad study. When these are put together even in the purest of motives and the greatest desire to win people to Christ, they will still lack an overall picture and are often missing various parts of the entire doctrine.

> In Acts 20:27, Paul [the apostle] was in Ephesus preparing the elders for his departure. These would be his final words to them [elders] and reminded them of how he had taught them everything. He had left nothing out. For I didn't shrink from declaring to you the whole counsel of God.
>
> Acts 20:27

He declared that he had delivered to them the whole counsel of God. Would not evangelism involve a part of that whole counsel? In Ephesians 4:11-12, Christians are to be in service to build up the body of Christ. This consists of evangelism which provides the numerical growth and edification which provides spiritual growth. The church has delineated much truth concerning edification, but it has neglected the critical doctrine of evangelism in its fullness.

> *Key Concept: There is a great need to present a full doctrine of evangelism.*

The Need for a Full Understanding

There are a number of major gaps in the church's current understanding of evangelism that this book addresses: the lack of a biblical framework for thinking about evangelism, the absence of several key concepts in evangelism, and an incomplete understanding of the critical biblical principles that govern the development of evangelistic methods.

As a result, in this book many questions will be answered to address these issues.

> Every Scripture is God-breathed and profitable for teaching, for reproof, for correction, and for instruction in righteousness, that the man of God may be complete [sufficient], thoroughly equipped for every good work.
> 2 Timothy 3:16-17

In 2 Timothy 3:16-17, Paul asserts to young Timothy that the Scriptures can answer any question in any area. What is true evangelism? Why should Christians share the gospel? What is the role of God in evangelism? What part does man play in the evangelistic encounter? What is the role of prayer in evangelism? What schemes might Satan utilize to oppose evangelism? What is the authentic evangelistic message that should be proclaimed to all? What is a true saving response to the evangelistic message? How should saints evangelize the unsaved in their individual lives and as a church? How will those who are evangelized react to the presentation of the gospel, both positively and negatively? How should the saints respond to different positive and negative reactions in their personal lives and the life of the church? Can Christians use the laws of the land to protect themselves?

> *Key Concept: There is a need to present a full and complete understanding of doctrine of evangelism.*

The Need for Careful Study

This book will put into the hands of any Christian, pastor, teacher, or church leader the tools necessary to understand the biblical doctrine of evangelism and its many applications to Christians. This was no small task to research and study. I did not read any books on evangelism until after the initial study. I basically read through the entire New Testament verse by verse identifying and categorizing every individual verse or passage which dealt in some way with evangelism. Categories were built from the individual verses, rather than a set of preconceived notions. These categories became the chapter and section headings. Bible passages were studied in their historical, grammatical, and scriptural contexts. Once my interpretations were complete, I compared them to the interpretation of other commentators both past and present.

Finally, I compared my personal interpretation of the all the biblical passages to the historical interpretation of the evangelical church. With this technique I often use, I imagine myself as an independent observer experiencing the events mentioned in the Gospels, Acts, and Revelation. When I read the letters, I attempted to read them as if I was a first century Christian, who knew nothing of the modern concept of evangelism. The categories with the framework that I will present grew out of the passages. After the initial study was finished and the framework complete, I compared my study with information in other books on the subject. There was some overlap, but most books focused on a specific method or aspect of evangelism without the whole framework.

I attempted to stay away from the typical study cycle of some in Christianity. Often times, when Christians desire to study a topic, they simply read a book about the topic. The book they read is usually based on a book or books someone wrote, whose foundation is on a book or books someone else wrote. This continues until all the information passed from book to book becomes extremely limited and incomplete. I have ventured away from this approach to broaden the church's understanding of this important doctrine.

As a result, this book will be no small task to read. I have referenced many verses of Scripture. I have been careful to present the content describing this important doctrine in as few words as possible, and it is loaded with truth. I have tried to be thorough concerning the basic framework and all components in the presentation of this important doctrine. Every aspect of this study touched on so many theological truths that they could not possibly be incorporated into this book. As a result, I often left a particular truth with a few proof texts that could be filled in with a simple concordance study. Other truths were explained and left for the readers to research on their own. Also, I have repeated many passages over and over viewing them from many different angles. Though this might be tedious at times to read, it is crucial to discovering every truth concerning this topic.

There are no personal stories. There is no humor or jokes. There is no attached websites or videos one can watch. There are no clever sayings or techniques that will make one smile or feel warm inside. This does not describe my journey with the Lord. There are no personal spiritual experiences which are portrayed, except by the biblical characters themselves. This is a nuts-and-bolts biblical framework on evangelism.

In 1 Corinthians 14:20, all believers are commanded to be mature in their Christian thinking.

> Brothers, don't be children in thoughts, yet in malice be babies, but in thoughts be mature.
> 1 Corinthians 14:20

This book is for those who want some of the meat (Deeper truths) of the Word of God which concerns the doctrine of evangelism. It is for those who desire the depth and breadth of God's thinking on the subject of sharing the gospel. The reading of this book will require much time, commitment, and meditation. Many verses might need to be referenced in God's Scripture, studied, and then passage cited. If you are capable, do not skip this step in your growth as a Christian and as an evangelist who shares God's Word.

SHARING THE GOSPEL: THE DOCTRINE OF EVANGELISM

In 1 John 4:4, John discloses to his readers that they are to test the spirits. His is my challenge to all my readers and a method by which God desires us to test truth. I want the readers to test the Spirit in me by the Spirit in them, in order to verify the truths that I disclose based on my careful study. In 1 Thessalonians 5:21, those in the church are exhorted to examine everything with care. I exhort my readers to do the same with this book. In Acts 17:11, the Bereans are described as nobler because they closely examined the Scriptures. I encourage my readers to be nobler and examine the many Scriptures I present to support my doctrinal statements.

This scrutiny is critical, since Christians share a message that brings eternal life. The proclamation of a wrong or incomplete gospel will lead unbelievers only to judgment and eternal destruction. Christians who have the desire or gifts to evangelize the lost cannot allow themselves to be moved by every book that comes along claiming to have some brand-new method for evangelism. Many of these books have not grown out of a careful reading and study of Scripture. This is so easy to tell because the authors will use commonly used Scriptures out of context, few biblical passages, or none at all. They do not defend their writings with the appropriate scriptural support.

Also, the church cannot allow anyone to add or subtract a portion of the gospel. Several of these books do this very thing because it fits their particular ministry, presentation, or the culture of their audience. Most of all, they want to soften the offense of the gospel. The good news will provoke and disturb most. We know this. In 1 Corinthians 1:23, Paul calls it a stumbling block to the Jews and offensive to the Greeks. Yet, according to the next verse, the called of the Lord Jesus Christ will fully embrace its power and wisdom. Since, Jews and Greeks will ultimately mock our good news, we should expect this kind of negative reaction.

A Final Comment

Readers will notice that the book is written in a simple, straightforward style. This framework is not presented with a large number of theological terms, complex philosophical thoughts, obscure vocabulary, or my personal opinions. This design is intended to focus all of the reader's attention on the Bible and what it teaches concerning evangelism. I am truly interested in allowing God to fully speak on this subject. The words He chooses to use through His inspired writers are to be the words that teach us as best that is possible before we add other terms for ease of comprehension or clarification. It is my way of remaining true to God and His words to us.

I leave you with Paul's final words to the elders in the city of Ephesus.

> Now, brothers, I entrust you to God, and to the word of his grace [Bible], which is able to build up, and to give you the inheritance among all those who are sanctified.
> Acts 20:32

In Acts 20:32, Paul commended the elders to the Lord and His Word. He was leaving them and would never return. He knew that they would have to commit themselves to the study of His Word and trust His guidance through the Holy Spirit. In the same way, I leave you to the Lord's guidance and the careful study of His Word. Read the book. Study the Scriptures contained within it. Share the gospel. Be prepared to be used by God. Watch for the fruits of your labor. Trust in His Spirit to lead you (2 Timothy 2:7). This will take faith on your part.

Key Concept: This is a "nuts and bolts" framework on evangelism for the mature.

SHARING THE GOSPEL: THE DOCTRINE OF EVANGELISM

Chapter 1

The Divine Plan

This plan that redeems was ordained in eternity past and fully revealed to man over thousands of years in the Old and New Testaments. It is an amazing story.

The Creation of Man

In Genesis chapter 2, God created the Earth, sun, moon, stars, the plants, and animals. After this, He proceeded to fashion His highest creation – man. In verse 7, Moses writes that God formed man out of the dust of the ground and then breathed into him the breath of life. As a result, man became a living being. The critical question then arises, "Why did God create man?"

The answers are found all over Scripture. Romans 8:29-30 indicates that Christians were given to the Son, so He might be the firstborn (the preeminent one) among a kingdom of brothers.

> For whom he foreknew, he also predestined to be conformed to the image of his Son, that he might be the firstborn among many brothers. Whom he predestined, those he also called. Whom he called, those he also justified. Whom he justified, those he also glorified.
> Romans 8:29-30

Men were primarily created to be the gift of a kingdom from God the Father to God the Son (John 3:35; Col. 1:15-18).

This brought forth the other purposes for which man was created. Those purposes are to give the Triune God glory (Ephesians 1:11-12), to experience fellowship with God (1 John 1:3; Genesis 3:8), to be holy and blameless before Him (Ephesians 1:4), to serve God (Genesis 1:26), to experience God's attributes (Romans 9:22), to rule over Earth (Genesis 1:8), to live in harmony with other men and nature (Genesis 1:29-31), and to exist forever and ever (Genesis 3:22).

Key Concept: Man was created to be a kingdom for God's Son and to glorify and serve Him.

The Fall of Man

At first, things went very well for man, as God and man walked and talked in the Garden of Eden. God had only given man one stipulation: if he was to continue to enjoy all that he had, he was not to eat of the Tree of Good and Evil (Genesis 2:16-17). The Serpent tempted and deceived Eve, and she ate of the fruit. Adam rebelled and ate the fruit also (Genesis 3:1-7). As a result, all mankind fell (1 Corinthians 15:22). No longer could man be a kingdom for His Only Son (Colossians 1:13), give God glory (Romans 8:8), fellowship with the Almighty (Genesis 3:24), be holy and blameless before the Holy One (Psalm 51:5; Romans 3:10-18), rule the Earth (Ephesians 2:2), live in harmony with men (Genesis 4:7-8; 1 John 3:12) or nature (Genesis 3:7; Romans 8:20-21), and most of all, live forever physically in his original body (Ephesians 2:1; Romans 6:23).

Man would die. Also, man came under the wrath of God (Romans 1:18; Ephesians 2:3; Hebrews 9:27). Man would now experience spiritual death and punishment for his sins in a hell of fire (Matthew 5:22), a place of unquenchable fire (Matthew 9:23), a furnace of fire (Matthew 13:42), a lake of fire

(Revelation 20:10), a place which was originally created for the Serpent of old and his evil demons (Matthew 25:41). When Christians encounter unbelievers, who appear as if all is well, they must remember these passages. All is not well; they are in a difficult and desperate situation due to sin.

> *Key Concept: Man fell, lost everything, and gained only wrath.*

The Redemption of Man

Man no longer functioned according to the purposes for which God had created him. The entire human race was now destined for a life of rebellion and an eternity of hell. As a result, instead of God destroying Adam and Eve, the plan of redemption came into effect. Before the very foundation of the world, this plan was worked out in eternity past in the mind of the Triune God (Ephesians 1:3-6, 11-12).

This plan took into account man's sin, though man did not have to, nor should he have, nor did God want him to, but God knew man would. God allowed man to sin and determined that His response would be to pour out onto man even more love, goodness, mercy, grace, wisdom, and blessing. This would bring greater glory to God and blessing to man (Ephesians 1:6).

God would display His attributes as He delivered man from his own rebellion and subsequent punishment.

> To the intent that now through the assembly the manifold wisdom of God might be made known to the principalities and the powers in the Heavenly places.
>
> Ephesians 3:10

In Ephesians 3:10, Paul indicates that God demonstrated His wisdom through the conception of such an incredible plan. He displayed His love as He sent His Son to die (Romans 5:8), His mercy in turning man away from the punishment of fire (Titus 3:5), His grace as He offered an eternity in heaven (Titus 3:7), His patience as He restrained Himself from the destruction of humanity (1 Timothy 1:16), and His eternal power as He destroyed the evil works of darkness (Hebrews 2:14) and death (1 Corinthians 15:55). Here is an important note: God even demonstrated His justice and wrath, which are also His attributes, as He condemned man to eternal punishment (Romans 9:21-23).

> *Key Concept: When man fell into sin, God's eternal plan of redemption took effect. This provided greater glory to God and blessing to man demonstrating all of God's attributes.*

The New Creation of Man

This wonderful plan not only gave God more glory, but it gave man more benefits. It did not simply restore man to his original state but gave to him a better and more excellent existence. Man would be given a new and better Earth to rule (Revelation 21:1) and have a closer fellowship with God through the Holy Spirit inside of him (1 Corinthians 3:16; Philippians 2:13). Man would be clothed in the holiness and righteousness of Christ becoming like Him (1 John 3:2-3), able to give God even more glory as the objects of His grace (Ephesians 5:18; 1 John 2:27), able to fellowship closely with each other (1 John 1:3-4), able to experience death with hope in Christ (John 5:29), given an immortal body (1 Corinthians 15:20-27), and all the riches that are in Christ (1 Peter 1:4). There is so much more that could be written concerning this abundant glory and benefits of the new creation.

All this was God's gracious and loving plan in response to man's evil rebellion. It had been determined that the Second Person of the Trinity would cloth Himself in humanity and come to Earth to pay the penalty for mankind's wickedness (Philippians 2:5-8; Isaiah 53:6).

In Romans 3:24, the apostle Paul asserts that redemption came through Christ.

> Being justified freely by his grace through the redemption that is in Christ Jesus.
> Romans 3:24

When Jesus came, He proclaimed this plan of redemption. After this, He recruited others to also proclaim this crucial plan (Matthew 28:19-20; Acts 1:1-8). Every Christian is to be an important part of this gospel recruitment. Christians will encounter those who do not know Jesus Christ and may be searching for Him (Matthew 7:7). These lost souls need to hear the plan of redemption and be saved.

Key Concept: The plan of redemption offered man a new and better state of existence.

Chapter 2

The Proper Proclamation

Christians have been given this message of creation, the fall, and God's redemption through Jesus Christ to proclaim. According to Hebrews 1:1-4, God communicated this plan to His people through the fathers and the prophets in the Old Testament. After a period of silence, God spoke through His Beloved Son, in the New Testament. This proclamation is described using several crucial Greek words filled with great meaning in the New Testament. Believers are told that they should announce it, preach it, comfort with it, proclaim it, testify of it, teach it, and deliver it.

Each word views evangelism from a different angle and presents to the Christian the awesome endeavor of sharing the gospel. To further enhance the understanding of this proclamation, these words will be compared to the Greek Septuagint. The Septuagint is the Hebrew Old Testament translated into the Greek language referred to as the LXX. The passages that contain the Greek words translated from the Hebrew will be presented. A fuller understanding of the meaning of the Greek words can be gleaned from what corresponding words in the Hebrew they translate and the context in which they are used.

The Announcement of the Plan

The good news is to be announced. The Greek word that is translated "announce" is used in many places in the LXX or the Septuagint. In its Old Testament use, the term that is translated "announce" has the connotation of a declaration from God by His messenger. It is used in 2 Samuel 15:13, when David's own servant came to announce to him that his son Absalom had won the hearts of the people of Israel. In Exodus 9:16, Moses tells Pharaoh that the Lord God will send many plagues upon Egypt to show God's power and announce His presence in the midst of the Hebrew nation. The Psalmists also utilized this word "to announce" God's holiness and righteousness (Psalm 22:30-31), His faithfulness (Psalm 30:9), His wondrous deeds (Psalm 71:17), and His steadfast love (Psalm 92:2). In Isaiah 42:9, God announces that He will bring new things through His coming Messiah.

In the New Testament, the Greek word is used in John 4:25 by the woman at the well. She declares that the Messiah, when He comes, will announce all things. In John 1:18, John explains that no man has seen God at any time, but the Lord Jesus has announced Him. Christ, as the divine messenger, has turned His sacred message over to His church. In 1 John 1:2-3, the apostle writes to his readers that the message they received from the Lord was announced (declared) to them. Now, His disciples are the messengers who are to go out and announce the divine message from God. The implication is that we, as Christians, are then called to do the very same thing. We must go to our spouses, children, extended family, friends, neighbors, co-workers and announce the plan.

In Acts 20:20, Paul told the elders in Ephesus that he did not ever shrink from announcing to them anything that was profitable.

> But declared first to them of Damascus, at Jerusalem, and throughout all the country of Judea, and also to the Gentiles, that they should repent and turn to God, doing works worthy of repentance.
> Acts 26:20

Then, in Acts 26:20, Paul told King Agrippa that he had kept announcing (declaring) the message (they should repent and turn to God - the plan of redemption) to those at Damascus, in Jerusalem, in the entire region of Judea, and even to the Gentiles. So, one facet of evangelism is an announcement by Christians on behalf of God that His beloved Son has come, and salvation is in Him. Christians are to go out into to the world and announce this sacred message and plan.

Key Concept: Christians are to announce the official message of God that salvation has come in Christ.

The Preaching of the Plan

The good news is to be preached. The Greek word that is translated "preach" is used in many places in the Septuagint. The word was used to speak of good news that a new era had begun. The word was used in 1 Kings 1:42 to refer to the good news that a king had been anointed and a new rule had begun. In Jeremiah 20:15, it's used to speak of the birth of a baby and the new life that had come.

The word's most significant use is in the preaching of a new era of salvation that would be brought by Yahweh and His Messiah. This would fulfill the longings of Israel and sinful man for joy, happiness, and peace. In Psalm 96:2, the psalmist exhorts his audience to sing and bless the name of God. They were to preach good tidings of salvation from day to day. In Isaiah 41:27, God assures His people, Israel, of their future redemption in the midst of present punishment. He would send a messenger of good news, the Messiah. In Isaiah 61:1, the pre-incarnate Jesus Christ is speaking and declares to Israel that He will come to preach the good news to the humble. At His coming, there would be a brand-new era that will arise - an era of salvation.

The Greek word is used similarly in the New Testament. In Luke 4:17-21, Jesus entered the synagogue on the Sabbath and stood up to read. The Lord read the passage from Isaiah which stated that the promised Messiah with the Spirit upon Him would preach good news. After this reading, Jesus told the congregation that this passage had at that moment been fulfilled in Him. He was preaching the good news that the era of the kingdom of God had begun. Mark describes Jesus as coming into Galilee preaching the gospel of kingdom of God (Mark 1:14-15).

In Acts 5:42, the apostles carried on this preaching every day in the temple and from house to house.

> Every day, in the temple and at home, they never stopped teaching and preaching Jesus, the Christ.
>
> Acts 5:42

In Acts 8:4, the saints were scattered from Jerusalem and went about preaching the good news. This news involved the message that a new era was beginning. When people are encountered in the lives of the saints, who are not Christians, they must realize these unsaved are desperate for a new era. They are dead in their sin (Ephesians 2:1), walk according to this current world and its prince (Ephesians 2:2), are sons of disobedience (Ephesians 2:2), live in the lusts of their flesh (Ephesians 2:3), and are children of wrath (Ephesians 2:3). They are filled with the cancer of sinfulness which is ruining their lives now and will destroy their lives beyond the grave.

When unbelievers become Christians, a brand-new era is ushered into their lives. This brand-new era is characterized by these lost souls becoming brand-new creatures in Christ (2 Corinthians 5:17), children of the true God (John 1:12), and alive together with Him (Ephesians 2:5). They can walk in newness of life (Galatians 5:16), experience peace with God (Romans 10:15), and find a true joy from the Spirit (Galatians 5:22). Most of all, they will have eternal life (1 John 5:11-12). Any Christian can obviously see how powerful the gospel is.

> *Key Concept: Christians are to preach that a new era of salvation has begun.*

The Comfort of the Plan

The good news is to comfort people. The Greek word that is translated "comfort" literally means to come along the side and help. Its various forms are used in many places in the Septuagint. It was used to speak of comfort and showing pity (Psalm 119:50) and of compassion and sorrow (Psalm 135:14). It refers to coming alongside others and encouraging them (Deuteronomy 3:24; Job 4:3). It involves the comfort that the gospel of salvation can bring. In Isaiah 40:1, God exhorts the prophets to comfort his people. They were to tell them of His great deliverance after His wrath had come.

In the New Testament, Jesus is called the Consolation of Israel by Luke as he describes the waiting of Simeon for the Messiah (Luke 2:25). In John 16:7, Jesus told His disciples that He would leave them and send another Comforter (the Holy Spirit). In verse 8, Jesus explains that this Comforter would bring conviction of sin, righteousness, and judgment. In other words, He would comfort them in the conviction of their sin with the gospel and then with the resultant plan of salvation preached. Sometimes, we can't be comforted if we do not understand the trouble we are in. If one is diagnosed with cancer when they did not know it and then given the proper treatment for it, then is the greatest comfort of all. It is even better that living in ignorance with disaster ahead.
In Acts 2:42, Luke describes Peter comforting the people.

> With many other words he [Peter] testified, and exhorted them, saying, "Save yourselves from this crooked generation!"
>
> Acts 2:40

At Pentecost, Peter continued to solemnly testify and exhort (comfort) the people to be saved. The gospel of Christ brings an amazing amount of comfort as people trust Jesus for their salvation.

In Acts 13:14-17, Paul arrived in Antioch of Pisidia and entered the temple. Since he was a rabbi, they asked him to give a word of exhortation (comfort), and Paul preached the gospel. He comforted them with the gospel. Paul told the Corinthians that his affliction was for their comfort and salvation. Comfort and salvation go hand in hand. The best example is found in 1 Thessalonians 2:7-12, where Paul tells the Thessalonians that he comforted them in the gospel as a mother nurses her newborn babes. Christians can bring great comfort with the gospel. What more comfort could one give then offering peace with God (Romans 5:1)? When those who do not know Christ come to Christians seeking advice in the hope of finding peace in their lives, they can find a true peace that is everlasting; this comforts.

> *Key Concept: Christians are to comfort others with the good news and hope of salvation.*

The Proclamation of the Plan

The good news is to be proclaimed. The Greek word that is translated "proclaim" is utilized in many places in the Septuagint. The Old Testament connotation for the word is to officially herald important news or announce an arrival of a dignitary. The word is used to speak of Moses proclaiming to the people that they had brought enough offerings for the tabernacle (Exodus 36:6). The new king, Josiah, had found a copy of the Scriptures in the temple. He then heralded the news, proclaiming that the people of Judah and Jerusalem were to bring to the Lord God the levy fixed by Moses, the servant of God (2 Chronicles 24:9). The official proclamation from the ruler and the binding character of his vital message demanded that the people comply.

Cyrus, ruler of the Persian Empire, made a proclamation that God desired for him to build a temple in Jerusalem and released all the Jews to return to their land if they desired (2 Chronicles 36:22-23). This was an official proclamation from a supreme ruler who was demanding obedience and perfect compliance.

The word is used of Jonah's proclamation from God to Nineveh, when he told them to repent, or God would destroy them in forty days (Jonah 3:4). This same word is used to proclaim God's future judgments upon the nations by the prophet Joel (Joel 3:9-13). The connotation is clear: Joel is heralding a message that the ruler of the universe will bring judgment on the nations. It is binding, and the nations are expected to respond. Zephaniah uses the word to speak of the cry of triumph at the future restoration and salvation of Israel as a nation (Zephaniah 3:14).

Zachariah proclaims the future coming of the king on a donkey who brings salvation and righteousness (Zachariah 9:9). The prophet is heralding the coming of a king bringing salvation. It was serious and binding upon his hearers, who were to respond with real repentance and acceptance of this message. Zachariah became the official herald of God with a powerfully binding announcement. How binding was it? It so binding that one's present temporal life and future eternal destiny would be affected forever and ever.

SHARING THE GOSPEL: THE DOCTRINE OF EVANGELISM

In the New Testament, Jesus was God's official herald, so God calls Him "My Servant" in Isaiah 42:1. Jesus declared that the Father had sent Him down from heaven (John 6:38). In Matthew 28:18, He proclaimed that He had all authority in heaven and on Earth. Jesus Christ came as God's official emissary to proclaim the message of redemption from the ruler of the universe. Jesus told His followers that He was speaking the things that He heard directly from God, His Father (John 8:26).

The message of Jesus came from the lips of God Himself, and it was a message of sin, judgment, and also salvation. In Matthew 4:17, the apostle Matthew describes the Lord Jesus as heralding (preaching) a message of repentance (judgment) and the imminent coming of the kingdom of God on Earth. This heralding ministry of Jesus was then turned over to His disciples. In Mark 6:7-12, the Lord called His disciples, gave them His authority, and sent them out to herald the good news of salvation. In Acts 8:5, Luke writes that Philip went into Samaria and proclaimed (heralded) Christ to the people.

In 1 Corinthians 1:23, Paul describes the proclamation of the disciples of Christ. This was a message from God, the king of the universe, brought by a group of heralds. That group not only encompassed the twelve but all the followers of Him. In 1 Thessalonians 2:9, though he had been working night and day, Paul told the church at Thessalonica that he had proclaimed (heralded) to them the gospel of God. In fact, Paul was one of His great heralds. He established most of the churches and wrote most of the New Testament.

> For you remember, brothers, our labor and travail; for working night and day, that we might not burden any of you, we preached to you the good news of God.
>
> 1 Thessalonians 2:9

In 2 Corinthians 5:20, Paul refers specifically to himself as an ambassador of God, as the apostle implores the Corinthians to be reconciled to Him. An ambassador would be a herald.

Christians must carry out this awesome responsibility. All Christians are ambassadors (heralds) of God in an alien and foreign land (Philippians 3:20). The saved are aliens and strangers upon the Earth (1 Peter 2:11), who herald a great message from a holy God. Christians proclaim a message of reconciliation to a people desperate for a solution to their problems. This message is a binding decree from the King of Kings that heralds judgment and eternal salvation.

This decree must be the starting point of a relationship with unbelievers. In Acts 10:42-43, Peter arrived at the home of Cornelius declaring that Christ is the one who will judge the living and the dead. Cornelius was to believe in Him and receive the forgiveness of sins. Peter was a herald for God.

Judgment and salvation were the message to herald. This message from the lips of a Christian becomes binding on all who hear. If they do not comply, they shall be punished in hell for all eternity. In Romans 10:16, Paul asks how people will believe if they have not heard. How will they hear if someone does not tell them? Christians can tell them. At times, unbelievers, who do not know our glorious Lord, will come to Christians asking for help and advice with a myriad of issues. These Christians must herald the message that the ultimate solution to every one of their problems begins with Jesus Christ, then provide biblical solutions to their many temporal problems.

> *Key Concept: Christians are to herald the official proclamation from their God of salvation with the binding character of the message demanding they comply with everything.*

The Testimony of the Plan

Christians are to bear witness of the gospel. The Greek word translated "bear witness" literally means to testify in a court of law, or to be a witness. In the Septuagint, the noun form is used to speak of a piece of evidence which calls to mind a particular event. The stones on which Almighty God wrote the Ten Commandments were also called the Tablets of Testimony (Exodus 31:18). Another name for the Tent of Meeting or Tabernacle was the Tent of Testimony (Exodus 29:4, 10). The Ark of God was also referred to as the Ark of Testimony (Exodus 40:3).

All of these objects were the evidence testifying to God's existence and His communication to man. The verb form is used in a legal sense all over the Old Testament. In the book of Numbers 35:30, it is used to speak of the witnesses in a murder trial. In Deuteronomy 19:15, Moses warns against the condemnation of a man based on insufficient testimony. This word always deals with certifiable, objective evidence, not simply unverifiable, subjective evidence. The concept of subjective feelings being used as evidence is foreign to the Old Testament. It had no place among the thinking of the Hebrews. One must keep this in mind when approaching the New Testament.

To bear witness or testify of the gospel meant to proclaim the gospel with evidence. Also, it meant to substantiate the claims of Christ with evidence. This is exactly what God intended and His Christ was meant to do. Throughout the Old Testament, God told His people, the Jews, He would send His Messiah, and they would know Him through signs. The Messiah would be born in the city of Bethlehem (Micah 5:2), from a virgin (Isaiah 7:14), receive vinegar to drink at His death (Psalm 9:21), and perform many miracles (Isaiah 6:1). This is just to name a few because there are many more. So, the purpose of the signs was to testify that Christ was the true Messiah. This was God's way of authenticating Him.

The signs bore witness and testified to man that He was the Christ of God. Jesus told His people that he had not come to abolish the law and the prophets but to fulfill them (Matthew 5:17). All throughout His ministry, He appealed to that evidence. Christ did not expect people to simply believe His words but to see His works and the prophecies that He fulfilled and would fulfill. In the book of Matthew 11:4-5, John the Baptist sent his disciples to confirm that Christ was indeed the Messiah. Jesus did not tell them to just believe His words. He told John's disciples to go and tell John that the blind see, the lame walk, and the lepers are cleansed. These indicators would attest to His true identity. The signs would bear witness and testify to His anointing. The Lord Jesus specifically stated that His works bore witness of who He was and that He had come from the Father (John 5:36). In John 10:24-25, the Jews came and asked Him directly if He was the Christ. Jesus told them to look at His works that they testified that He was the Christ.

This bearing witness and testifying was turned over to His disciples. In Acts 1:8, as Jesus was leaving the Earth, He taught His disciples that they were to be His witnesses. They were to testify of what they had seen and heard about Jesus. The sermons that the apostle Peter preached which began in Acts 2:14, Acts 3:12, and Acts 4:8 clearly demonstrate that Peter did provide powerful evidence that Jesus Christ was the Messiah through the Lord's mighty works and fulfilled prophecy. What is more important is that they were actually the eyewitnesses to these things.

John declares in 1 John 1:2 that the apostles proclaimed what they had heard, seen, and touched concerning Jesus, the Word of Life. They were eyewitnesses.

> And the life was revealed, and we have seen, and testify, and declare to you the life, the eternal life, which was with the Father, and was revealed to us.
>
> 1 John 1:2

This is a true testimony. When Christians proclaim the plan, they are to bear witness of the good news. The Christian is to share the testimony of actual eyewitnesses, miracles, and fulfilled prophecies of the Lord to demonstrate Christ's true identity. This is the witness that would bring salvation to the unsaved. Often times, Christians are told to speak of their personal experience or their journey with God. Though this is admirable, it is not biblical. In fact, any committed cultist or member of any religion could recount a great experience. God desires a testimony of facts found in the Scriptures.

> *Key concept: Christians are to share the testimony of the eyewitnesses, the miracles, and the fulfilled prophecies of the Lord Jesus to demonstrate Christ's true identity bringing salvation to their hearers.*

The Teaching of the Plan

The good news is to be taught. The Greek word translated "teach" literally means to extend the hand for acceptance. A teacher extended his hand with instruction and the student accepted it. In the Septuagint, the term was used to denote instruction with life applications. It entails the many truths of the Scriptures. In Deuteronomy 4:1, 10, and 14, it is used of God's instruction to His people. The teaching concerned His history with His people and His many commandments. In Deuteronomy 11:19, the word is also used to speak of the Jewish history of God interacting with His people. Why?" So, people would not fall into any idolatry. The many nations of the world which were around them had a wealth of gods for the wicked element of God's people to choose from.

Anyone who reads the New Testament will see that Jesus taught the people and instructed them concerning the many truths the kingdom of God (Matthew 5-7). In Matthew 4:23, the apostle Matthew records that Jesus was teaching in the synagogues and proclaiming the gospel of the kingdom of God all throughout Galilee and the surrounding area. Jesus was teaching many truths beyond just the good news.

In Matthew 11:1, the Lord departed to teach and preach in the cities.

> When Jesus had finished directing his twelve disciples, he departed from there to teach and preach in their cities.
>
> Matthew 11:1

Jesus taught the gospel. He also explained many different aspects of it especially in regard to the fruits one bears once one is saved. In Luke 24:27, Jesus taught the two on the road to Emmaus the detailed truths concerning the Messiah in the Old Testament. This would have been included identifying Himself as the Messiah and the signs that would accompany Him. The disciples were to do the same.

The gospel presentation involves much instruction from the Bible. In Matthew 28:19-20, a passage known as the Great Commission, the Lord told His followers "to make disciples." The term translated "disciples" literally means learners. The concept of evangelism is not telling people to accept Christ tacked on at the end of a sermon, but it is the teaching of the Word concerning the plan of redemption and then making a plea for acceptance. This is very important for the Christian. When an unbeliever comes to a Christian for help, a simple plea for salvation will not be enough. The unbeliever should be taught from the Scriptures the true gospel and entreated to accept Jesus Christ as Lord and Savior as a result. No one should ever take a short cut when it comes to the good news of Jesus Christ. It is pure and must never be altered in any way. Time, offense, or ignorance cannot be allowed to block the full presentation of the plan of redemption. Christians must realize this important principle.

> *Key Concept: Christians should extend their hands in careful instruction to share the gospel.*

The Deliverance of the Plan

The gospel is to be passed on from one person to the next. The Greek word translated "deliver" literally means to hand something down, to pass something on, or even to deliver something to another. In the Septuagint, fathers are exhorted in Psalm 78:3-4 not to hide the knowledge of God from their children. These fathers were to deliver to the next generation the holy praises of God. God set up memorials, testimonies, and celebrations all throughout Israel's history, so the next generation would set their hope on Him. The Lord did not want his divine works forgotten as their fathers stubbornly had done.

The New Testament uses this word and concept often. In 1 Corinthians 11:2, Paul lauds and commends the church for holding firmly to the traditions delivered to them. Later in the letter, he again uses the word when he reminds them that he delivered to them the gospel (1 Corinthians 15:3). This gospel which was handed down to the apostles has been handed down to all believers to deliver. Luke opens his book writing to Theophilus that those who were witnesses handed the gospel down to him, and he was in turn handing it down to the man Theophilus and all Christians (Luke 1:1-2). Of course, they in turn will hand it over to us.

In 1 Corinthians 9:16-17, Paul writes that he delivered the gospel to them out of compulsion. This spiritual obsession has a divine origin that could not be denied.

> For if I preach the Good News, I have nothing to boast about; for necessity is laid on me; but woe is to me, if I don't preach the Good News. For if I do this of my own will, I have a reward. But if not of my own will, I have a stewardship entrusted to me.
> 1 Corinthians 9:16-17

It was a stewardship entrusted to him. Now, Christians have this critical stewardship entrusted to them. They can spend hundreds of hours with unbelieving friends, neighbors, or co-workers, but if they never "deliver" the gospel to them, what have they really done? This beloved person will perish and spend an eternity without God.

James says that a man does not know what his life will be tomorrow, for his life is but a vapor which appears for a time and then vanishes away (James 4:14). Christians can help many individuals fully become as prosperous emotionally, financially, psychologically, and intellectually as they could be, but they will still fade away. The church's gospel will allow men to fade away into an eternity of blessing, rather than condemnation.

> *Key Concept: Christians are to deliver the gospel that was handed down from Christ to the apostles and now to the church.*

Chapter 3

The Proper Motivation

All around the saints are broken people. Christians are to see through all the physical, emotional, psychological, and intellectual suffering and to their real spiritual pain first. All people are caught in the grip of spiritual death. In Ephesians 2:1, Paul says that those without Christ are spiritually dead in their sins and their trespasses. In Romans 6:16, Paul states that they are slaves to sin, which results in spiritual death. Christ sends every believer into the spiritually dying world with the only solution that can heal them from their greatest ill, which is the gospel of Jesus.

After His resurrection, Jesus told his disciples that as His Father had sent Him into the world, so He sent them (John 17:18). Christians have been sent with the gospel; there is no other cure. The salvation of the unsaved must be the priority of God's children. Jesus told his disciples that He was the way, truth, and life that all men and women must come to God through Him (John 14:6). People must be told this.

Some Christians may feel inadequate to share the gospel. Others may be unwilling to take the time or make the effort to share the good news. Christians can easily fall into the slumber of not witnessing and merely hope that unbelievers come to Christ based solely on their examples! How will they come to Christ, if no one tells them? Most Christians just bring the unsaved into the church and hope the pastor will save them when he preaches his sermon.

Unfortunately, many of the pastors of today have only a morning sermon on Sunday to share the plan of redemption.

How many people could they possibly reach, even if, they shared the true gospel every Sunday for over forty years? Evangelism is every believer's responsibility.

In Romans 9:1-3, the apostle described the great sorrow and grief that filled his heart for his unbelieving Hebrew brethren in the nation of Israel.

> I tell the truth in Christ. I am not lying, my conscience testifying with me in the Holy Spirit, that I have great sorrow and unceasing pain in my heart. For I could wish that I myself were accursed from Christ for my brothers' sake, my relatives according to the flesh.
> Romans 9:1-3

Paul would have gladly been condemned for the sake of His lost countrymen. The apostle possessed a powerful passion for the salvation of souls, especially those caught in the same plight as him. The saints may feel great compassion for the brokenness of the people they encounter, but it must first be for their salvation and then for their temporal lives on Earth. In 1 Corinthians 9:19, the apostle claimed that he cared so much for the salvation of all people that he made himself a slave to all. He gave up his Christian liberty in some areas so they would not be offended and more would come to Christ.

He told the church in Thessalonica that he was mistreated at Philippi. Yet, he pressed on to preach the gospel to them against much opposition (1 Thessalonians 2:2). Paul was impelled to act. He declared to the Corinthians that he had absolutely nothing to boast about because he was under compulsion to preach the gospel (1 Corinthians 9:16).

The Scriptures provide reasons why Christians should be compelled to proclaim the redemptive plan. These reasons clearly cover the critical part evangelism must play in time spent with unbelievers. The saved cannot deny or dismiss this critical responsibility away. It is a powerful and exciting challenge for all believers. Remember, it is not to be a burden thrust upon people from the pulpit. God never intended this. Yet, Christians must realize that they are deeply indebted to the ones who took their responsibility to share the gospel.

Key Concept: The Bible presents many reasons why Christians should share the gospel.

The Glory of God

The theme of the universe, the reason for which all things were created, was, and is, and always will be, to give God glory. In Psalm 29:1-2, King David proclaims that all should ascribe to the Lord glory and strength. He must be given the glory that is due His name. David indicates that the Lord God by His very nature deserves glory. In Psalm 145:3, the psalmist proclaims that the Lord is magnificent and is to be greatly praised. The Lord is so grand, so awesome, and so powerful that He deserves praise from every human being on Earth (all of His creation). Yet, there is a vast majority of unsaved people who cannot glorify Him in words or actions!

In John 5:23, Jesus declared emphatically, if one does not honor the son, one does not honor the Father who sent Him. Those who have not heard the gospel cannot know Christ and cannot glorify God. In Romans 3:23, Paul sets forth the problem when he states that all men have sinned and have fallen short of God's glory. If one has not been cleansed with the blood of the Lamb, he cannot give God glory (1 John 1:7). Without faith in God through Jesus Christ no one can please God (Hebrews 11:6). This is such a critical understanding for all Christians who may look upon the world as innocent.

SHARING THE GOSPEL: THE DOCTRINE OF EVANGELISM

Every day, God is faced with a massive sea of humanity, numbering in the billions, who will not and cannot give him the honor, praise, glory, and exaltation worthy of his person. Yet, Christians through the power of Christ can remedy such a despicable and horrendous situation. Christians can do this by proclaiming the plan to the small, but significant portion of humanity could be found in their schools, neighborhoods, workplaces, and cities.

Through their witness, they can bring someone into the kingdom of God producing a lifetime of glorifying God in thought, word, and deed. Through the process of sharing the gospel, coming to Christ, and living a holy life afterwards, God receives a tremendous amount of glory and honor. In 2 Corinthians 2:14-16, Paul pronounces that in every place he shares the gospel a sweet aroma is sent to God giving Him glory. In Romans 15:9, the apostle explains that when Christ accepts people (saves them), even though they are all sinners and deserve nothing, the Lord God will receive glory and honor. Why? God demonstrates His great mercy.

In 2 Corinthians 4:15, when Paul proclaimed the gospel and people came to Christ, they responded with the giving of thanks to God.

> For all things are for your sakes, that the grace, being multiplied through the many, may cause the thanksgiving to abound to the glory of God.
> 2 Corinthians 4:15

This gave the Lord glory. In Ephesians 2:7, Paul asserts that those who come to Christ will be forever trophies of God's grace. When Christians display God's grace, He is glorified. In Ephesians 1:6, 12, and 14, this apostle, who was sent to the Gentiles, affirms that all Christians were redeemed for God's glory. Then, the saints can spend a lifetime giving God glory through praying (John 14:13), living righteously (Philippians 1:9-11), doing good deeds (John 15:8), confession of sin (Luke 23:41), seeking unity with all the brethren (Romans 15:5-7), sharing the gospel (Galatians 1:23), and suffering for Christ (John 21:19).

Christians have the great privilege of bringing people into a relationship with God, which will produce a lifetime and eternity of glorifying Him. Since all believers seek to glorify God in everything, then bringing others to Christ will satisfy this great longing. What a blessing for Christians to be able stand before their God and Father and glorify Him through the bringing of others into His kingdom to do the same!

Key Concept: When Christians share the gospel and bring others to Christ, it glorifies God.

The Command of Christ

Christians are commanded to proclaim the gospel. This is obvious, but it is a critically essential in living the Christian life. During Jesus Christ's time on Earth, He issued many commands. One of them is found in Matthew 28:19-20. Here, Matthew records the final words of our Lord before He must depart from the Earth. Jesus begins by acknowledging that He has complete divine authority. In that very authority, He commands His followers "to make disciples" of Him (main verb: make learners), by going (proclamation of the gospel), baptizing (belief with its sign), and then teaching (obedient lifestyle, building up in the faith).

In Mark 16, they were commanded by their Lord to travel throughout the entire world and proclaim the gospel. In verse 15, the author provides this additional detail.

SHARING THE GOSPEL: THE DOCTRINE OF EVANGELISM

> He said to them, "Go into all the world, and preach the Good News to the whole creation."
>
> Mark 16:15

Jesus also exhorted His disciples to speak in the light what they had heard from Him in the darkness. His followers were entreated to declare what had been whispered in their ears upon the housetops (Matthew 10:27). The good news is not God's private little message that He gave to His Son Jesus and His followers alone. It is for public consumption. It should also be spoken in the light and shouted from the roofs of homes (an ancient custom for announcing good news). If the Lord commands it, the saints are to do it.

In Jude 1:22-23, Jude essentially commands believers to proclaim the plan, when he states that all believers are to show mercy (a command) to some doubters and to save (a command) still others from the fire. Jesus explains to His disciples that loving Him involves obeying Him. This means keeping His commandments (John 14:15). One of the many commandments of Jesus was to share the good news. We do not often hear this preached, but it is true.

God's children are compelled to share the gospel of the Lord Jesus with all their unbelieving friends, neighbors, co-workers, and fellow students. The specifics of who, when, and where is left up to each individual believer as they desire. What is not left up to the believer is to live a Christian life without ever sharing the good news of Jesus Christ with anyone. He wants us to do it. This is not to be a burdensome command but one all believers carry out with joy. We have all the freedom in the power of the Spirit to choose when, where, and how often.

> *Key Concept: When Christians share the gospel and bring others to Christ, they obey His command.*

The Call of God

Christians are called by God to proclaim the plan. This is not just a serious command but a high calling. In Romans 1:6-7, in Paul's opening words to the Christians at Rome, he puts forward the concept that Christians are called to belong to Jesus Christ and are called to be His saints (Romans 1:6-7). This word "call" means to call out, to summon. What does this "calling" involve? What attitudes or actions spring from this call?

According to 1 Corinthians 1:9, Paul states that Christians were called into fellowship with His Son.

> God is faithful, through whom you were called into the fellowship of his Son, Jesus Christ, our Lord.
> 1 Corinthians 1:9

The word translated "fellowship" means partnership or joint participation. Believers were called into joint participation with His Son. This entails so much more than just personal time with Christ. What is the Son of God doing that involves a saint's participation? He is calling those who were written in the book of life before the foundation of the world to Him. Then Jesus is building them up in the faith (Ephesians 1:15). This is essentially evangelism and edification. These are the two pillars of the church (Ephesians 4:11; Acts 2:41-42).

Christians are to be regularly involved in edification, but it must begin with evangelism. After His resurrection, Jesus conveyed to His disciples that the Father had sent Him into the world to proclaim the kingdom of God. Jesus was now sending them to do the exact same thing. Sharing the gospel is a responsibility of all who fellowship with Christ. It is one way we participate [fellowship] together with Him.

In 2 Corinthians 5:18-19, Paul describes it clearly when he explains that the Lord God reconciled or restored the union with the world through Christ. The Lord then gave him the word of reconciliation, the gospel, commissioning him as an ambassador of Christ to the world. Christians have the same commission (calling) of proclaiming the plan in order to reconcile the unsaved. His ambassadorship is not the same as his apostleship and extends to all believers.

Key Concept: When Christians share the gospel and bring others to Christ, they fulfill the high calling of God.

The Characteristic of Christians

Proclaiming the gospel is a characteristic of Christians. In Acts 1:8, the Lord revealed that the disciples would receive power when the Holy Spirit came upon them. This would result in a very powerful testimony of Him all throughout the region and beyond to the farthest reaches of the Earth. He informed them that they would be His witnesses. This was not up for any negotiation but instead would happen. In essence, their testimony of His Word would be a common characteristic of their lives.

One of the clearest statements concerning this important quality can be found in Matthew 5:14-15. In this passage, the Lord Jesus is speaking to the Jews as a nation and reaffirms to them something they already should have known; they were lights to the world. Now, they should begin acting like God's light in the darkness of unbelievers. These people are desperate to experience His love, mercy, and grace.

The concept of light in the Scriptures always entailed the revelation of God's truth or holy living. This is diametrically opposed to the darkness which spoke of Satan's lies or evil living. To be a light to the world meant to show forth God's truth and holiness to the world, in other words, the gospel. When God's people, the Jews, rejected Christ, He established the church to take on that mantle. This mantle is an amazing opportunity to participate in something truly meaningful.

Paul validated this truth to the church at Philippi, when he declared that they appeared as lights in the world and were to be holding forth the Word of Truth.

> Do all things without murmurings and disputes, that you may become blameless and harmless, children of God without blemish in the midst of a crooked and perverse generation, among whom you are seen as lights in the world.
>
> Philippians 2:14-15

In Philippians 2:14-15, Paul writes this injunction in a matter-of-fact tone. This is what all Christians are to do. They are to be lights in their world. Believers should live in harmony, without disputes or grumbling, and with holy habits in the midst of a world that is perverse, sinful, and crooked.

In John 12:35-36, Jesus refers to Himself as the light of the world and those who believe in Him as sons of light. When unsaved people come into the lives of Christians (the light), they come enveloped in complete darkness (Colossians 1:13) and are constantly stumbling in total blindness (1 John 2:11). Christians are to be the light shining through that darkness with the good news. This good news will place them on the path of light where they will not stumble in lies and sin any longer. Christians may not always display this characteristic due to a rebellious flesh (Romans 7). This flesh will desire to criticize unbelievers in their minds and be uncompassionate.

SHARING THE GOSPEL: THE DOCTRINE OF EVANGELISM

> *Key Concept: When Christians share the gospel and bring others to Jesus Christ, they evidence the genuine character of Christians.*

The Result of Maturity

Proclaiming the plan is a natural outgrowth of maturity. Paul affirms that Christians are to build themselves up into a mature man. This spiritual maturity must measure up to the stature of the fullness of Christ (Ephesians 4:13-14).

In Ephesians 4:15, Paul explains that Christians should no longer behave like children, who are tossed back and forth by false doctrines, but they are to speak God's truth in love.

> But speaking truth in love, we may grow up in all things into him, who is the head, Christ.
> Ephesians 4:15

This critical concept of "speaking the truth" must encompass the sharing of the gospel. This is the first truth anyone must know. Is it not? In Jude 1:17-21, the author describes clearly the spiritual growth process. He identified the elements of this growth as building oneself up in the faith, praying in the Holy Spirit, keeping oneself in love, waiting for Christ, and having mercy on those who doubt. Then the author issues the command that they are to save some by snatching them and pulling them out of the fire (Jude 1:23).

This refers to evangelism; the fire is hell (Matthew 18:9). Sharing Christ and bringing them into the kingdom snatches them out of that fire. The apostles had been trained by Jesus before and after His resurrection and had spent much time with the Lord. They had grown and matured in the faith resulting in a dynamic witness for Christ (Acts 3:4-12). Their maturity was expressed in their growing desire to share the gospel as they became more like Christ in His compassion, mercy, and grace. As they are filled by the Holy Spirit more and more, Christians should commit themselves to sharing the gospel more and more (Ephesians 5:18).

> *Key Concept: When Christians share the gospel and bring others to Christ, they display their maturity in Christ.*

The Divinely Chosen Method

Proclaiming the good news by Christians is God's chosen method of evangelism. There are many ways in which God could have ordained to bring people into His kingdom. Yet, He decided to have His followers share His good news. In Galatians 3:1-2, Paul challenges his readers to remember that they were all saved by hearing accompanied by faith, not by works. This is what the Judaizers had said. The Galatians had heard the gospel from Paul, and they had believed. In Romans 10:14, the apostle questioned the Romans as to how unbelievers could call upon the Lord, if they had not heard. Then, how could they hear without a preacher? A preacher going out to proclaim the gospel is the method of God. This preacher, who heralds the gospel, is the average believer.

There are numerous ways in which God could reveal His plan, but he chose the simple sharing of the gospel by His followers. This sounds almost trite but a critical distinction. God desires for His good news about His Son coming to Earth and dying for our sins to be shared person to person. People are to be talking and sharing with other people. Jude demands that Christians earnestly contend for the faith that was delivered once and for all to the church (Jude 1:3). This "contending' involves people to people encounters.

SHARING THE GOSPEL: THE DOCTRINE OF EVANGELISM

Christians now take the Scriptures and share the plan.

> And how will they preach unless they are sent? As it is written: "How beautiful are the feet of those who preach the Good News of peace, who bring glad tidings of good things!"
> Romans 10:15

Paul asserts in Romans 10:15 that those who bring the glad tidings of salvation have very beautiful feet. It is the feet that must be used to approach the unsaved. What a blessing it would be to say at the end of a day, "The Lord made my feet beautiful today!"

The proclamation of the good news was always shared in the Old Testament from person to person as well. Abraham's son heard it from Abraham. Isaac proclaimed it to Jacob. His sons heard it from him. The people of Israel heard it from Moses and the other prophets. The saints in the first century heard it from other Christians, who had heard it from the apostles. They then told others.

In Matthew 16:18, Jesus declared to Peter that He, Christ, would build His church. Christ is the one who causes numerical growth in the church. In Revelation 1:10-20, John views Christ walking among lamp stands, which represent the churches. This description portrays the Lord ministering and building up His churches. In Colossians 1:18, the apostle emphatically declares that Jesus Christ is the head of the church, and He has the preeminence above all. The question then arises, how does Christ build His church numerically? The church experiences numerical growth through sharing the gospel.

Two familiar passages teach this critical truth: Matthew 28:19-20 and Acts 1:8. Here He announces to his disciples that they are to be His witnesses and are to make disciples throughout the entire world. In 1 Corinthians 3:6, the apostle explains to the saints in Corinth that they should not group themselves according to the person who brought them to Christ. Paul may have planted the seed of the gospel, but Apollos watered, and God caused the growth (1 Corinthians 3:6).

The Lord God causes people to receive the gospel unto eternal life; no one else. God builds His church as Christians are faithful to bear witness of it; no one else. Witnessing churches are growing churches. Witnessing ministries are growing ministries. This is the New Testament pattern. This is shown powerfully through the actions of the early church, which is found in Acts 5:42-6:1. In this passage, the saints proclaimed that the Lord Jesus was the Messiah, and God kept increasing their numbers.

The growth plan of Jesus was incredibly simple: people are to proclaim the good news of Jesus with other people also. The saints should be spending time sharing the gospel with unsaved people wherever they go. It will be eternally devastating for an unbeliever to spend much time with a believer or believers and never hear the gospel. This damns that person to eternal condemnation.

> *Key Concept: When Christians share the gospel and bring others to Christ, they demonstrate God's only plan to bring others into His kingdom.*

The Chosen Await the Proclamation

Those who have been chosen are awaiting the coming of Christians. Why? They must share the gospel with them. Who else will? In Ephesians 1:3-4, Paul opens his letter by describing the tremendous blessings that Christians possess. These divine blessings come to those chosen by God before the foundation of the world. In Colossians 3:12, the apostle calls Christians "the ones who have been chosen of God." In 1 Thessalonians 1:4, he specifies that his readers are beloved by God, chosen of Him. Christians must acknowledge that all around them are the elect waiting for their proclamation.

Paul reiterated this concept of believers being "chosen" to young pastor Timothy.

> Therefore, I endure all things for the chosen ones' sake, that they [the chosen] also may obtain the salvation which is in Christ Jesus with eternal glory.
> 2 Timothy 2:10

In 2 Timothy 2:10, Paul encouraged Timothy to remember that Paul had endured many difficulties for the sake of those who had been chosen. He would endure anything that they might find salvation in Christ (2 Timothy 2:7-10). He saw the potentially chosen in every unbeliever he encountered. He was willing to suffer any difficulty, endure any hardship, and handle any persecution in order to proclaim the plan to the chosen. He knew he would have to share the gospel with everyone, since the chosen could not be identified by Paul.

Christians must realize that people, who come into their lives, might have their names written in God's book of life. Could they have walked into our lives to hear the good news (Philippians 4:3)? It is so easy to ignore and pretend that it is someone else's responsibility, but what if God brought them into our path because He wants us specifically to have the privilege of sharing the gospel with these particular people? Is this at all a possibility? It is important that all Christians at least consider that this could actually be the case.

Key Concept: When Christians share the gospel and bring others to Christ, they have brought the elect, who were waiting for the proclamation, into the kingdom.

The Exaltation of Christ

The church has been given as a gift to the Son from God, the Father, for His exaltation and glory. This we will do now and for all eternity.

> For whom he foreknew, he also predestined to be conformed to the image of his Son, that he might be the firstborn among many brothers. Whom he predestined, those he also called. Whom he called, those he also justified. Whom he justified, those he also glorified.
> Romans 8:29-30

In Romans 8:28-30, Paul recounts God's purpose for His Son. He is to be the "first-born" of many brethren. The Lord is to be preeminent among a great host of brothers and sisters. Christians were predestined, called, justified, glorified, and conformed to Christ's image for this purpose.

In Colossians 1:18, the saints in Colossae were taught that Christ is the head of His body (church). He is the beginning and first born from the dead. As a result, Christ will have first place in everything. This first place speaks of exaltation and glory. Earlier in the same letter, it was presented that all things had been created for Jesus Christ and through Jesus Christ (Colossians 1:16). In his letter to the Philippians, Paul declares with great excitement that every knee will bow, and every tongue will confess that Jesus Christ is the Lord and Master of all (Philippians 2:9-11).

In John 3:35, John the Baptist proclaimed that the Father loved the Son and gave all things into His hand. All that one sees is given as a gift to Christ from the Father. In John 10:29, Jesus confirmed this when He told His followers that His Father, who was greater than all, had given His disciples to Him. No one could snatch them out of the Father's hand.

The church must realize that the unbelievers will either bend the knee in salvation or judgment. In either instance, Christ will be glorified. Therefore, receiving Christ must be the first step for Christ's exaltation now and at His coming.

> *Key Concept: When Christians share the gospel and bring others to Christ, Jesus will now receive the exaltation the Father desires for His Son.*

The Stewardship of the Proclamation

The gospel is a stewardship that has been entrusted to the church. This stewardship is the church's main priority. The church is always to be proclaiming the plan of redemption. In 1 Corinthians 4:1-2, Paul declares that he saw himself as God's steward of the mysteries of Jesus Christ requiring Him to be faithful to that task.

> For if I do this of my own will, I have a reward. But if not of my own will, I have a stewardship entrusted to me.
> 1 Corinthians 9:17

In 1 Corinthians 9:17, Paul asserts that God had entrusted a stewardship to him. This godly servant knew that he would be held accountable for his faithfulness to this conservancy. Now this critical guardianship is entrusted to the church of Jesus Christ. How do we know this? In 1 Timothy 3:15, the apostle describes the church as the pillar and support of the truth. Think of a whole congregation's hands being up in the air supporting God's truth as pillars. This is what we are.

In 2 Timothy 1:13-14, Paul encourages Timothy to hold onto the pattern of sound words that he had heard from Paul. These sound words (doctrine) had been committed to him and were to be guarded by him in the power of the Holy Spirit who had indwelt him. In chapter 2, verse 2, Paul commanded his son in the faith, Timothy, to commit all that he had taught him (the doctrine) to faithful men, who would teach it to others. This stewardship was to be passed down.

In 2 Timothy 2:15, Paul alluded to this stewardship of the truth, when he pronounced that Timothy was to be handling the Word of God properly, as a diligent workman who was not ashamed of his use of it. In this same letter, Timothy was to use the Word of God to correct, rebuke, and instruct with patience and carefulness (2 Timothy 3:16), while he preached in season and out of season (2 Timothy 4:2).

This stewardship of the truth had to do with the mystery mentioned in 1 Timothy 3:16. In this passage, Paul states that the mystery of godliness is that God was revealed in the flesh, justified in the spirit, seen by angels, proclaimed unto the nations, believed in the world, and received up in glory. Is this not the very essence of the gospel? The only aspect left out is repentance for sin. Outside of this (which can easily be implied (our recognition of sin in His presence), all of it is there in that set of divine truths. Guarding these truths from error and sharing them is our stewardship.

So, what does this mean to the average believer? Well, if Christians are indeed the church, then all the followers of Christ are the many pillars and supports of the truth both individually and corporately. They do not volunteer for this crucial stewardship. Instead, it is one of the foundations of

Christian living. This is why believers must do everything to preserve the gospel and its message among them. They are not to allow it to be changed, watered-down, or perverted.

> *Key Concept: When Christians share the gospel and bring others to Christ, they display faithfulness to the stewardship of the truth.*

The Need of the World

The world is desperate for the proclamation of the plan of redemption. Consider the condition of those who come into a Christian's life and do not know Christ. First, they are born in rebellion to God. David declared in Psalm 51:5 that he was brought forth in iniquity and conceived in sin. Man is born with a sin principle which is an innate propensity to sin. In Romans 7:14, Paul felt such a conflict within himself that he described it as being of the flesh, sold into bondage to sin.

Second, unbelievers live lives devoted and committed to sin. The unsaved live by sinful values and attitudes resulting in sinful actions. In Romans 6:17, Paul describes this sinful lifestyle, when he declares that the Roman Christians were slaves to sin in their former lives before Christ. In Ephesians 2:2, Paul describes the constant sin of the unsaved by stating that they walk according to the course of this world, which is according to the Devil, the prince of the power of the air, and are sons of disobedience. When people do not know Christ, they are following the Devil and his ways. Though they may not realize they are his slaves.

Third, Satan's kingdom is called the domain of darkness in Colossians 1:13. Every unbeliever lives in this domain and behaves in this deep darkness.

> If we say that we have fellowship with him and walk in the darkness, we lie, and don't tell the truth.
>
> 1 John 1:6

In 1 John 1:6, the apostle John calls this walking in darkness. Therefore, they are spiritually dead. In Ephesians 2:1, the apostle Paul reveals to the Ephesians that they had been dead in their trespasses and sin before coming to the Savior. Then in verses 17-18, he explains this spiritual condition as being completely futile in their thinking, having no understanding of spiritual things, and alienated from the eternal life that is found in God.

The Scriptures describe with many details this terrifying condition that unbelief produces. These poor people have no forgiveness of sins (Colossians 1:14). They are unrighteous (Romans 3:10), children of God's wrath (Ephesians 2:3), and captive by their own desires (Galatians 5:19-21). They have problems but no real solutions to their difficulties (James 1:2-4). They have human friendships but no bond that is eternal and spiritual (1 Corinthians 12:25).

When true believers come to Christ through the power of the Holy Spirit, their whole lives change. Christ transforms them from rebellion to praise (Ephesians 1:12), turns them from a life totally devoted to sin to a life devoted to holiness (Romans 7:24-25), and turns them from captivity to sin to freedom in the Holy Spirit (Romans 8:9-10). They are made spiritually alive (Ephesians 2:5) and given the forgiveness of sins (Acts 10:43). These children of wrath become children of God (John 1:12). They are declared righteous before the Lord God (Romans 5:19). With this new relationship will come the outpouring of the numerous fruits of the Holy Spirit which are His love, joy, peace, patience, kindness, goodness, faith, gentleness, and self-control (Galatians 5:22-23).

The person who does not know the Lord must live a life centered on sinful values, motivated by sinful attitudes, and committed to sinning as a pattern of their lives. Christians know that He is the solution to every problem, the answer to every dilemma, and the way of coping with every difficulty (Philippians 1:20). As a result, in all their relationships with unbelievers, the sharing of the good news must come first. Trouble will never leave a life filled with sin that is destined for judgment. These dear people are desperate for salvation in the Lord Jesus which will meet their innermost longings and outer most needs.

> *Key Concept: When Christians share the gospel and bring others to Christ, they bring alive those who were dead in sin.*

The Judgment to Come

The previous point dealt with unbelievers in his present life and condition, but without Christ their future eternity is worse. The intense emotional, psychological, physical, and intellectual torment that they may feel while on this Earth is nothing compared to what awaits them at death.

In Romans 2:12-16, Paul presents a very important fact: all men will be judged. The Jews will be judged with the law and by the law in the Scriptures. The Gentiles will be judged without the written law and by the law within them. This law is the conscience. Both will be judged by a law. No man will escape judgment out of ignorance of God's law. Paul discloses to the Romans that unbelievers are storing up for themselves wrath for the day of God's righteous and holy judgment. This will be a time of tremendous anguish, agony, torment, and pain. This will be a day that will bring eternal judgment and condemnation.

> But according to your hardness and unrepentant heart you are treasuring up for yourself wrath in the day of wrath, revelation, and of the righteous judgment of God; "who will pay back to everyone according to their works."
>
> Romans 2:5-6

In Romans 2:5-6, the author declares that they will be judged according to their deeds. Basically, these will be compared to God's law and judgment will come. Every day unbelievers remain in their unbelief; they sin again and again storing up additional wrath for the Lord's judgment day. Every single day becomes a day of unbelief and increasing wrath for their evil deeds.

In Revelation 19:11-15, the apostle John compares the Day of Judgment upon the world to a winepress crushing grapes. The winepress was simply an enclosure, where grapes were placed to be crushed under the feet of men. When Christ returns and pours out His wrath, men will be crushed under His powerful and mighty feet. This judgment will occur world-wide at the second coming of Christ and individually at the great white throne.

In Revelation 20:12-15, John writes that he saw death, Hades, and the sea give up their dead, both great and small. Each one stood before Christ's white throne and books were opened in which were written all their works. Each person was judged according to each and every sin. Can anyone imagine being judged for every single sin one commits in a lifetime? All those whose names were not written in the book of life were cast into a lake of fire.

This is a truly frightening future for those who come to believers in friendship or for counsel, comfort, or solace. It cannot be wished away or ignored; rather, it must be faced.

Those we know or who come to us for help must have the good news preached to them at this important moment no matter what the world may say. They need deliverance from eternal condemnation and judgment. We should resist the fleshly fears that sometimes pervade us in these situations and trust God.

> *Key Concept: When Christians share the gospel and bring others to Christ, they prevent the unsaved from experiencing the judgment to come.*

The Destruction of Satan's Works

At the fall of man, God promised Satan that he would be dealt a crushing blow upon the head by the seed of Eve (Genesis 3:15). The blow came at the resurrection of Christ (her seed) as He ultimately rendered Satan powerless. As the world comes to an end, Satan will be thrown into a lake of fire ending his influence and power forever (Revelation 20:10). Until this time, Satan is allowed to continue his evil ways, but he is powerless over believers. He can only control them, if they allow him too (Ephesians 4:27).

Since the Devil fully controls unbelievers as their father (John 8:44) and the world they live in as its prince, these people must come to Christ for Satan to be fully rendered powerless in their lives. Christians should share the gospel in order to destroy the works of the Devil in the lives of the unsaved.

One of his works is physical death. As people come into the kingdom of God, they are no longer held in the fearful lifelong bondage of death. In 1 Corinthians 15:54-57, Paul asserts that believers have victory over death through the resurrection. Since Christians have been freed from sin and now have the victory of eternal life, Paul declares that death has lost its sting! In 1 John 3:8, John emphatically states that the Son of God came upon the Earth for the purpose of destroying the numerous works of the Devil. The Devil has been attempting to ruin everything God has done since He created man. Christ came to annihilate these evil works.

> Since then the children have shared in flesh and blood, he also himself in the same way partook of the same, that through death he might bring to nothing [render powerless] him who had the power of death, that is, the Devil.
> Hebrews 2:14

In Hebrews 2:14-15, the author writes that Christ rendered the Devil powerless, the one who had the power of death. Death was this evil being's ultimate weapon, and he lost it at the resurrection.

In John 16:33, Christ declared that he had overcome the world. Christ had overcome the system that Satan controls upon the Earth. How? Believers no longer are controlled by its evil system through the lusts of the flesh. They have the power necessary within them through the Spirit to resist sin and find victory in Christ. This is taught in such passages as Romans 6:17-19 and Galatians 5:16-18.

The apostle John declares that this constant accuser, his world system, and his false prophets no longer have any power over believers. In 1 John 4:4, the apostle encourages his readers to stand against the influence of false prophets. Why? The God, who is in them, is greater than the Devil (implied), who is in the false prophets. In 1 John 5:4, John writes that Christians, who are born of God, have overcome the world. The entire world system of Satan no longer has a death grip of lust and temptation on them.

In 1 John 5:18, John announces that people who are born of God do not continually sin. Why? God keeps them, and they cannot be touched by the Evil One. Satan no longer has power over them. When unbelievers come to Christ, they are freed from the evil clutches of all these terribly destructive enemies. Many of the problems of people are derived from these adversaries.

As Christians encounter the unsaved everywhere they go, they ought to proclaim the gospel of Jesus Christ and release these spiritually poor people from the clutches of the Devil. They must find freedom from his cleverly devised, wicked, and evil system of lies and false beliefs. Of course, this can only be fully accomplished through the Spirit's power.

> *Key Concept: When Christians share the gospel and bring others to Christ, they release them from the power of the Devil.*

The Joy of Heaven

When the plan of redemption is proclaimed and someone is saved, there is great joy in heaven. In Luke 15:2-7, Jesus speaks of this rejoicing in the Parable of the Lost Sheep. He describes the joy in heaven when one sinner comes to Christ What an amazing thought? The angels rejoice over a human being becoming a Christian. As the lost come to believers for relief from their ultimate spiritual burden of their sin and unbelief, Christians should proclaim to them the good news of Jesus Christ. This news will release them from the sin and its bondage which holds them captive.

When they turn to Jesus as their Savior and Lord, those in the heavenly places rejoice with great and exceeding joy. The angels find happiness in the salvation of mankind.

> When she found it, she calls her friends and neighbors, saying, "Rejoice with me, for I have found the drachma which I had lost." Even so, I tell you, there is joy in the presence of the angels of God over one sinner repenting.
>
> Luke 15:9-10

In Luke 15:9-10, Jesus tells a powerful story about a lost coin. A woman lost one coin, even though she had ten. She lit a lamp, swept the floor, and looked diligently for the coin. When she had found it, she called together all her friends and rejoiced with them. Here, Jesus asserts that the angels of heaven rejoice over one repentant sinner in the same way. This concept of the angels rejoicing in heaven when someone comes to receive Jesus Christ as Savior and Lord can be such a great motivator for sharing the gospel. When believers are deciding to share, they might imagine the myriads of angels who will be rejoicing in heaven if that person receives Jesus as Savior and Lord.

> *Key Concept: When Christians share the gospel and bring others to Christ, there is joy in heaven.*

The Blessing of Proclamation

As Christians proclaim the gospel of Jesus, they will bring upon themselves great blessing. Jesus professed in Matthew 5:9 that peacemakers are blessed, for they shall be called sons of God. The word "blessed" denotes happiness and joy. In the Beatitudes, Jesus is describing the characteristics of those in the kingdom of God and the blessedness that they have in Him.

One of those characteristics is peace-making. Jesus was speaking spiritually of those who bring others to peace with

SHARING THE GOSPEL: THE DOCTRINE OF EVANGELISM

God through the Lord. Peacemakers are proclaimers of the gospel of peace (Ephesians 6:15). In that peacemaking, there is great joy. In that peacemaking, Christians demonstrate to the God, the world, the angels, and themselves that they are truly His. This is part of the fruit that comes from a true branch from the Vine of Christ (Matthew 7:20). It will be one of the ways Christians demonstrate their faith by their works (James 2:18).

There are many other blessings involved in sharing the gospel. In Philippians 1:12-13, Paul was a prisoner in chains awaiting trial before Caesar. This was the worst situation of his life, yet God was still using him in mighty ways. He was chained night and day to members of the Praetorian Guard and took this opportunity to share the gospel with them. Many became believers. As he encountered those of Caesar's household, the plan was proclaimed and many of them came to Christ. The saints in Rome were awakening from their spiritual slumber and becoming bolder in their witness for Christ. The entire city was hearing the good news through one chained prisoner (Philippians 1:14). As a result of this, Paul declared that he rejoiced and would continue to rejoice (Philippians 1:18). Though the Philippians were miserable about Paul's situation, they needed to see it from God's side.

There is blessing in seeing God work through a believer. There is blessing in watching someone come to Christ. There is blessing in viewing a supernatural work of God. There is blessing in observing people's lives change. There is blessing in knowing that someone has been snatched from the fire of hell. There is blessing as Christians become spiritual parents and rejoice in their children's birth and growth as they share the gospel and disciple them to be like Christ.

Paul describes himself to the Corinthians as their spiritual father because he proclaimed the good news of Jesus Christ to them and established their church (1 Corinthians 4:15). Joy comes in all the fathering, nourishing, and encouraging of spiritual children. What joy would it be to fellowship with one's spiritual children (Romans 15:32; Philippians 1:4; 2:17)!

In 1 Thessalonians 2:19, Paul cried out that the church of Thessalonica was his hope, crown, and joy.

> For what is our hope, or joy, or crown of rejoicing? Isn't it even you, before our Lord Jesus at his coming?
> 1 Thessalonians 2:19

This blessing would be at the coming of the Lord Jesus. This is the future aspect of the blessing of the proclamation of the gospel. Believers will be rejoicing together with those who have come to Christ through their ministry. These are just a few of the many blessings for those who share the gospel. Can Christians imagine the joy they would feel to enter into God's heaven and see all the people that they had shared the gospel with perhaps come up to greet them?

> *Key Concept: When Christians share the gospel and bring others to Christ, these saints will experience the present joy and blessing of God, and His future joy and blessing.*

Chapter 4

The Role of God

As Christians proclaim the gospel, God is also at work. It takes a dynamic interaction between God and man to bring others to the gospel. In the Great Commission, Jesus told his followers to go out into all the world and make disciples for Him. This was their part. Then He asserted that He would be with them always, even to the very end. That was His part (Matthew 28:19-20). Sharing the gospel was always meant to be an interaction between God and man. Both participate as a team in the evangelistic encounter. The Lord God desires believers to have the privilege and responsibility of sharing His good news; he does not need them to do it.

Throughout the New Testament, as one carefully studies the various evangelistic encounters, it becomes obvious that there is an important interaction between God and man. The Father has designed it so that man works with Him as He endeavors to bring people into the kingdom of His Son. There are numerous examples of this in the New Testament. In Acts 2:1-6, it was God who sent a sound like the wind and brought the multitude together. In verse 14, it was Peter who preached to the gathered crowd.

In Acts 3:6, it was the power of God that healed the lame man, and it was Peter who took the divine opportunity and shared the gospel. When the crowd had gathered, if Peter had not preached, no one would have been saved. Yet, more importantly, if Peter had preached without God bestowing His grace, mercy, and power on the hearers, no one would have been saved. No person becomes a Christian and enters eternal life without God's work.

> In Acts 4:8, God [Father] filled Peter with His Holy Spirit, and the apostle spoke the gospel in boldness to the Sanhedrin. Then Peter, filled with the Holy Spirit, said to them, "You rulers of the people, and elders of Israel."
>
> Acts 4:8

Both must be present for the world to be saved. This is how God has designed it. In Acts 6:3-8, it was the Lord who filled Stephen with the Spirit, faith, wisdom, grace, and power to share the gospel. Yet, it was Stephen who preached Christ to the people. In Acts 8:26-40, it was God's Spirit who readied the heart of the Ethiopian court official of Candace and sent Philip miraculously to him. It was Philip who started the initial conversation, preached Jesus, and baptized him.

In Acts 10:1-5, God worked on the heart of Cornelius and moved him to send for Peter. In Acts 10:10-16, God sent a vision to Peter showing him there was no longer clean and unclean, but all who believe would receive the Spirit. Then in Acts 10:23-24, the apostle Peter journeyed to Caesarea and preached the gospel to Cornelius and to all in his household. Then, it was the Lord who brought them to Himself.

Of course, there are the incredible missionary journeys of the apostle Paul. The Lord sent him (Acts 13:1-2), guided him (Acts 16:6-8), empowered him (Acts 13:9), and brought miraculous results through him (1 Corinthians 3:6). Yet, also acted in this great divine and human drama. He planned and took the journeys (Acts 13:4), followed the Spirit (Acts 16:9-10), preached the plan of redemption (Acts 16:14), then taught and nurtured those who believed in obedience to the gospel (1 Thessalonians 2:8).

In evangelism, God and man play different roles, have different responsibilities, and perform different functions. It is crucial that Christians understand these functions. Any misunderstanding can leave believers immobilized, anxious, and discouraged. It can rob the saints of the joy that any evangelistic encounter was meant to bring. If a Christian shares the gospel, God will produce the growth. A reliance on God brings joy, confidence, and boldness. The role of God will be discussed first in this chapter concerning the proclamation. The next chapter will discuss the role of man.

Obviously, God plays the crucial role in the proclamation of the plan of redemption. It is His power that is always at work. When people's lives are miraculously changed, praise and thanksgiving is offered up to Him. It is about Him.

Key Concept: Evangelism involves an interaction between God and man and God has the main role.

The Ordination and Planning of God

The redemption of man was God's design from eternity past. In Ephesians 1:3-4, Paul opens his powerful letter with a description of the many blessings the saints have in Christ. In fact, he explains that we have every spiritual blessing in the heavenly places. Believers should consider that one of the most important of those blessings was their election itself When did this election occur? Paul asserts that it was before the foundation of the world was laid. Before God created the Earth, Christians were chosen to be redeemed by the Lord Jesus Christ. Man's salvation and redemption was ordained by God. It was His idea. How this is actually worked out in the trinity is a mystery.

In Ephesians 1:5-6, Paul instructs the church in Ephesus that believers were predestined to be God's adopted sons through His Son, the Lord Jesus Christ.

> Having predestined us for adoption as child-ren through Jesus Christ to himself, according to the good pleasure of his desire, to the praise of the glory of his grace, by which he freely bestowed favor on us in the Beloved.
>
> Ephesians 1:5-6

This adoption was through Christ and is according to His will and His kind intention, which is to the praise and glory of His grace. God wanted to demonstrate His grace and the plan to redeem man was conceived. Paul disclosed to the church in Corinth that there is only one true God, the Father, who was the originator of all things (1 Corinthians 8:6). This includes the plan of redemption.

> *Key Concept: God's role in evangelism involved His creation of the plan and predestination of those who would be redeemed before the world began.*

The Revelation and Fulfillment in Christ

God's redemptive plan was to be revealed through Christ. In the letter of Hebrews 1:1-2, the author of Hebrews makes this crystal clear. He certifies that God revealed His plan in the past through the patriarchs and the prophets and now reveals Himself through His only Son. The New Testament is simply the revelation about the Father revealed in the Son written down by the apostles and others.

Jesus declared to the Jews that His teaching was not His own but God's who had sent Him (John 7:16).

> Jesus therefore answered them, "My teaching is not mine, but his who sent me."
>
> John 7:16

Jesus was continually disclosing everything that was being revealed to Him by His Father. In John 1:18, the beloved apostle confesses that no man has ever seen God at any time; Christ, the only begotten of God in His bosom, has explained Him. The explanation of the Father and His plan is found in the words and actions of Jesus Christ. In John 14:8-11, when Philip asked the Lord to show them the Father, Jesus was astonished. How could Philip have been with Jesus for so long and not realized that He was one with the Father? If they had seen Him, they had seen the Father.

Redemption was fulfilled in the Lord. In Matthew 5:17, Christ declared that He did not come to abolish the law or the prophets. Instead, he came upon the Earth to fulfill them. In Christ Jesus, the entire law of God was completely and totally fulfilled, so He went to the cross as a fully righteous, unblemished lamb. In Luke 24:44-47, after His resurrection, Jesus visited some of His disciples and explained to them, once again that He must fulfill all that was in the Law of Moses, the Prophets, and the Psalms. Then, the Lord opened their minds to show them that He had to die, rise, and bring redemption to man.

These important truths were found in the Scriptures and shown to them. Salvation was accomplished on the cross. When the Father had ordained the plan in eternity past, then His only Son came to Earth and proclaimed and fulfilled the plan. What a wonderful mutual interaction of the Father with the Son and the Son with the Father! The many facets of how all of this was determined and established within the Godhead are a wonderful mystery yet to be revealed to His people. In 1 Corinthians 13:12, Paul said that one day the saints will know as they are known, perhaps then.

> *Key Concept: God's role in evangelism involved His Son revealing and fulfilling His plan.*

SHARING THE GOSPEL: THE DOCTRINE OF EVANGELISM

The Witness and Testimony of the Spirit

In John 15:26-27, Jesus gave one of His final discourses to the disciples. He explained to them that the Holy Spirit was coming from the Father to bear witness Him (the Son). God ordained the plan, Christ proclaimed and fulfilled the plan, and the Holy Spirit was to convict people of their sin and convince them to believe in the plan. In John 16:7-11, Jesus explains the role of the Spirit concerning this testimony of Christ in the world. The Spirit convicts of sin, righteousness, and judgment. In the context, these terms have a deep, rich meaning. The Greek word that is translated "convicts" has the dual meaning of convicting and convincing. First, the Holy Spirit convicts unbelievers that their unbelief is false, which is the sin that will condemn them. Then, He convinces them that Jesus is the Christ, which saves them.

Second, the Holy Spirit convicts the unsaved world of the insufficiency of their self-righteousness to save them. Then, He convinces them that Christ's righteousness is sufficient for their salvation. This was the responsibility of Jesus while on Earth, but He is now with the Father, so the Holy Spirit must assume the role. Third, the Spirit convicts the world concerning the lie of the Devil. Their judgment of Jesus as a false messiah (the lie) is untrue. Instead, the Spirit convinces unbelievers that Jesus is the Christ, who brings eternal life. The Spirit testifies and bears witness of Christ. This is a very critical role. He works quietly behind the scenes.

In 1 John 5:5-8, John records that there are three witnesses to the deity of Jesus Christ.

> For there are three who testify: the Spirit, the water, and the blood; and the three agree as one.
>
> 1 John 5:7-8

The water, which alludes to the baptism of Jesus, testifies of His deity because God Himself declared Jesus was His Son. The blood, which alludes to His death, testifies of His deity because He rose from the dead proving Christ is the Son of God. The Holy Spirit testifies of His deity because He is the Spirit of truth revealing and confirming the deity of Jesus. Christians should be assured that the good news they are sharing, was ordained by God, proclaimed and fulfilled in Christ, and is currently being testified by the Spirit. This is a powerful and encouraging biblical truth. As the Christian is witnessing to the unsaved, God's Spirit will be at work.

> *Key Concept: God's role in evangelism involves the Spirit convicting the world of sin and convincing them to believe in Christ.*

The Election of Those Who Believe

Another role God plays in the evangelism process is the choosing of souls to be a part of the kingdom being given to His Son. Before the foundation of the world, the Lord God chose or elected every believer that He desired to be saved. In Ephesians 1:4, Paul conveys the truth that God chose all Christians in Him before the foundation of the world and predestined them for adoption as children. Colossians 3:12 again states that believers are chosen of God. God knows every person who will come to His Son because He chose them before the foundation of the world. It is these chosen or elected saints who will respond to the proclamation.

Often, Christians are worried about making a mistake in the presentation, but those chosen will respond. Others try and soften the discussion of sin thinking the unsaved will reject the gospel because it is too harsh. They are mistaken. The chosen will respond to the powerful work of the Holy

Spirit in their hearts as they hear the Word of God preached to them (the gospel).

In Acts 13:48, Luke wrote that Paul preached and as many of those who were appointed to receive eternal life believed.

> As the Gentiles heard this, they were glad, and glorified the Word of God. As many as were appointed to eternal life believed.
> Acts 13:48

Paul disclosed to Timothy that saints have a holy calling by God's grace given to them before time eternal (2 Timothy 1:9). To Titus, another companion in ministry, Paul declared that he was a servant and an apostle according to the faith of God's chosen ones (Titus 1:1). This is clear.

God appoints some to eternal life, and they are the ones who respond to the gospel. God does the calling and those who had been chosen will believe. All throughout the cities are people chosen of God who have not yet heard nor have believed. The Lord will bring these individuals into the lives of Christians to be saved. Christians must share the gospel with all because they cannot determine who might be called.

> *Key Concept: God's role in evangelism involved the choosing of Christians before the world began.*

The Sending of Christians to Proclaim

God sends all Christians into the world to proclaim the plan of redemption. This is another important role He plays in the evangelistic process. It was God's idea to utilize man to share His good news. It was God's Son who commanded His followers to go and make disciples (Matthew 28:19).

Just before His ascension, the Lord repeated this mandate once again. This time with the promise of the power of the Holy Spirit associated with it.

> But you will receive power when the Holy Spirit has come upon you. You will be witnesses to me in Jerusalem, in all Judea and Samaria, and to the uttermost parts of the Earth.
> Acts 1:8

In Acts 1:8, the Lord promised His disciples that they would receive power from the Spirit. After this, they were to be His witnesses in Jerusalem, Judea, Samaria, and throughout the entire world. In John 20:21, Jesus told His disciples that as the Father sent Him, He was sending them.

Do these exhortations include the average Christian? Of course, otherwise, the true gospel would have died out with the apostles. The exact opposite was true. Immediately, the Christians were out sharing the good news everywhere, and the church grew in leaps and bounds (Acts 2:41,47). God's mandate applies to all believers in all churches throughout the entire Earth.

Though scattered from persecution, Christians in the first century still proclaimed Christ (Acts 8:4). It now becomes the privilege of Christians today to do the same. The saints do not have to be compelled by persecution to share what is in their hearts and on their minds. They must see themselves as divinely sent to share that truth. When a Christian shares the gospel, he does it as one sent from the King of Kings and Lord of Lords (Revelation 19:16).

> *Key Concept: God's role in evangelism involves the sending of Christians to proclaim His plan.*

The Provision of Opportunities to Proclaim

God provides opportunities for his followers to proclaim the plan. Throughout the New Testament, God was active in directing the many evangelistic activities of the apostles and His church. Time and time again, they were provided with opportunities to proclaim the plan.

In Acts 2:2-6, God brought the sound of a wind and drew an immense crowd for Peter to share the gospel. In Acts 8:26, an angel of the Lord sent Philip to the road from Jerusalem to Gaza. There an angel directed him to an Ethiopian eunuch puzzling over a passage of Scripture, and Philip shared the gospel. The eunuch, one of the elect, was waiting (though he did not know it) for God to send a believer into his path with the gospel.

In Acts 13:2, the Holy Spirit told the church at Antioch to set apart Paul and Barnabas for ministry.

> As they served the Lord and fasted, the Holy Spirit said, "Separate Barnabas and Saul for me, for the work to which I have called them."
> Acts 13:2

The Holy Spirit directed them all throughout their journeys, leading them every step of the way. At the end of that first missionary journey, Paul gathered the church together and told them of how God had opened many doors of faith to the nations (Acts 14:27). The apostle credited the Lord for creating the opportunities for the gospel to go to the world. In Acts 16:6-16, they traveled through the large regions of Phrygia and Galatia and the Holy Spirit would not allow them to preach in Asia. They attempted to enter Bithynia, but the Spirit would not allow it. Then Paul had a vision that God desired him to go into Macedonia and followed it.

Over and over, God had put Paul in the right place at the right time. God will do the same for every Christian who desires to witness for Him. God will create opportunities by opening doors into situations for the gospel to be preached. Those Christians sharing the gospel should watch for these open doors. As will be discussed later, Paul asked the saints at Colossae to pray that God would open a door for the Word (Colossians 4:3). As a result, all Christians should be praying for open doors for the good news and watching for them to occur. Praying and watching are critical elements in the evangelistic process. In Psalm 5:3, David writes he will pray to the Lord and then eagerly watch for His response. Christians are to do the same regarding evangelism.

Key Concept: God's role in evangelism involves the providing of opportunities to proclaim the plan.

The Provision of Wisdom to Proclaim

Most Christians do not share the gospel because they are fearful that their presentation will be inadequate. This was the fear of Moses, when God told him to speak to Pharaoh in Exodus 4:10-12. He complained to God that he had never been eloquent of speech. He could not collect his thoughts fast enough to speak. When he did speak his words would not come out fast enough or smoothly enough. Then, the Lord explained to Moses that that he had made his mouth and the speech of all people. He had made his ears and the hearing of all people. Whether they could hear or speak, mute or deaf, it was all Him. God would give Moses wisdom as the leader spoke the words God had given him to speak.

In Luke 12:11-12, Jesus told his disciples that they were not to worry when they were proclaiming the plan before the governing rulers and authorities.

> When they bring you before the synagogues, the rulers, and the authorities, don't be anxious how or what you will answer, or what you will say; for the Holy Spirit will teach you in that same hour what you must say.
>
> Luke 12:11-12

They knew the truth. The Lord prepared His disciples and trained them to share His good news (Luke 24:40; Acts 1:1-3). Once trained, the Holy Spirit would guide them as they spoke that truth. Is this not true for every Christian today? This is a promise upon which all Christians can depend. This is a promise that should bring confidence to His saints.

Christians should be fully prepared at any time to present the basic truths of the gospel. In the very moment of sharing the gospel, the Holy Spirit will take over. He will use the biblical truths of whatever words they speak to bring people to Christ. Of course, the better prepared Christians are the more truth the Spirit has to work with in the unbeliever's life.

In Ephesians 6:19, Paul enjoins the saints to pray that the right utterance would be given to him as he opened his mouth to preach and teach the Word. Christians are to know the Word and rely on the Spirit to use that knowledge in the lives of the unsaved. Christians don't have to depend on clever techniques of persuasion but the simple truths of God's Word as His Spirit works. In 1 Corinthians 2:1-2, Paul acknowledged the fact that he did not come as the world did in superiority of speech or wisdom but simply proclaimed the testimony of God.

Then Paul asserted that he purposely determined to know nothing, but Christ crucified. The testimony of God is found only in His Word. Christians need to stay within the bounds of the Scriptures. Paul exalts the Thessalonians because they accepted his word as the Word of God, and it did its work in them who believed (1 Thessalonians 2:13). Christians need to stay within the scope of the Scriptures, and the Spirit will use the Scriptures to do its work in those who do not know Christ. Believers do not depend upon their own powers of persuasion, clever stories, or cultural hipness. They will speak the wisdom of God, which will be foolishness to the Gentiles or a stumbling block to the Jews but the power of God to those being saved (1 Corinthians 1). Herein lies the key to the wisdom of the gospel; it is God's not man's.

> *Key Concept: God's role in evangelism involves the provision of wisdom through His Spirit as the plan is proclaimed by Christians according to His Word.*

The Opening of Hearts to Believe

For people to believe in the gospel and receive the Lord, God must open up their hearts. In Acts 2:47, Luke declares that the Lord Jesus was adding to their number day by day. Christians can bring the good news, but the Holy Spirit must open their minds. Unbelievers are blinded in their spiritual eyes (2 Corinthians 4:4), cannot understand spiritual things (1 Corinthians 2:14), and are hardened in their hearts toward Him (Ephesians 4:19). God must change this through His Spirit. Luke describes the Lord Jesus opening the minds of His disciples, so that they could understand the Scriptures (Luke 24:45).

In John 6:44, Jesus declares that no one can come to Him unless the Father draws Him. Jesus brought the Word, and the Father through His Holy Spirit opened their minds. Paul declares the good news of Christ came to the Thessalonians not just in words but in the full conviction, in the Spirit, and in power (1 Thessalonians 1:5). Once again, Paul brought the

Word, but the Holy Spirit opened the minds. This opening of the minds involves the softening of their hearts, the removal of all their spiritual blinders, and the enlightening of their minds to understand the gospel.

In Acts 16:14, Paul preached to a woman named Lydia, a seller of purple fabrics, in Philippi. He always depended on the Spirit to work in the hearts of his listeners. He knew he could not do this work on his own. Human effort cannot compensate for the supernatural work of the Spirit.

> A certain woman named Lydia, a seller of purple, of the city of Thyatira, one who worshiped God, heard us; whose heart the Lord opened to listen to the things which were spoken by Paul.
> Acts 16:14

Luke discloses that the Lord opened her heart to listen to the things which Paul spoke.

Key Concept: God's role in evangelism involves the opening of the hearts and minds of unbelievers in order for them to believe.

The Accomplishment of God's Purpose

All unbelievers who are called to Christ will come to Him despite any contention or opposition from the world system, or even the unwillingness of Christians to share the gospel in a particular encounter with unbelievers. Often, Christians may worry that they missed opportunities to witness due to fear or inattentiveness which may lead to the loss of eternal life for some. This is needless worry because the Lord God is a sovereign God over all things, even this.

The Lord God is an omnipotent and sovereign God, who calls the unsaved to Himself. The Lord will work in any and every situation to bring them to His Son. If God desires, they will come. There is nothing an unbeliever in his resistance, a saint in his unwillingness, the world in their antagonism, or the Devil and demons in their opposition can do to thwart someone from entering the kingdom, if God wills. Whatever God desires will happen. God Almighty is omniscient (all-knowing), omnipresent (everywhere present), omnipotent (all powerful), eternal (always has existed), and immutable (never changes). This guarantees His sovereignty over every person and situation we could encounter.

God has declared from ancient times that all His purposes come to pass.

> Declaring the end from the beginning, and from ancient times things that are not yet done; saying, My counsel shall stand, and I will do all my pleasure.
>
> Isaiah 46:10

God declares in Isaiah 46:10 that His purpose will always be established, and He will accomplish all His good pleasure. In Daniel 4:34-35, after Nebuchadnezzar had returned from his punishment of insanity for his arrogance, he lifted up his eyes to heaven and blessed God. He declared that God acts according to His will in the host of heaven, the angels, and among the people on the Earth. No one can stop Him. In other words, God does exactly what He desires anytime He desires it. In Psalm 135:6, the psalmist reiterates this very concept, when he writes that Yahweh does whatever He pleases in heaven, on Earth, in the seas, and all the oceans. This would include the Christian's evangelistic encounters, would it not? In Hebrews 11:6, the author describes God as only being pleased when people come to Him in faith.

SHARING THE GOSPEL: THE DOCTRINE OF EVANGELISM

Even if Christians are willing and share the gospel, there isn't a mistake, a blunder, anything the Christian can do that can stop someone from coming to Christ, if it is God's will. Also, if God is indeed sovereign, He knows the kinds of blunders Christians are capable of making, before He sends the unsaved into their paths. In Psalm 139:4, David utters that even before there is a word on a believer's tongue, the Lord knows it. Most Christians think that they need to bring the seeking unbeliever to someone else better qualified to share the gospel. This is not needed. God can compensate for the bumbling or ineptness Christians may have in sharing. God desires for all believers to share, not a professional few. He will do the rest.

Key Concept: God's role in evangelism involves the salvation of souls in spite of any mistakes in the presentation of the plan a Christian might make.

Chapter 5

The Role of Man

Not only does God have a part in the proclamation of the plan, but man does too. As has been studied earlier, if God wanted to use a vehicle other than people to proclaim the plan, He would have, but this is His divine approach. God has a very active role in bringing people to His Son Jesus so does His church. He requires every individual in the church to participate. As the saints present the gospel (man's part), they rely on God's work in the person's heart through His Holy Spirit (God's part).

In 1 Peter 2:9, Peter explains to his readers that they are a chosen race, a royal priesthood, a holy nation, and a people for God's own possession.

> But you are a chosen race, a royal priesthood, a holy nation, a people for God's own possession, that you may proclaim the excellence of him who called you out of darkness into his marvelous light.
>
> 1 Peter 2:9

For what purpose? Believers are a kingdom of people whose purpose is to proclaim the excellence of the God who drew them out of darkness into His wonderful light. Could the followers of Jesus Christ demonstrate what God has done for them in a more glorious way than to proclaim all the ways in which God is excellent?

Key Concept: Though God has the primary role to play in the plan, man also has an important role.

SHARING THE GOSPEL: THE DOCTRINE OF EVANGELISM

The Need to Know the Plan

Christians cannot fulfill their responsibility in evangelism, if they do not know the plan that they must share. In Luke 9, the disciples had been with Jesus for quite a while and the time came for some missionary work. In verses 1-6, He sent them to preach the gospel throughout the villages in the area giving them power over demons and disease. This implies that they had knowledge of the good news that they were proclaiming. These followers of Jesus understood the good news of the kingdom.

This is rather obvious, yet many Christians do not really know the simple truths that must be proclaimed to preach the gospel. Jesus had taught all of them the plan. In Luke 8:1, the disciples listened to and watched Jesus go from city to city proclaiming His gospel. Prior to their own departure, Jesus preached the parables to the multitude and explained them in private to His disciples (Luke 8:9-10).

In Matthew 10:27, Jesus declared to his disciples that they were to speak in the light and on the housetops what they had heard in the darkness and whispered in their ears.

> What I tell you in the darkness, speak in the light; and what you hear whispered in the ear, proclaim on the housetops.
> Matthew 10:27

Jesus was proclaiming to them the mysteries of the kingdom of God. Once learned, they were to share it everywhere. The mysteries were to be declared for all to hear and see. For the disciples to accomplish this task, they would have to listen and learn everything the Lord had taught them about the gospel. Similarly, Christians must learn the key elements of the good news and proclaim them to all.

After His resurrection, the Lord spent much of His time teaching and training His disciples in the gospel. In Luke 24:45-47, Luke reveals that Jesus met with His disciples and explained what had been written about His suffering, dying, and rising again on the third day in the Holy Scriptures. Repentance for the forgiveness of sins was to be proclaimed in His Name to all nations. Luke reiterates this again, when he writes that Christ showed Himself alive by many proofs for over a period of forty days to His disciples and spoke to them about God's kingdom (Acts 1:3).

Christ taught His disciples the gospel, its many facets and truths, and all of its proofs until He was taken up to be with God the Father. Christians must know the key points of the gospel, the Scriptures to back them up, and have enough knowledge to answer questions. People have nowhere else to find the truth except to go to Christians. If Christians do not know these truths and proofs, where will the unbeliever go? They are to be found nowhere else in the world.

Key Concept: Man's role in evangelism involves the learning of the plan of redemption.

The Choice to Proclaim the Plan

God commands Christians to proclaim the plan, but they must respond to that command. Believers must choose to take their role and responsibility for sharing the gospel. The New Testament is filled with saints responding to God's command by presenting the good news. In Acts chapter 2, after the Holy Spirit had come upon those at Pentecost, which was manifested by tongues of fire, Peter preached a great sermon. This sermon was not the only preaching that went. According to verse 1, there were 119 other people in the upper room who received the miracle. He describes that the one hundred and nineteen also began speaking in other languages the mighty works of God (Acts 2:1-4). They were basically testifying of God's work in Jesus.

In Acts 6-8, Luke speaks of the evangelistic ministries of two great men of faith, Stephen and Philip. Yet, in Acts 8:4, Luke mentions that the Christians, who were scattered due to persecution, went about preaching the Word. Though the impact of these two men was great, it would never have equaled the impact of these scattered Christians taking their responsibility and proclaiming the plan.

Once Paul, the apostle, had planted a church in a city, he usually left. Who won others to Christ and built the church? The saints in that church did this. They were responsible for carrying the presentation of the gospel to the next level. This involved the evangelism of the entire city.

In 1 Thessalonians 1:8, Paul writes how much he rejoiced over the dynamic witness of the Thessalonians.

> For from you the Word of the Lord has been declared, not only in Macedonia and Achaia, but also in every place your faith toward God has gone out; so that we [Paul and others] need not to say anything.
> 1 Thessalonians 1:8

He applauds them because the gospel had gone forth from them into Macedonia, Achaia, and many other places. Those believers did not just leave the responsibility for evangelism up to the chosen twelve apostles. They themselves chose to share their newfound faith with others and live it before all.

When God sends those searching for Christ into the path of believers at work, school, or in their neighborhood, those believers must accept their own responsibility and share the gospel. Christians could provide unbelievers with a helping hand, some clothes, food, money, or some other resource, but without the gospel, these people will never have eternal life. A warm meal cannot save one's soul. Also, Christians cannot just leave it up to pastors. When unbelieving friends, acquaintances, or even strangers come to Christians for help that help must include the gospel.

> *Key Concept: Man's role in evangelism involves the Christian choosing to proclaim the plan.*

The Opportunities to Be Taken

In the first century, God created many opportunities for a Christian to proclaim the eternal plan of redemption. When God brings evangelistic opportunities, believers must act. The Spirit of God is constantly working in people's lives to bring them to Christ. He must lead them into the path of a believer to bring them into the kingdom. In Romans 10:13-15, Paul argues that people cannot believe unless they hear, and they cannot hear unless they have preachers - us.

In Acts 8:29-30, Philip was sent by the Holy Spirit to the Ethiopian eunuch.

> The Spirit said to Philip, "Go near, and join yourself to this chariot." Philip ran to him, and heard him reading Isaiah the prophet, and said, "Do you understand what you are reading?"
> Acts 8:29-30

The Scriptures were opened, but Philip had to take it from there and preach the gospel. Had Philip refused, out of fear or lack of motivation, the eunuch would have had to come to Christ through another preacher.

In Acts 10, Cornelius received a dream from God and sent for Peter. When the apostle Peter arrived at the house of Cornelius, everyone had gathered to hear his message. God had set up the entire opportunity. Yet, Peter had to actually travel to the home of Cornelius and share the gospel with him. The opportunity God provided had to be taken. This is man's role in evangelism. Man must act in the preaching of the gospel for someone to be saved. This is and has always been God's way.

In Acts 9:15-16, God told Paul through a prophet, whose name was Ananias that Paul would speak before governors and kings. When Paul was finally arrested in Acts 21:33 in Jerusalem, God began fulfilling that prophecy and opening up opportunities to share the gospel. In Acts 22:1, he spoke before the Roman centurions and a gathering of the Jews.

In Acts 23:1, he proclaimed his message before the Jewish counsel. In Acts 24:10, Paul spoke before Governor Felix. In Acts 25:6, Felix left Paul in prison, and Paul preached the gospel to Festus, Felix's next successor. In Acts 26:1, Paul was sent to King Herod Agrippa, leader of the Jewish nation, and preached the gospel. Paul was able to share the good news with the highest Jewish official.

Yet, the Lord God was not done, in Acts 28:16, Paul was sent to Rome to speak before the emperor (Philippians 1:12). In each instance, the apostle had to make a conscious choice to take the opportunity that God had given him and share the gospel. Paul could have chosen not to proclaim the plan, and the Book of Acts would have been written differently. Many opportunities will be brought to Christians to share (God's role), but they must proclaim the gospel (man's role).

Key Concept: Man's role in evangelism involves the Christian taking the opportunities God provides to proclaim the plan.

The Opportunities to Be Made

Not only are Christians to take the opportunities that God provides to share the gospel, but they are to make their own opportunities to share the gospel. In Acts 3:1-4:4, Peter and John saw the lame man begging in the temple. When they healed the man, a large crowd gathered. Peter preached the gospel, which brought over 5,000 people to Christ. Peter created this opportunity to share the gospel by healing the lame man. He knew a crowd would be gathered. In Acts 4:5-11, the apostles were taken into custody and brought before the Sanhedrin. Rather than remaining silent, Peter created an opportunity and shared the good news.

In Acts 5:29-32, after many in Jerusalem were healed of their infirmities, the apostles were dragged in before the council and commanded by them not to preach. After being miraculously released, they went out preaching the gospel in defiance of the council's command. They would obey God, rather than man. They were once again arrested. This time Peter preached the good news. He created an opportunity as they stood before the council.

In Acts 6:5, Stephen was called a man "full of faith and the Spirit." In verse 8, he is described as being "full of grace and power." In Acts 6-7, we discover that besides being one of those in charge of feeding all the widows in the Jerusalem church, he had a ministry of sharing the gospel. Stephen went about preaching the good news and performing many miracles. Some responded positively and some debated. Yet, he continued creating opportunities to evangelize. Those who could not cope with the wisdom convinced the Jewish authorities to arrest him. When he stood before the council, he merely turned that into an opportunity to speak of Jesus. Though we cannot do the miracles today that they did then, what a great example to follow!

This instigated Saul to begin his persecution of Christians in Acts 8. When this occurred, many Christians ran for their lives.

> Therefore, those who were scattered abroad went around preaching the Word.
> Acts 8:4

In Acts 8:4, what happened next? Everywhere they traveled, these Christians created opportunities to share the gospel. They did not wait around for God to hand deliver a situation for them to speak. They shared the good news of the Lord Jesus Christ with anyone who would listen.

During his persecutions, Saul was converted on the road to Damascus. Sometime after, Saul, who became Paul, began his three missionary journeys recorded in Acts thirteen and described through the rest of the book. Each of his journeys involved many opportunities Paul made to share the gospel.

Paul's strategy was simple: go into the synagogue or into the marketplace and present the good news to anyone who would listen (Acts 17:17). Christians need to do the same. The Lord does not direct every single evangelistic encounter as He did with Cornelius or the eunuch. Most of the time, evangelistic opportunities were simply created. The gospel can be brought into many situations, with some forethought or prayerful consideration. This can be done before or as the situation is unfolding. One way to do this is to start small and practice fitting the fact that one is a Christian into the conversation or even asking if they attend church directly or believe in a religion. The actual sharing of the gospel in its entirety may come later with the same individuals or others.

> *Key Concept: Man's role in evangelism involves the Christian making many opportunities to proclaim the plan in a variety of situations.*

Chapter 6

The Role of Prayer

Prayer is one of the most effective and powerful tools for bringing people to Christ. Unfortunately, it is probably the most neglected method utilized in evangelism. The saints should pray consistently and persistently for the unsaved. Prayer can and will move the hand of an all-powerful God. Since the Bible is filled with examples of prayer having very powerful effects on the lives of people and nations. Why not the salvation of souls?

In James 5:16, James wrote that the prayer of a righteous man is powerfully effective.

> Confess your offenses to one another, and pray for one another, that you may be healed. The insistent prayer of a righteous person is powerfully effective.
>
> James 5:16

Prayer can unleash divine power. In Genesis 18:22, when Abraham prayed for Lot, his life was spared from the fire of Sodom and Gomorrah. In Exodus 14:10, when Moses prayed for God's people to be delivered from Egypt, God parted the Red Sea. In Exodus 15:25, when Moses cried out to God for the starving Hebrews, God provided manna from heaven.

In 1 Kings 17:1, When Elijah, the prophet, prayed for the rain to cease in judgment upon God's people, it did not rain for three-and-one-half years. In 1 Kings 18:38, When Elijah asked God to consume his water drenched offering before the 850 prophets of Baal and Asherah, fire came from heaven and burned up his offering while leaving theirs untouched. In Daniel 9:3, when Daniel, the prophet, prayed for Israel's release from Babylonian captivity, God delivered His people through King Cyrus (Ezra 1:1-4). In Luke 1:13, when the priest Zacharias prayed for his barren wife, she conceived John the Baptist. In Acts 12:5, when the saints prayed for Peter who was guarded by trained soldiers in a prison, he was rescued by an angel.

The prayers of believers can be an effective and powerful means for accomplishing the work of God. In 1 Corinthians 2:1-3, Paul tells the Corinthians that his gospel did not come to them in persuasive words of man's wisdom but "in power and the Spirit." Power through the Spirit can be unleashed through prayer. In 1 Thessalonians 1:5-6, Paul rejoices and thanks his God and Father for the Word coming into their lives in power through the Holy Spirit. This power could produce a mighty witness for the Lord throughout the whole region.

In 2 Thessalonians 1:11-12, Paul discusses the persecution that resulted from their witness and prays that God would grant them power in their work of faith. The main work of faith was their witness for Christ. Here Paul is praying that their witness would go forth in power. Prayer has a definite role in evangelism. It can provide power to save.

> *Key Concept: Christians should pray for God's power to work as they share the gospel.*

The Priority of Prayer in the Proclamation

Prayer is very important in evangelism. Prayer should be involved intimately and intricately in every aspect of sharing the good news. This importance is described in two different ways. First, praying for the salvation of others is an essential part of prayer. Second, praying for the salvation of others is an essential part of evangelism. These are two sides of the same gospel coin. The personal and congregational prayers of the saints must involve evangelism and the salvation of the unsaved. To win others to Christ begins on one's knees.

First, evangelism is an essential part of prayer. Whenever saints pray, they should include prayer for the salvation of the unsaved and for those who share the gospel. Prayer for all the physical needs of unbelievers is important, but prayer for their eternal destiny should be the priority. In Matthew 6, the Lord's disciples approached Jesus and asked Him how to pray. In verses 8-13, Jesus composed a prayer that included the salvation of the lost.

In Matthew 6:10, Jesus commands them to pray that His Father's kingdom will come.

> Let your kingdom come. Let your will be done, as in Heaven, so on Earth.
> Matthew 6:10

According to Jesus, an essential element of one's prayer life is a request that the Lord God establish His kingdom. God will build His church upon the Earth. How does God build His kingdom? In Colossians 1:13, the apostle Paul declares that the unsaved, who become Christians, are transferred from Satan's domain of darkness to the kingdom of Christ. The kingdom of Jesus is the kingdom of God.

Any time a believer shares the good news of Jesus, and an unbeliever receives Jesus Christ as Savior and Lord, then the kingdom of our God is advanced. Why? Christians comprise this kingdom. Believers are its temple, priests, and building blocks (1 Corinthians 3:17; 1 Peter 2:9; Ephesians 2:21).

SHARING THE GOSPEL: THE DOCTRINE OF EVANGELISM

Therefore, to pray for the kingdom of God to come, one is praying for believers who are sharing the gospel and for unbelievers who are being saved. In Romans 10:1, Paul cried out that his heart's true desire and prayer was for the Jews to be saved. This prayer for their salvation was a prayer for the advancement of the kingdom.

Second, prayer is an essential part of sharing the gospel. Whenever we proclaim the plan, we need to pray. In Luke 5:15-17, the author describes the ministry of Jesus as healing the people and proclaiming the kingdom of God. He was out teaching the multitudes and confronting the Pharisees. Then he would often slip away to pray. What would have been the subject of His prayers? He was praying for His ministry which was proclaiming the gospel (evangelism).

In Mark 1:35, Jesus left His disciples early in the morning to pray.

> Early in the morning, while it was still dark, he rose up and went out, and departed into a deserted place, and prayed there.
>
> Mark 1:35

The disciples came and told Him that many were looking for Him, but the Lord desired to preach to the towns nearby. Obviously, He prayed for His Father to bless His preaching in the towns where he shared the gospel. In Acts 6:4, Paul described the work of the apostles as the work of ministry and prayer. The primary ministry of the twelve apostles was evangelism. Preaching and praying go hand in hand.

Christians need to be constantly preaching and praying. As has been seen earlier, preaching and praying was done by regular, ordinary saints, not just the pastor and church staff. These are the pillars of ministry.

Key Concept: Evangelism is an essential part of prayer, and prayer is an essential part of evangelism because it can move the hand of God.

The Reasons for Prayer in the Proclamation

There are many reasons why one should be proclaiming the plan and praying for the salvation of others. First, saints are encouraged and exhorted to pray for the salvation of souls. In 1 Timothy 2:1-2, Paul discusses with Timothy how people are to conduct themselves in the church. He urges Timothy to have the saints pray for all men and kings in authority, so that the saints may lead quiet, peaceful lives in godliness and dignity. In verses 3-4, Paul writes the reason. The entreating, prayers, petitions, and thanksgivings, which were on behalf of all men, were for their salvation. Christians are to clearly be praying for the salvation of souls.

Second, when believers pray for the salvation of others, it pleases God. In that same passage, Paul asserts to his fellow worker that this is good and acceptable to God. To pray for the salvation of all men is a good thing and God accepts it. Why? It pleases Him.

Third, God desires people to be saved. Once again, in that same passage, Paul gives the reason that it is acceptable to God because He desires all people to come to a saving knowledge of Him. Peter told his readers that God is patient and does not wish any to perish, so the second coming of Christ had not occurred yet (2 Peter 2:9). God is delaying the coming of His only Son because He wants more people to become His children.

Fourth, prayer for the unsaved is the natural result of a burdened heart. In Romans 9:1-3, Paul declares his burden for the salvation of the Jewish people. It brought him great sorrow and constant grief. In Romans 10:1, this deep burden poured forth in prayer for these people.

> Brothers, my heart's desire and my prayer to God is for Israel, that they may be saved.
> Romans 10:1

He was so troubled that he would trade his own salvation if he could see his Hebrew brothers saved.

Fifth, prayer is the natural result of a kindred heart. In that same passage, Paul calls the Jews his brethren and his kinsmen according to the flesh. Paul felt a human bond to the Jews. He was born of their nation (Acts 22:3). Christians are to take all of these reasons for prayer in the proclamation of the gospel to heart. Petitions for the salvation of others should be an important part of a Christian's life of prayer.

> *Key Concept: Christians ought to please and obey God by praying for the salvation of others out of a burdened heart.*

The Content of Prayer in the Proclamation

The Scriptures clearly delineate the content of prayer that involves the evangelistic process. First, Christians are to pray for the salvation of particular souls. This concept has been discussed. Second, believers are to pray for an open door to share their testimony. In Colossians 4:2-3, Paul requests the Colossians to ask God for an open door to the gospel. As was seen previously, the Father creates opportunities for Christians to witness for Him. That is God's part. The part Christians play is to pray for those very opportunities to be created. Also, these prayers should be made by Christians on behalf of their fellow believers, not just for themselves. Paul was asking for prayer on his own behalf because he wanted many people praying for him.

Third, Christians should pray for God's wisdom in their witnessing. In Colossians 4:4-6, Paul exhorted the church at Colossae to pray so he would know how he ought to speak. Then he discussed being wise toward outsiders and having speech that is gracious, seasoned with salt. Not only are the saints to pray for opportunities to speak, but the wisdom to be gracious and kind.

Fourth, Christians are to pray that the gospel will spread rapidly. Paul encourages the Thessalonians to pray that God would multiply his evangelistic efforts and spread the Word quickly (2 Thessalonians 3:1). Fifth, saints are to be praying for great boldness. Paul entreated the church to request God to give him courage in sharing the mystery of the gospel of Jesus Christ (Ephesians 6:19).

Sixth, believers are to pray for additional workers to share the gospel.

> Then he said to his disciples, "The harvest indeed is plentiful, but the laborers are few. Pray therefore that the Lord of the harvest will send out laborers into his harvest."
> Matthew 9:37-38

In Matthew 9:37-38, the Lord gazed out at all the people and saw crops of souls ripe for harvest. He asked his disciples to pray that the Lord of the harvest would send out workers to share the gospel. Christians need to be praying that the Lord Jesus would provoke their own hearts and the hearts of other Christians to share the gospel with the lost around them. Churches need prayers to reach those far away.

SHARING THE GOSPEL: THE DOCTRINE OF EVANGELISM

Key Concept: Christians must pray for the souls of the unsaved, open doors into their lives to share, wisdom as to how they ought to speak, the gospel spreading rapidly, boldness, and additional workers.

Chapter 7

The Schemes of Satan

Satan is in control of this world (John 12:31). This serpent will not allow unbelievers to leave his evil domain without a fight (Colossians 1:3). His strategy is to oppose all efforts at sharing the gospel. In Ephesians 6:10-20, Paul asserts that every day his minions direct his wicked schemes against all the saints who evangelize. Then he entreats believers to put on the full armor of God. This was not only for each other but for his boldness in proclaiming the plan.

Paul wrote to the Thessalonians that he had a great desire to see them.

> But we, brothers, being bereaved of you for a short season, in presence, not in heart, tried even harder to see your face with great desire, because we wanted to come to you - indeed, I, Paul, once and again - but Satan hindered us.
> 1 Thessalonians 2:17-18

In 1 Thessalonians 2:17-18, he described how he wanted to come to them more than once, but Satan thwarted him. Paul knew the schemes and flaming missiles of the Devil aimed toward those who know Jesus Christ. He also knew the evil intentions and battle plans directed at those who were about to enter the kingdom. When Christians become committed to witnessing to as many people as possible, or simply on a regular basis, Satan will take notice.

Satan is a powerful evil angelic being. In Scripture, Satan is called the Great Dragon or the Serpent of Old (Revelation

12:9), the Prince of the Power of the Air (Ephesians 2:2), the Evil One (1 John 3:12), and the Father of Lies (John 8:44) as well as other designations. As Christians present the gospel, they may battle this formidable, supernatural adversary. Satan has developed some specific strategies or schemes in his wicked attempt to build a kingdom of his own and to become higher than the Most High (Isaiah 14, Ezekiel 28).

His approach is found in 1 Peter 5:8, where Peter declares that Satan is the adversary, who behaves like a roaring lion seeking someone to devour. Would not the perfect target be all Christians who are sharing the gospel and pulling people out of his dark kingdom? Here are several of the schemes Satan has developed in his wicked opposition to evangelism.

> *Key Concept: Evangelism involves a raging battle with Satan and his demons for the souls of men.*

The Destruction of Man's Original Relationship

The Devil was instrumental in destroying man's original relationship to God. Had he not done this, there would be no need for evangelism. In Ezekiel 28:12-15, the prophet writes a lamentation concerning the king of Tyre, but it is obvious that he is talking about the evil influence behind the man.

Lucifer was an anointed cherub, who was blameless in his ways and perfect in beauty and wisdom. God placed Lucifer in the Garden of Eden. He was there with Adam and Eve. The story of the fall in Genesis 3 is well known by most. Satan appeared in the form of a serpent and deceived Eve into partaking of the forbidden fruit. Then in rebellion, not deception, Adam ate. Then man fell from grace. Satan was relentless. He would not rest in his rebellion. He continued to work as he went after Adam's children.

In Genesis 4, this deceiver was behind the slaying of Abel. Though the Devil is not mentioned, he influenced Cain.

> Unlike Cain, who was of the evil one, and killed his brother. Why did he kill him? Because his works were evil, and his brother's righteous.
>
> 1 John 3:12

John writes in 1 John 3:12 that Cain murdered Abel because he was of the Evil One. By the time of Noah, the entire world had been corrupted by the Devil (Genesis 6:5). In Ephesians 2:1-3, Paul argues that those who do not know Christ are dead in their sins, walking according to the course of this world, according to the Devil, living in the lusts of their flesh, and doing his desires.

This is what occurred before the flood. These people were simply living according to the Evil One. They sinned and sinned to such an extent that God obliterated them from the Earth (Genesis 6:5-8). God eventually bound Himself with a covenant so He would not do it again and again and again as men continued to sin (Genesis 8:21). Unsaved people are in the same condition today. They still sin continually. Their relationship with God does not exist. They desperately need the gospel of Jesus Christ preached to them.

> *Key Concept: Satan was instrumental in destroying man's relationship with God producing a need for evangelism.*

The Creation of an Opposing World System

In Isaiah 14:4-21, Isaiah is speaking to the King of Babylon and then addresses Satan who is behind his actions. In this passage, he declares that the Devil wanted to be like the Most High God. Essentially, Satan wanted the kingdom that was being created for the Son! After Lucifer enticed Adam to fall and he did, man's relationship with God ended. Then Satan's relationship with man began. As a result, all fallen people became Satan's children (John 8:44) and entered into his domain of darkness (Colossians 1:13). He became their prince (Ephesians 2:2).

In 1 John 5:19, John informs his readers that they are from God, but the world lies in the power of the Evil One.

> We know that we are of God, and the whole world lies in the power of the evil one.
> 1 John 5:19

After man was thrown out of Eden, Satan began molding unbelievers into an evil system opposed to God expressed in the many nations and societies on Earth. This system was designed to make Satan the god of men and to prevent them from coming to the Lord (2 Corinthians 4:4; James 4:4). John echoes this theme when he insists that his readers not love the world and the things in the world, which were the lust of the eyes, flesh, and boastful pride of life (1 John 2:15-16).

Satan's evil world system will culminate in the coming of the man of lawlessness. This wicked ruler will come in the power of Satan performing signs and wonders and unite the entire world against God. It will terminate when the Devil is thrown into the Lake of Fire (Revelation 20:10) and the Earth is destroyed (2 Peter 3:10).

When Christians share the gospel, they are dealing with people who are trapped by their own lustful desires and the pride that proceeds from following after the Devil. They are trapped in a system opposed to the gospel (2 Timothy 2:26).

This system keeps them from Christ.

> *Key Concept: Satan has developed a world system opposed to the gospel to keep man ensnared by him.*

The Attempt to Destroy the Messiah

Satan attempted to destroy the Messiah who would fulfill the plan of redemption. It began with Herod. After speaking to the wise men, he determined that the Messiah must have been born within two years of their arrival. Herod ordered all the Hebrew children who were under two years of age to be slaughtered (Matthew 2:1-20). Was the Devil behind this? Of course, he was. The next recorded incident occurred at the temptation.

In Matthew 4:1-11, the Devil appeared to Christ in the wilderness and tempted Him in His humanity. He wanted to give the Lord Jesus a very easy and simple way out from the pain and torment of the coming cross. This would destroy God's eternal plan of redemption. Then, during His ministry the Lord was constantly hounded by the Jewish leaders, who endeavored to destroy His witness. They constantly accused Him of teaching doctrines contrary to Moses (Matthew 19:3-9), breaking the law (Matthew 12:1-7), and doing the works of demons (Matthew 12:24).

These men pursued Jesus so they could find something to bring against Him. The leaders watched Him and watched Him. Finally, when the chief priests, Sadducees, Pharisees, scribe, and elders could find absolutely nothing against Him, they brought false witnesses against Him. When these false witnesses couldn't even agree among themselves as to what he did, they finally demanded that Jesus declare Himself to be the Son of God. When He did, they claimed blasphemy against their God (Luke 22:70-71). When they took Him to Pilate and the Romans, they claimed he was seditious.

In John 8, the Lord goes to the heart of the issue.

> You are of your father, the Devil, and you want to do the desires of your father. He was a murderer from the beginning, and doesn't stand in the truth, because there is no truth in him. When he speaks a lie, he speaks on his own; for he is a liar, and its father.
> John 8:44

He pronounced that they were of their father the Devil. They were being used by Satan to destroy Jesus Christ's work and ministry. Unfortunately, the serpent had fooled them into thinking they were serving God.

Key Concept: Satan attempted to destroy the Lord who is at the center of evangelism.

The Attempt to Influence the Disciples

The Serpent sought to influence the disciples of the Lord. In Matthew 16:22-23, Jesus declared that He would suffer, be killed, and then be raised up on the third day. Peter strongly disagreed. He declared that this would never happen to the Lord. Christ's reply was to rebuke the Devil, who had been behind Peter's foolish remark.

In Luke 22:31-32, Christ told Peter and the other disciples that Satan had asked the Father permission to sift them like wheat, and it had been granted to him by God. The disciples would be scattered, but there was something special planned for Peter. Before sunrise he would be challenged and deny

Christ three times. The Devil had his attention on the Lord's disciples and destroying them as the Lord was arrested.

> The Lord said, "Simon, Simon, behold, Satan asked to have you, that he might sift you as wheat, but I prayed for you, that your faith wouldn't fail. You, when once you have turn- ed again, establish your brothers."
> Luke 22:31-32

Then Jesus comforted Peter with the knowledge that He had prayed for him. After he turned back to the Lord, Peter was to strengthen his brothers. This was fulfilled in the denial of the Lord three times (Luke 22:34).

Satan's ultimate attempt was his possession of Judas, one of the twelve, who betrayed the Lord (John 13:27). Judas was used to aid the Jews in killing the Lord to stop Him (Psalm 22:11-13). This only led to victory in His resurrection. Satan had bruised the Messiah on the heel, and Christ had crushed him on the head, as was predicted (Genesis 3:15). The saints may face similar attacks of the Devil.

> *Key Concept: Satan attempted to influence Christ's disciples to oppose Jesus and may do the same to Christians.*

The Blindness of Men toward the Gospel

Satan blinds men to the light of the gospel. Paul describes how the Devil has blinded the minds of the unsaved and put a veil over them. They cannot see the light of the good news and the glory of the Lord that it brings (2 Corinthians 4:4-5). The apostle John reiterates this theme of light and darkness and the blinding of men.

In 1 John 2:11, John compares the state of unbelievers to walking in darkness. As they walk, they do not know where they are going. Why? They cannot spiritually see the things of the Lord.

> But he who hates his brother is in the darkness, and walks in the darkness, and doesn't know where he is going, because the darkness has blinded his eyes.
>
> 1 John 2:11

The darkness has blinded their eyes. It is interesting that the Serpent's evil kingdom is entitled "the domain of darkness" (Colossians 1:13). This fallen angel dwells in darkness and so does his children who have been spiritually enveloped in the blackest of night. Christians are the light of Christ holding forth the Word of Light in their world (Philippians 2:15-16). In Romans 2:19, Paul explains that believers are a guide to these blind people and a light in their darkness. In 1 John 2:11, the apostle describes unsaved as stumbling around in the darkness from the blindness of Satan. They need saints of Christ to bring the light.

> *Key Concept: Satan blinds the unsaved, so they will not respond to the gospel.*

The Preparation of an Opposing Plan

Throughout history, Satan created his own false messiahs (Luke 21:8), devised his own false gospels (2 Corinthians 11:4) and sent his own false prophets to proclaim his lies (Matthew 24:11). His counterattack against Jesus Christ, His gospel, and His apostles are his own counterfeits. He has his minions everywhere in religious and non-religious disguises attempting to confuse and hide the true light of Christ.

In 2 Corinthians 11:14-15, Paul asserts that Satan disguises himself to look like an angel of light. The word light refers to truth and holiness revealed. It has a moral and a doctrinal aspect to it. Its opposite is evil and error (darkness).

> And no wonder, for even Satan masquerades as an angel of light. It is no great thing there- fore his servants also masquerade as servants of righteousness, whose end will be according to their works.
> 2 Corinthians 11:14-15

He dresses himself up to look like a messenger of the truth and dresses his servants up like ministers of righteousness. His strategy is simple. While the true light is shining, he will put up false lights all around the true one. These false lights in the guise of attractive messiahs and prophets will teach doctrines that cater to men's lusts. This is why there are so many false religions.

In 1 John 4:5, John declares that the spirits behind all of these false religions are from the world. They speak as from this system and the world listens to them. Those who do not know the Lord are listening to them. When true Christians inevitably encounter the unbeliever, Satan will be trying to draw them away with his own false prophets and religions.

Key Concept: Satan has created many false gospels, messiahs, and prophets to fool the unsaved.

The Perversion of the True Gospel

Not only does the Devil propagate his own gospel but attempts to pervert the true gospel. In Galatia, false teachers had crept into the church claiming the Gentile Christians had to become circumcised and keep certain tenets of the law to be saved. Paul asserts in Galatians 1:6-7 that this was not just a different gospel but an alteration or perversion of the true and real gospel. This was not a different gospel but a heresy or altering of the true one.

In 2 Peter 2:1, Peter spoke of false prophets who had come and had secretly introduced destructive heresies.

> But false prophets also arose among the people, as false teachers will also be among you, who will secretly bring in destructive heresies, denying even the Master who bought them, bringing on themselves swift destruction.
> 2 Peter 2:1

In Acts 20:30, Paul warned the elders at Ephesus that men would rise from among them and speak perverse things (an alternate gospel). In Jude 4, Jude, the half-brother of Jesus, describes some ungodly men who had secretly crept into the church. They turned the grace of God into indecency and denied the Savior. These were perversions of the gospel.

In 2 Timothy 2:17-18, Paul describes the empty chatter and ungodliness of Hymenaeus and Philetus. They claimed the resurrection had already occurred, which had affected the faith of some Christians. He was worried that their error (perversion of the gospel) would spread much like gangrene. There will be those who present themselves as true Christian evangelists but will pervert the truth of God. The church has experienced this throughout its history.

This is designed by the deceiver to confound people, thus, obscuring the true gospel of Jesus Christ. The unbeliever will have difficulty discerning who is presenting the "real" truth and who is not. Yet, God provides His Holy Spirit to anyone seeking after His truth. He will enable them to discern the Truth (John 15:26-27). He will remove the dark blinders on their eyes (2 Corinthians 4:4). He will open their hearts.

Key Concept: Satan has sent false teachers into the church to pervert the true gospel.

The Disruption of Evangelistic Efforts

Satan disrupts the saint's evangelistic efforts. This serpent accomplishes this evil activity in many different ways. Paul was sent a difficult thorn in the flesh, which could have been his eyesight or even false teachers. He called this "thorn" a messenger of Satan in 2 Corinthians 12:7. Satan might send someone to counteract what Christians say, such as Elymas, the magician. This worker of evil interrupted Paul's gospel testimony to Sergius Paulus in Acts 13:8. Followers of Christ must be aware of this and even anticipate it.

The Evil One can send one of his emissaries to wrongly associate with believers, such as the demon-possessed slave girl in Philippi. She followed after Paul and his companions everywhere they went making declarations about them. She would shout that they were the servants of God proclaiming the way to salvation. This was a true statement, but the Devil was attempting to associate their ministry with her wicked fortune telling. This would confuse people and dim the light of the gospel. People would think Paul and his companions were just like her. Perhaps, the people would also think she was legitimate because she was authenticating them. Paul simply cast the demon out of her. (Acts 16:16-18).

In 2 Thessalonians 2:1-2, this fake god, this accuser of the brethren, will attempt to send false believers into the paths of those with whom true Christians are sharing the gospel.

> Now, brothers, concerning the coming of our Lord Jesus Christ, and our gathering together to him, we ask you not to be quickly shaken in your mind, nor yet be troubled, either by spirit, or by word, or by letter as from us, saying that the day of Christ had come.
>
> 2 Thessalonians 2:1-2

These false believers will have a false gospel to deceive the true ones. He will slander these Christians and shed doubt on much of their credibility (Galatians 1:10, 2 Corinthians 11:5), or persecute, mistreat, and harass them (Philippians 1:27-30). He controls a myriad of demons to carry out these disruptions. Revelation implies that one third of the angels fell with the Devil (Revelation 12:4-9). John warns believers about these very spirits who were behind the false messages they were receiving.

The church was to test the spirits to see if they were from God (1 John 4:1). Paul declares that some Christians will fall away and follow after the teachings of deceitful spirits and demons (1 Timothy 4:1). Believers should be very careful in their associations with others as they share the gospel. Some might have been sent by the Devil as one of his schemes to interrupt their presentations of the truth.

> *Key Concepts: Satan will oppose the efforts of the saints to proclaim the plan.*

The Response to the Role of Satan

How do Christians fully respond to these strategies of the Devil? Many of the following Christian responses have been mentioned before in other contexts but are pertinent here. First, Christians cannot afford to be ignorant of the Devil's schemes or they will allow him to outwit them. They must acknowledge and understand the real battle that will rage as they share the gospel (1 Corinthians 9:24).

Second, believers should never underestimate the work of Satan in an unbeliever's life. The unsaved are in the Serpent's snare and held captive by him (2 Timothy 2:26). Third, the saints in Christ should know that Satan is not omnipotent, omnipresent, or omniscient as their God is. Yet, he is still an extremely powerful angel (2 Thessalonians 2:9-10; Job 1-2). Fourth, believers should not overestimate Satan's power, or underestimate God's sovereign control (Job 1-2).

Fifth, Christians should rely upon God's Spirit while they witness.

> You are of God, little children, and have overcome them; because greater is he who is in you than he who is in the world.
> 1 John 4:4

In 1 John 4:4, John explains to his readers that the Holy Spirit in them is greater than the Serpent who is in the world. No matter what the Devil and his demons can throw at believers while witnessing, they can handle it through the power of the Holy Spirit. Sixth, bearing witness of the plan is the responsibility of the Spirit. Believers only need to present the plan the Spirit will do the rest (John 15:26-27). Seventh, the saved must use their spiritual armor to fight the battle for the souls of men and women. Paul asserts that his readers must put on their spiritual armor and stand firm against the schemes of the Evil One (Ephesians 6:11).

Eighth, those who share the good news should anticipate persecution (John 15:20). Witnessing can bring a wide range of negative responses, which should not only be expected but accepted as part of the reality of sharing the gospel (Acts 5:41, Philippians 3:10). Ninth, Christians should bathe their presentation of the good news in prayer (Ephesians 6:18-19). It is prayer that can protect them or help them endure harm. Tenth, the saved must remain close to God in order to resist the Devil in their witnessing. He will endeavor to find any weakness to exploit (James 4:7-8). The apostle John refers to it as abiding (remaining) in Him (1 John 2:27-28; 3:24).

Christians must take this knowledge about the Devil to heart. They should not be foolish enough to think that Satan is going to allow them to walk into his domain, proclaim the plan of redemption, and win his subjects to Christ without opposition. There will be a battle for the souls of those who hear the gospel. In Ephesians 6:12, Paul declared that his struggle was not against real flesh and blood but against powers in the heavens.

Was Paul not speaking to the average believer when he declared this truth? Like Paul, are all Christians to have a ministry of evangelism to the world and edification to the church? Then, believers will face the powers of darkness and must be ready. The saints will battle against the many levels of demons that encompass the forces of the Evil One. They should be of good courage because victory is theirs.

> *Key Concept: Christians are to respond to Satan by being knowledgeable of his schemes, anticipating his opposition, and relying on the Holy Spirit's power for victory in the battle for souls.*

Chapter 8

The Proper Message

Why do thousands receive the Lord in a great evangelistic crusade, yet few join or remain in a church for any length of time? Why does the church appear to be growing in size in leaps and bounds, but the saints don't seem to be maturing in Christ? Why do many seem to come to Christ when they are young, fall away in their teens, then later rededicate their lives to Christ? Was this actually their initial salvation? Why do some who claim to receive the Lord never change? Why do others spend their Christian lives receiving Christ over and over again?

Why do still others have a very dramatic conversion with weeping and great joy then fall away a short time afterward? Why do others claim to know Christ, yet produce little or no fruit year after year? These questions become all the more relevant in the light of several Bible passages which speak of the change that occurs, when someone moves from darkness into light (John 3:20; 11:10; 1 John 2:9-10).

In Matthew 9:37, Jesus Christ compared the whole world to a field ready for harvest.

> Then he said to his disciples, "The harvest indeed is plentiful, but the laborers are few."
> Matthew 9:37

Why does much of the wheat harvested seem so weak and brittle? In John 3:3, the Lord compared salvation to being born again. Why do many "born again" Christians appear so frail, weak, and immature in their faith, never growing up in

Christ? In 2 Corinthians 5:17, Paul declares that those who become Christians are new creations. The old things have passed away and new things have come. Why do some people appear to have little "new things" and are still filled with the "old things"? In John 1:12, the people who become Christians are called the children of God. They now belong to the family of God. Why then do many after only a few months forsake their new family and return to the Devil (1 John 3:10)? Were they in God's family or not?

These questions have various answers. Certainly, Satan is prowling about like a roaring, hungry lion seeking as many saints as possible to devour (1 Peter 5:8). Certainly, there is mounting pressure from the world to stay within its realm of influence. In James 4:4, James sternly warned his readers not to be friends with the world system. This would be spiritual adultery and hostility toward God. Also, there is a real battle within Christians against their flesh. In Romans 7:23, Paul recognized this when he described the waging of war within him. His mind was in constant battle with his flesh. He desired good and his flesh desired evil. Though these are acceptable answers, they do account for the sheer lack of any spiritual fruit whatsoever.

Consider another reason: they were not saved at all. There was no harvest of wheat in the first place. These unhealthy spiritual births of "newborn babes in Jesus Christ" were not births at all. Those who demonstrate only the deeds of the old creation had never become new. Some will appear to be Christians when they are not.

There is no real battle against the Devil, the world, or the flesh because they simply are not saved. Jesus presents this very concept when He speaks of the narrow road. There will be some who call Him Lord on judgment day and will not enter His kingdom. They may have prophesied in His name, cast out demons in His name, and even done mighty works, but he will tell all of them to depart for He never knew them (Matthew 7:22-23). How is this possible? Can some claim the name of Christ and not be one of His? Yes!

It is not enough to just name His name or serve Him; one must have a genuine, saving faith. This involves trusting in Him and Him alone for their salvation and living for Him. In 1 John 2:19, the apostle describes this phenomenon. Some in the churches claimed to be true Christians and had departed. This exodus prompted similar questions by the believers. John denounced those who had left as never really being a part of the true church. They were not saved at all. Paul told the Corinthians that there were to be divisions in the church to identify the saved from the unsaved (1 Corinthians 11:19). James asserts that even the demons believe Jesus is the Son, but true saints demonstrate their faith through their good works (James 2:18-19).

Why does this happen? The key resides in the fact that a saving relationship comes from the presentation of a true gospel and a proper response to it. Sometimes, people do not hear the true gospel, so they cannot respond in a true saving way. The preaching of an incomplete, distorted, or different gospel will only result in a message that cannot save. This aberration produces virtually no harvest, no new birth, no new creation, and no adoption as sons. Unfortunately, those who respond may think they are saved, when they are not.

Once again, this was the particular case of those described in Matthew 7:22-23. Numerous Christians, including some leaders, may not even know the key components that must be in a gospel message to bring an unbeliever to a saving knowledge. All of these critical elements must come directly from the Bible, not emotion or experience. To put "Jesus in one's heart" is hardly the true gospel message of salvation. To accept Christ as Savior is only a part of the true good news. To love Jesus is important but will not admit someone into the kingdom of His God. Others might be sincere about their faith in Jesus but be sincerely wrong. They believed in the wrong Jesus, or false gospel message, or gave only a partial response. When the members of many cults come to the door of Christians today, they claim they have "accepted Jesus into their hearts." Have they? No, they have not.

When Paul preached in the Berean church in Acts 17:11, they responded to him by searching the Scriptures to see if what he was saying was true. Then, they reacted in saving faith. The proper proclamation of the gospel must come out of Scripture, not Scripture plus other writings. Neither will inspirational stories, emotional appeals, meaningful music, and spectacular events or presentations save, only the true gospel proclaimed through the power of the Spirit saves. This chapter will elucidate the essential elements of the good news of the proclamation of the plan of redemption. Then, the responses to the gospel that bring eternal salvation will be considered in another chapter.

> *Key Concept: Christians who fall away from the faith may never have been Christians at all having heard an incomplete gospel or made an inadequate response.*

The Declaration of the Kingdom

The message begins with a declaration of the kingdom of God. Christians should begin by identifying themselves as believers and explaining briefly the redemptive plan of God discussed in chapter one. This would include the three parts discussed: the creation of man in order to create a kingdom of priests to God's Son (John 3:35; Colossians 1:16; John 17:2, 6,

7,9,12); the temptation of man and his fall (Genesis 3:1-7; 1 Timothy 2:14), the plan to redeem man through Jesus Christ (Ephesians 1:7, 14; Colossians 1:14), and the eternal life that comes (John 6:40,47,68; 1 John 5:11-12). This presentation of the redemptive plan is called preaching the kingdom of God in the New Testament writers (Matthew 3:2; 9:35; Luke 4:43).

Jesus then passed on this ministry of proclamation to His disciples.

> "As you go, preach, saying, 'The Kingdom of Heaven is at hand!'
>
> Matthew 10:7

In Matthew 10:7, Jesus calls His twelve disciples and gives them the commission to preach the kingdom of heaven just as He was doing. This is reiterated and described in many places in the New Testament (Luke 9:2; Acts 8:12; 14:22; 19:8; 28:31). Once the gift of the kingdom from the Father to the Son is explained, then it should be offered to the unbelievers to whom the Christian is speaking. They should be asked if they desire to become a part of God's Kingdom on Earth and then into eternity. Do they want eternal life now?

> *Key Concept: True evangelism involves proclaiming and offering the kingdom of God.*

The Proclamation of Sin and Judgment

Proclaiming sin and judgment is absolutely critical when the gospel is shared. Today, many people believe they are basically good and will be in a better place when they die. Others believe that they do not have to worry about death because somehow it will all work out to a happy conclusion. Still others simply do not concern themselves about death because they feel nothing can be done to prevent it. Some have decided that they will not worry since no one knows what will happen anyway. These denials cannot change the reality of their judgment and condemnation for a lifetime of sin or even one sin for that matter (James 2:10). Those who have not received Christ, thus appropriating His death on the cross for their sins, will not be saved from this judgment. Unfortunately, this life is not a fairy tale with an imaginary, happy ending. This reality must be declared to unbelievers. Yes, it is offensive, but much more offensive would be an eternity of hell and punishment.

In Romans 3:10-11, Paul explains that there is no one who is righteous or understands God. In Romans 3:23, he asserts that all have sinned and fall short of God's glory. This sin brought God's condemnation. Romans 1:18 describes the wrath of God, which is revealed in heaven against man's sin and unrighteousness. John the Baptist spoke about judgment from sin. Every evangelist who preached in the book of Acts spoke of this condemnation. They never left it out.

In Acts 14:15, Paul arrives in Lystra and heals a lame man. Then, he and Barnabas are hailed as gods. Paul is given a chance to speak and entreats them to turn from their useless and vain worship of idols. In Acts 17:30-31, Paul travels to Athens and he preaches that they must repent of their sin for judgment is coming. The apostle Paul preached the gospel which included continually indicting people for their sin and proclaiming a coming judgment. Sin is the major issue facing man and with it comes judgment and condemnation.

In Acts 26:18, the apostle Paul is preaching the gospel to King Agrippa and explains that belief in Christ will bring the forgiveness of sins and an inheritance in heaven. How can Christians speak of forgiveness without first speaking of sin and judgment? Without sin what is one saved from?

This cannot be replaced by the proclamation that Jesus can fulfill the felt needs of people. To ask people to place their faith in Jesus Christ because the Lord will satisfy all their needs is preaching contrary to the message of Jesus and the apostles. God does not always fulfill one's felt needs. Often, Christianity brings persecution and trials from the Devil, the world (society), and the flesh. Often, one's life becomes more complicated with more problems because he is now moving against the flow of the whole world. Some will say that Jesus did miracles to fulfill needs to prepare people for the gospel. Jesus performed miracles primarily to substantiate His claims. This is a critical distinction!

Believers must remember that Revelation ends with the judgment of unbelievers. This judgment can only be avoided through a gospel that proclaims it.

> I saw the dead, the great and the small, standing before the throne, and they opened books. Another book was opened, which is the book of life. The dead were judged out of the things which were written in the books, according to their works.
> Revelation 20:12

Revelation 20:12 describes a terrifying judgment of every sin an unbeliever has ever committed. Christians who share the gospel must address personal sin and its resultant judgment to see their desperate need for salvation. This does not mean an evangelist has to deal with specific sins. This will be done by the conviction of the Spirit. So then, what does it really profit a man, if he gains the whole world (has all his needs fulfilled), but he loses his soul?

> *Key Concept: True evangelism involves proclaiming that all men have sinned and all men will be judged.*

SHARING THE GOSPEL: THE DOCTRINE OF EVANGELISM

The Proclamation of Christ as God

There is no true gospel message without the proclamation of Christ as the true God. The essential message of the Lord is that He is the Son of God and equal with God in His deity. In John 8:58, Jesus told the Jews that before Abraham was born, He existed (I Am). This is a direct claim to be the God or Yahweh (I Am) of the Old Testament. The Jews knew this. In verse 59, they took up stones to kill him for blasphemy. In Mark 14:61, Jesus stood before the Sanhedrin. When asked if He was the Christ, the Son of the Blessed One, He replied with the "I Am." This was the designation of Yahweh of the Old Testament. The high priest's response was the tearing of his robes to signify blasphemy. Declaring oneself as the Son of God was a pronouncement of deity. In John 10:30, when Jesus declared that He and the Father were one (essence), He was proclaiming His deity.

The apostles also proclaimed the deity of Jesus.

> Let all the house of Israel therefore know certainly that God has made him both Lord and Christ, this Jesus whom you crucified.
> Acts 2:36

In Acts 2:36, Peter, as he was speaking before the multitude at Pentecost, declared that Jesus was both Lord and Christ. In Acts 3:14-15, Peter healed the lame man and proclaimed Jesus as the Holy and Righteous One and the Prince of Life. These were all designations of His deity. In Acts 4:12, Peter boldly announced to the Sanhedrin that only in the name of Jesus could one be saved! This can only be done by deity. In Acts 8, the eunuch from Ethiopia was reading a messianic passage from Isaiah. Philip revealed that it referred to Jesus as the Messiah. This was the proclamation of His deity. From chapter nine through the entire book, Paul receives Christ and preaches His deity. Luke's book of Acts has numerous examples which Luke provides.

Now, Christ's humanity is assumed but critical. Though Christians must proclaim the Lord's deity, they may have to declare that He was also fully human, if it becomes an issue. Most have no problem with Jesus being a man of history. Jesus Christ was fully God and fully man. This belief in His full humanity as essential to saving faith was declared when aberrations of this truth rose in the church (1 John 4:2; 2 John 1:7; Hebrews 5:7; Philippians 2:7).

> *Key Concept: True evangelism involves proclaiming that Christ is the Son of God, one with the Father.*

The Proclamation of Christ as Savior

Jesus must be proclaimed as the Savior of the world. In Luke 19:10, Jesus Himself said that He had come to save all those who were lost. In Matthew 1:21, an angel of the Lord told Joseph to name the baby in Mary's womb Jesus because He will save His people from their sins. In Romans 5:8-11, the apostle wrote that Christians were saved by His death on the cross, justified by His blood, reconciled to God, and also delivered from the wrath to come.

Paul told the Corinthians he desired only to preach Jesus Christ and Him crucified (1 Corinthians 2:2). Jesus was His humanity and Christ was His deity. The cross spoke of Jesus being the Savior. In Colossians 2:13-15, Paul declared that though believers were dead in their sins, Christ made them alive. Jesus forgave all their trespasses and took all of the ordinances of God which was against them and nailed them to the cross. All of their sins, whether they are in the past, in the present, or in the future, are forgiven.

Yet, this is not enough. Jesus must be proclaimed as the only Savior and the only way to heaven.

> Jesus said to him, "I am the way, the truth, and the life. No one comes to the Father, except through me."
>
> John 14:6

In John 14:6, Jesus told his disciples that He was going into heaven to prepare a place for them all. When Thomas asked what the way was to get there, Jesus testified that He was the way, truth, and life. Then Jesus pronounced that no one came to the Father, except through Him. In Acts 4:12, Peter preached to the Sanhedrin that Christ had the full authority to save. He asserted that there was no other name that men could call upon to be saved.

In John 5:23, Jesus explicitly stated that unless He was honored as the Son, no one could honor the Father who sent Him. Christ is to be proclaimed as only Savior of the world. As Christians share the gospel, they must let the unsaved know that Christ died for all their sins on the cross and is the only way to heaven. Often, believers are accused of being too narrow in the faith, when it was actually Jesus Himself who claimed to be the narrow way. They simply proclaim what He said!

> *Key Concept: True evangelism involves proclaiming that Jesus Christ is the only Savior of the World.*

The Proclamation of Christ as Lord

Jesus must be proclaimed as Lord. This speaks of Christ's authority in relationship to His people. It speaks of entering into a relationship of obedience with Jesus Christ. He is not only the Savior but also the Lord. The key word referring to Jesus in the New Testament is "Lord," and it literally means master. The proclamation of the gospel involves declaring Jesus as Lord as well as Savior. In Matthew 3:3, the author describes John the Baptist as preparing the way for the Lord. In Matthew 7:20, Jesus refers to Himself as Lord. In Matthew 28:18, Jesus asserted that all authority had been given to Him on Earth and in heaven. This refers to His Lordship overall. There are numerous passages where the Lord declared and demonstrated His full authority over nature (John 6:16-21; Mark 11:12-20), disease (Matthew 4:23-24; Luke 6:17-19), sin (Mark 2:5; Luke 7:49), evil angels (Matthew 8:16), and death (John 11:17-44; Luke 7:14). His Lordship is a critical part of the message of the gospel and cannot be left out.

In Acts 2:36, Peter declared that all of Israel needed to know that God had made Jesus both Christ and Lord. Both terms are used. In Acts 4:33, Luke describes the apostles' proclamation of the gospel. He speaks of them witnessing to the resurrection of the Lord. Here again, Jesus is proclaimed as Lord which is an essential part of the gospel message.

In Acts 11:20, witnessing is termed "preaching the Lord Jesus."

> But there were some of them, men of Cyprus and Cyrene, who, when they had come to Antioch, spoke to the Hellenists, preaching the Lord Jesus.
>
> Acts 11:20

In Acts 13:12, the gospel is called the preaching of the Lord. In Ephesians 1:20-23, Paul asserts that Christ is the Lord of all. He is the only one with the authority to save, judge, and rule forever. Jesus is the only one with the right to demand allegiance and command obedience. This is a crucial element of the gospel because it produces the obedience that is the foundation of the true Christian life.

In James 2:17, the brother of Jesus declared that true faith without works is dead, being by itself. Faith always brings forth obedience. Jesus told his followers that the proof of a saint's true discipleship would be the bearing of much fruit (John 15:8) and would be the natural result of their love for Him (John 14:23). John the Baptist told his audience to bring forth fruit in keeping with their true repentance (Matthew 3:8). Fruit proves this true repentance. The Lordship of Jesus must be declared to bring forth not only true repentance but obedience. The knowledge that Jesus is Lord produces the fruit of obedience as Christians submit themselves to Him.

Key Concept: True evangelism involves proclaiming that Christ is Lord.

The Defense of Christ as God

In the gospel message, the presentation of evidence for the deity of Christ is a given. Jesus proved His deity through the performance of many signs and miracles, the fulfillment of prophecies (both Old Testament and His own), and His resurrection from the dead. Of course, His resurrection was his greatest miracle and fulfillment of prophecy.

First, Jesus performed numerous miracles to confirm His deity. In Matthew 4:23, the apostle records that the Lord preached the gospel and healed the sick. This was His usual method of evangelism. The Lord would proclaim His deity and prove it through miracles. In Matthew 11:4-6, when John the Baptist sent his followers to inquire as to Christ's deity, Jesus spoke of the miracles that He performed: He healed the sick, made the lame walk, the blind to see, the deaf to hear, and the mute to speak. In John 5:36, the Lord challenged the Jewish people to consider the works (miracles) He had done as a testimony to His deity.

Second, Jesus fulfilled numerous prophecies in order to demonstrate that He was the Son of God. The Lord fulfilled most Old Testament prophecies through God's providence (Micah 5:2; Psalm 72:10; Jeremiah 31:15; Hosea 11:1; Isaiah 9:1-2). Others, Christ fulfilled intentionally and deliberately (Luke 4:21; John 2:22; 13:18; 17:12; 19:28). He also predicted events that would occur that were fulfilled in His final week (Matthew 26:1-2, 6-12; John 3:14-15; 8:28-29; 12:23-24).

Third, Jesus resurrected from the dead to demonstrate His deity. This fulfilled many prophecies and proved His deity. His resurrection was predicted in the Old Testament (Job 19:25-26; Psalm 16:8-11; 22:19-24; Isaiah 53:10-11) and it was fulfilled with evidence in the New Testament (1 Corinthians 15:5-11; Matthew 28:9-10). Luke begins Acts by stating that the Lord appeared to His disciples after His resurrection for a period of forty days and provided many proofs that He was truly alive from the dead (Acts 1:3).

Before His resurrection, Christ proclaimed to the Jewish people that He would fulfill a critical prophecy from their Scriptures which would be a sign for them identifying Him as the true Messiah. The prophecy was the sign of Jonah. As Jonah was in the sea creature three days and three nights, so would He be in the Earth three days and three nights. The implication was that as Jonah was spewed forth onto the sand, so would Christ be spewed forth from the Earth and rise from the dead (Matthew 12:39-40; 16:4; Luke 11:29). This was an important element in His gospel message.

On other occasions, He predicted His own resurrection. Jesus declared that if they destroyed the temple, He would rebuild it in three days. Jesus was referring to His death and resurrection. This analogy confounded the Jewish people because they thought the Lord meant their physical temple. Yet, this prediction was often mentioned in His preaching. This is obvious because the prophecy was so well known.

The knowledge of this prediction about the temple was so widespread, it was used by the false witnesses against Jesus at His trial as words of sedition against the Jews (Matthew 26:61; Mark 14:58). These words were a part of the insults by the people walking by Jesus while He was on the cross. They mentioned this prediction demanding He prove He was the Son of God by coming down from the cross (Matthew 27:39-40; Mark 15:29). John acknowledges that when Christ had risen from the dead, the disciples remembered this prophecy and believed in Him. This was an important element in His message (John 2:18-22).

In Luke 24:25-27, there were two on the road to Emmaus who encountered the risen Christ, but they did not know it. These two men were confused as to who Christ was and the events that had just unfolded in Israel. Jesus rebuked them because they did not believe the prophets and what had just been fulfilled concerning His suffering and resurrection. The chastisement did not happen because they did not know; it occurred because they didn't believe. These prophecies were well known in Israel. Then, He explained how Jesus had fulfilled many of the prophecies in the Old Testament. Later, He revealed Himself to them, and they went immediately to His disciples. They described what happened and declared that Jesus was indeed alive. This proclamation of fulfilled prophecy and the physical proof that He had risen from the dead was extremely important to the Lord.

Not only did Jesus proclaim His deity and demonstrate it through His miracles, His fulfillment of prophecy, and His resurrection, but His disciples were told to proclaim what they had seen in Him. They were commanded to share His message and the proofs of His deity to those in Jerusalem, Judea, Samaria, and all the Earth (Acts 1:8). This is exactly what they did. He told them they would be His "witnesses." They were simply to share what they had seen and heard.

John, the apostle explains this commission by Christ to his readers in 1 John 1:1-2.

> "That which was from the beginning, that which we have heard, that which we have seen with our eyes, that which we saw, and our hands touched, concerning the Word of life 2 (and the life was revealed, and we have seen, and testify, and declare to you the life, the eternal life, which was with the Father, and was revealed to us)."
>
> John 1:1-2

The disciples heard Christ's message and saw His many miracles and His fulfillment of numerous prophecies. They talked and walked with Him after His resurrection. He gave them many convincing proofs. All of this was experienced by all their senses. They saw Him with their own eyes, heard Him with their own ears, and touched Him with their own hands. Then they merely declared Christ, His message, and these proofs to everyone they encountered. The four gospel writers appealed to the miracles, fulfilled prophecies, and the resurrection in their evangelistic messages.

Since Christians today are not eyewitnesses, what should they do about confirming and defending the faith? Consider Luke, who also was not an eyewitness. Yet, in Luke 1:1-4, the author explains that he investigated carefully all that had happened from actual eyewitness accounts. This way his readers would know with certainty that Christ was the Son of God. Christians should study carefully these proofs and use them in their gospel presentations as Luke did.

> *Key Concept: True evangelism involves proclaiming Christ's miracles, fulfilled prophecies, and most of all the resurrection which confirms His deity.*

The Proclamation of a Relationship with Christ

Christ isn't simply an historical man of the past, nor is He a distant God of the present but the God-Man, risen, alive, and desirous of a real relationship with people. The essence of Christianity is not just obeying a list of precepts but, more importantly, following a person in a relationship with Him. Though the Scriptures do not utilize the word relationship, it assumes it. John distinctly said in 1 John 5:11-13 that if one has (possesses) the Son, one has (possesses) eternal life.

In Matthew 7:23, Jesus speaks of the end, when some will come to Him and call for Him as Lord. He will say that they are to go away because He never "knew" them. The word "know" in that passage means an experiential knowledge which is more than intellectual. The Septuagint uses this key Greek term to characterize the intimacy between a man and woman. It is a relational knowing. Christians know of many historical figures, but they do not have a have a relationship of love, faith, and obedience with them. Some grow up with some knowledge of Jesus but do not trust Him as Savior or obey Him as Lord. They know only "of Him."

In Revelation, Jesus discusses His relationship with two churches. In Revelation 2:4, the Lord accuses the church at Ephesus of departing from their first love. Their motivation in their persistence and endurance was no longer love for

Him. True Christians are in love with Jesus Christ. This is an authentic relationship. In Revelation 3:16, Jesus charges the church in Laodicea with being lukewarm. They were neither hot nor cold toward Him. In verse 20, He offers those in the church a relationship with Him when he proclaims that He is standing at the door and knocking. If people in the church "hear" His voice and "open" the door, Christ will "dine" with them. These are relationship words.

In 1 John 1:3, John indicates that he proclaimed the gospel to them so they could fellowship with Jesus Christ.

> That which we have seen and heard we declare to you, that you also may have fellowship with us. Yes, and our fellowship is with the Father, and with his Son, Jesus Christ.
>
> 1 John 1:3

Fellowship speaks of a relationship. In Matthew 22:37, when He was asked about the greatest commandment, the Lord declared that it was to love God with all one's heart, soul, and mind. In Mark 12:30, Mark adds some additional aspects of this love, "'You shall love the Lord your God with all your heart, and with all your soul, and with all your mind, and with all your strength.' This is the first commandment." Is this not a description of a meaningful relationship? When Christians share the good news, they are actually offering a real relationship with Jesus Christ and with His Father. No one can bypass Jesus Christ and go to the Father directly. In John 5:23, Jesus says that honoring Him honors the Father. One cannot have a relationship with almighty God apart His Son. They come as a package with the Spirit.

> *Key Concept: True evangelism involves proclaiming a love relationship with Jesus when one receives Him as Savior and Lord.*

SHARING THE GOSPEL: THE DOCTRINE OF EVANGELISM

The Proclamation of Faith Alone

Another element in the proclamation of the gospel is the declaration that only faith in Jesus Christ alone saves. This is apart from works. People cannot work their way into God's heaven. Good works are always a result of salvation. Over and over, Jesus declared that one must believe in Him to be saved.

> For God so loved the world, that he gave his one and only Son, that whoever believes in him should not perish, but have eternal life.
> John 3:16

In John 3:16, Jesus told Nicodemus that whoever believes in Him will have eternal life. In John 4:39, John describes the salvation of the Samaritans, who had been brought to the well by the Samaritan woman, as believing in Him. In John 6:29, Jesus told His listeners that they must believe in Him who God sent. In John 6:35, Jesus declared that He was the bread of life, and they must believe in Him for eternal life. Research in a concordance of the biblical word "believe" in the Gospel of John by itself will yield passage after passage which emphasizes belief alone.

The apostles claimed that belief was the essential element, not works. In Acts 4:4, Luke describes those who were saved as those who had believed. In Acts 5:14, Luke declares that multitudes had believed. In Acts 8:37, when the eunuch from Ethiopia heard the gospel, he confessed that he believed that Jesus Christ was the Son of God. Peter preached to Cornelius that anyone who believes in Christ receives forgiveness of sins. In Acts 16:36, Paul told the Philippian jailer and all of his household that they must believe in the Lord Jesus Christ to be saved. Over and over, belief in Jesus Christ alone is proclaimed. Works were always a result, the fruits of belief.

The Lord Jesus spoke often concerning the producing of fruit in keeping with true faith. In Matthew 13:23, the Lord compared believers to good seeds that always produce the fruit of righteous deeds by their faith. In John 15:2, Jesus compares Himself to a vine and His true followers as those branches which produce fruit. If His branches abide in Him, they will bear much fruit because apart from Him they can do nothing (John 15:5). This is different than submission to Christ as Lord. The submission to Jesus as Lord is the saving response and obedience is the result.

Key Concept: True evangelism involves proclaiming salvation by faith alone with works as a result.

The Proclamation of Water Baptism

An additional element that is often left out in discussions of salvation messages is the teaching that Christians must immediately respond to their salvation by being baptized. Baptism in water does not save. God desires new believers to proclaim their new faith in Christ to the world through water baptism. It must become the initial response a believer makes in His obedience to Christ as Lord of his life.

Water baptism was continually declared and practiced as the initial response after someone becomes a Christian. One believes, and then one is baptized. When John the Baptist prepared the people for the coming Messiah, he proclaimed that all should repent and be baptized (Matthew 3:6, 11; Mark 1:5; Luke 3:2-3; John 1:26). In fact, John preached at the river Jordan, so he could baptize all those who responded immediately after their repentance. This was John's pattern.

There are many examples where water baptism is claimed as the initial response to salvation. In Acts 10:47, once the

Holy Spirit had entered into Cornelius and his household, indicating belief in Christ, Peter ordered them to be baptized and they were. In Acts 8:35-36, Philip is sent to the Ethiopian eunuch and shares the good news with him. As soon as the eunuch believes, he asks Philip to be baptized.

> Philip opened his mouth, and beginning from this Scripture, preached to him Jesus. As they went on the way, they came to some water, and the eunuch said, "Behold, here is water. What is keeping me from being baptized?"
>
> Acts 8:35-36

How did the eunuch know that he must be baptized? Philip explained this during his gospel presentation.

In Acts 22:16, Paul describes his baptism by Ananias. As soon as Paul's blindness was removed by the prophet, he demanded that Paul rise and be baptized. In fact, he asked Paul why he was delaying. Here this prophet proclaimed the baptism that was to proceed immediately after faith in Jesus Christ. Baptism follows but does not save.

Then what is baptism, its purpose, and why is it so closely linked to salvation? The Lord Jesus Christ desires for His people to announce their newly obtained salvation to the saints and the world through the outward sign of baptism. Therefore, baptism was to be practiced in public for all to see. The immersion in the water was to signify that they had died to their old lives and been raised to new ones through Christ's death and resurrection (Romans 6:4). This becomes the concluding remarks in one's gospel presentation. Though not often done, it is the biblical pattern.

Another important purpose is to have new saints publicly identify themselves with others in His church, the body of

Christ (1 Corinthians 12:13). Wherever the unsaved travel in the world, they should constantly be viewing new Christians being baptized by believers in public view. This means in numerous streams, lakes, rivers, and oceans not in buildings that cannot be viewed by all whether they know the person or not. People should see the outward sign of other people being cleansed from sin and becoming brand-new creations. This is the testimony of baptism the Lord God demands. Then those same people should be able to watch the old lives of those being baptized pass away and their new lives come as they live righteously for Him (2 Corinthians 5:17)! This is exactly what the people in the first century saw.

Since water baptism should proceed immediately after salvation, some have mistakenly thought it was an actual element of the salvation process. This could not be further from the truth. Baptism does not save. It is the outward sign of the believer's inward faith. It was always proclaimed in the good news as the first act of faith after salvation. As a result, Christians should proclaim the gospel and explain the concept of baptism within it. Then they should urge the new Christian to be baptized as soon as possible for the world to see.

Key Concept: True evangelism involves proclaiming water baptism as the first response to salvation.

Chapter 9

The Proper Methods

The good news can be presented and shared in a variety of ways and for many different reasons. These methods and motivations can honor or dishonor the Lord. Some believers have the mistaken notion that the gospel can be presented with any motive or method as long as "people get saved." This could not be further from the truth. Paul encountered many people who shared the gospel in shameful ways and with unrighteous motives and condemned them.

The first is found in Philippians 1:15-18. Paul describes a group of people who were sharing the gospel due to envy, rivalry, and selfish ambition. These evangelists wanted to see more people come to Christ and create a status above Paul in the Roman church. Paul exposes their selfish motives and condemns them. The gospel of Jesus Christ is a divine message of self-sacrifice and glorifying God, not a human message of selfishness and glorifying oneself.

What Christians think and why they share the gospel is important to God. The second through eighth are found in 1 Thessalonians 2:3-6. Here, the apostle Paul describes several other improper attitudes or presentations as he contrasts his method of holy preaching of the good news with those who had wicked motives and inappropriate presentations toward the Thessalonians.

Second, the true gospel should be presented without error according to the truths in the Scriptures. Third, saints are not to announce the plan with impurity but with pure motives. Fourth, the gospel should not be shared in deceit or with trickery but in truthfulness. Fifth, believers should not seek the favor of men in the presentation of the gospel but seek the approval of the Lord. The offense of the gospel cannot be removed.

Sixth, saints should not evangelize by relying on flattering speech but proclaim judgment for unbelief and salvation for belief. Seventh, the gospel should never be presented with a pretext for greed or for personal gain. The gospel should bring the gain of salvation for those who hear. Eighth, the gospel should never be heralded for personal glory but for the glory of the Almighty.

In 1 Corinthians 2:1-5, the apostle Paul describes several more inappropriate motives or behavior in the sharing of the gospel. Ninth, the gospel should not be presented in such a way as to appeal to the wisdom of man. The gospel is the wisdom of God and stands alone. Tenth, the gospel should not be shared in cleverness of speech. The Holy Spirit uses the simple message to convince and convert unbelievers not human persuasion.

In 2 Corinthians 2:17, Paul discloses the eleventh one. The gospel is not to be a money-making device, which is sold like various wares. The apostle never shared the good news like others who were simply peddling the Word of God. In 1 Thessalonians 1:5-7, the inspired writer discloses two more principles which govern motives and behavior. Twelfth, the good news should not be preached out of an unrighteous lifestyle but out of a devoted holy life, providing many good examples to follow. Thirteen, the good news should not be shared out of pity or disgust but from love and affection as a nursing mother cares for her babies.

These are important considerations for Christians, who are constantly being recruited for a wide variety of so-called evangelistic efforts. As a result, there are great temptations to fall into one of these offenses. These errors ought to be carefully studied and avoided at all costs. There are specific ways in which God desires His gospel to be proclaimed in Scripture. This is the key: God alone chooses how He wants His good news to be presented. The methods and motives in which the gospel is to be proclaimed are more important than the results of the proclamation. God does most of the work in salvation, and He desires things done His way.

> *Key Concept: The gospel is to be proclaimed without any envy, error, impure motives, deceit, flattering speech, greediness, desire for personal gain or glory, or dependence on human wisdom and cleverness of speech, but in holiness and love seeking the favor of God alone.*

An Individual Responsibility for the Proclamation

Every believer should take their proper responsibility for proclaiming the plan of redemption. God's perfect plan for evangelism is very, very simple. It has several basic steps. A church sends out an evangelist or missionary into an area where there are no Christians (or just a few). The evangelist or missionary wins people to Christ and equips the saints to win others to Christ. He might move on or remain. He then turns over the church to the pastor-teacher who equips the saints for the work of the ministry in the church.

The evangelist is a gifted believer in the church who wins people to Christ. In Acts 21:8, Philip is called an evangelist and went out and shared the gospel all over Samaria. Paul explains to Timothy that he needs to accomplish the work of an evangelist (2 Timothy 4:5). This young pastor was to go out and share Christ and bring them back into the church or establish a new church with these new believers. Besides this crucial responsibility, the evangelist must equip individual saints for evangelism in their own community, region, and even to the remotest parts of the Earth.

In Ephesians 4:11-12, Paul discusses exactly how Christ builds His body with the pastor-teacher and evangelist.

> He gave some to be apostles; and some, prophets; and some, evangelists; and some, shepherds and teachers; for the perfecting of the saints, to the work of serving, to the building up of the body of Christ.
> Ephesians 4:11-12

Christ's church should grow through spiritual reproduction and the mutual ministry of the saints. This is accomplished through the equipping by these two gifted leaders in the church. The evangelist and pastor-teacher are to equip the saints for the work of service to build up the body. A biblical evangelist equips the saints for the work of service outside the church and the pastor-teacher inside the church. Saints being equipped by an evangelist is absolutely essential in God's pattern of growth.

Then, the saints take over in the evangelistic process. This is found all throughout the book of Acts. In Acts 13:1-4, the church at Antioch sent Paul and Barnabas out to win people to Christ and plant churches. They went to Seleucia, then Cyprus (Acts 13:4). They preached the gospel in Salamis (Acts 13:5) then onto the island of Paphos (Acts 13:6). Then they traveled to Perga, and from there to Antioch of Pisidia (Acts 13:14). After these cities, Paul ventured into Iconium, Lycaonia, Lystra, Derbe, and the surrounding region (Acts 13:51-14:5). After he finished up in Derbe (Acts 14:20), he went back to those same cities, checked on their progress, exhorted them, and appointed elders (Acts 14:21-23). From this point, how did the churches grow? Did they find friends going to another church and attract them to come to theirs? No, they went out sharing the gospel.

The same process also occurred in the city of Philippi. In Acts 16, Paul enters Philippi and begins to preach the gospel (verses 11-13). He won Lydia to Christ (verse 14), possibly a demon-possessed fortune-telling slave girl (verse 18), and definitely the Philippian jailer. With them came the entire household of that jailer (verses 31-33). This was the core of the church. How did the church grow from a small handful of people? Obviously, those saints shared the good news. What else would they have done? They would not have waited for Paul to return and share the gospel again. Later, he went back to check on them (Acts 20:1-6).

The clearest example of saints sharing the gospel is found in Acts 17:1-10. Paul arrived in Thessalonica, preached the gospel and won people to Christ. Due to persecution, he stayed only a short time. He then left Timothy to equip all of them. What happened next is marveled at by the apostle. In 1 Thessalonians 1:8, the gospel had sounded out from them all over Macedonia and Achaia and everywhere their faith went. They were totally on fire for Christ and took their individual responsibility for sharing the gospel.

Notice, there are no examples of saints inviting them to church for the pastor to share the gospel with them. The saints went out from the church and shared the gospel. The evangelist equipped the saints to do this. The pastor-teacher was to equip the saints for ministry in the church.

> *Key Concept: Christians should share God's gospel with the world as they are trained, supported, and encouraged by an evangelist in their local church.*

An Individual Personal Evangelistic Strategy

In the New Testament, there are examples of many saints who simply went about proclaiming the gospel in a simple, upfront way. In Acts 8:4, Luke writes that those who were scattered due to Saul's intense persecution went about and preached the gospel. The saints were scattered and shared the gospel. In the letter of 1 Thessalonians 1:8, Paul tells the church the Word of the Lord was declared in Macedonia and Achaia and wherever their faith toward God had gone out. Christians were sharing the gospel. Every New Testament example demonstrates a simple up-front presentation.

There are other saints (including the apostles) who had a personal evangelistic strategy. They desired to establish a regular plan of action. This usually consisted of determining to whom they would witness and how they would make the opportunity to present the gospel.

Matthew delineates the evangelistic strategy of John the Baptist in Matthew 3:1-6. John went about in the wilderness of Judea, dressed in camel's hair, eating locusts and honey, and proclaimed that the kingdom of God was at hand. Why? John was a prophet (Matthew 11:9) and took a Nazarite vow to live a life of purity and devotion to God (Luke 1:13-15). This did not allow for the drinking of wine or the cutting of hair. John desired also to live an austere life as a witness to others which explains the camel's hair and his wilderness living. This contrasted John with the false and overindulgent leaders of the day. Then he proclaimed the coming Messiah.

The Lord had His own personal strategy of evangelism, which He followed His entire ministry. In Matthew 4:23, this method is described. Jesus would travel to a city. First, He entered the synagogue and preached. Then, He went into the streets, healing people, and proclaimed the kingdom of God.

> Jesus went about in all Galilee, teaching in their synagogues, preaching the Good News of the Kingdom, and healing every disease and every sickness among the people.
>
> Matthew 4:23

Paul's strategy was very similar. In Acts 17:1-2 and verse 17, Luke discloses that Paul's custom was to enter a city and begin preaching in the synagogue. Then he would go out into the marketplaces and proclaim the gospel. Why did Jesus (John 3:2) and Paul (Acts 22:3) have similar evangelistic strategies? They were both recognized as rabbis. A visiting rabbi was allowed to speak in the synagogues. They went to the streets during the week to reach the Gentiles also. In the streets and market places much discussion of events, stories, religion, and politics occurred.

Peter's strategy is described in Acts 3:1-11. Peter simply healed and preached. He was not a rabbi and did not go into the synagogues. Why was Peter the one who preached to the multitudes that gathered at Pentecost (Acts 2:14), after the healing of the lame man (Acts 3:12), and to the Sanhedrin (Acts 4:8) to name just a few? There were other apostles with him, but he was the spiritual head of the group. Also, he was a powerful speaker and willing to take bold steps for Christ.

Since Stephen and Philip were both Hellenistic Jews (Jews living in the Greek culture), they were able to minister to the Greek speaking peoples. Stephen preached to his people group while Philip proclaimed the gospel to the Samaritans, a similar group, (half-Jew, half-Greek). Since they possessed supernatural abilities, they both performed mighty miracles before they shared the gospel. They differed in that Stephen had a more public ministry (refuting the Jews in public and speaking before the Sanhedrin) and Philip a more private and personal ministry (sharing with Simon and the Eunuch).

Apollos had a gifted intellect, was a powerful orator, and was mighty in the Scriptures. Since he was unafraid of large crowds, he frequently debated the Jews in public. He was able to refute their arguments for all to see (Acts 18:24-25). As one can see from these examples, they all had strategies, but their strategies were different. These approaches were based upon their language, backgrounds, gifts, and abilities.

The Church should equip the saints to share the gospel. The saints can then develop their own strategies to proclaim this amazingly good news. Perhaps those who are orphans may share the gospel and minister to orphans. Maybe those who may have experienced a teen pregnancy might be the perfect people to bring the gospel to teens who are pregnant. Would they be able to relate to them? Yes, they would.

Those in various professions could use their achievements as opportunities to give God glory and then share the good news. An actor, musician, athlete, physician, or entrepreneur might share they're gratefulness for God's help when they achieve something. As they stand before an audience or are asked by others, the gospel could be shared.

Some think if they mention God that this is sufficient, but it is not. The Lord Jesus is the central focus of the good news. To simply mention God, they may bring to people's minds the god they believe in, which may or may not be the true God. Instead, it could be a god of their false religion or some god of their own making (Romans 1:23), essentially an idol. This does not bring God glory. Some believers in a church who may have the same language, backgrounds, gifts, and abilities could come together to evangelize as a team.

> *Key Concept: Christians should develop personal evangelistic strategies around their gifts, talents, abilities, backgrounds, ethnicities, and desires.*

A Potential Evangelistic Encounter

The apostles viewed almost every situation as a potential evangelistic encounter. Sometimes, they would create the opportunities to share the gospel. Other times, they took the opportunities when they came from the Spirit.

In Acts 2, the day of Pentecost arrived, and the disciples were in the upper room praying. Suddenly, the Spirit came. There was the sound of a violent wind and a manifestation of tongues of fire rested above each one. This drew a big crowd. What did the apostles do? Peter and the others took this crucial opportunity that God had presented and shared the gospel. They took the opportunity when it came.

In Acts 3, Peter and John encountered a crippled man as they went into the temple to pray. When he asked for alms, they instead healed him. It isn't too difficult to assume that a lame man now walking would draw a large crowd. Once the crowd had gathered around this amazing event, the apostle preached the gospel. He made the opportunity to share the gospel. Previously, we saw that the miracles of Jesus drew crowds which created opportunities to preach the gospel. They were primarily to confirm His deity but also gathered the crowds He needed to further His message.

In Acts 4, the apostle Peter was arrested and then brought before the Sanhedrin. Peter took the opportunity that was given to him and preached the gospel. In Acts 6-7, Stephen was arrested and dragged in before the Sanhedrin because he preached the gospel. This gave him another opportunity to preach it again to his accusers which he took. In Acts 10, the Lord told Cornelius to send for Peter. Peter was given an opportunity from the Lord, and he took it. He traveled to Caesarea and proclaimed the good news of Jesus Christ to Cornelius and his entire household.

SHARING THE GOSPEL: THE DOCTRINE OF EVANGELISM

In Acts 16, Paul was arrested and imprisoned in Philippi. When an Earthquake occurred, rather than escaping for his life, he utilized the situation to win the jailer and his whole household to Christ. This was not an opportunity that he planned. It was an opportunity he took. It is interesting that Paul allowed himself to be beaten and imprisoned, though He was a Roman which made this illegal. Perhaps, he sensed God was at work and let the situation play itself out. In Acts 21:27, the Jews claimed Paul had allowed a Gentile to enter the holy temple, and he was arrested. Consequently, Paul took the opportunity to share the good news with the crowd. From there, he preached the gospel to a series of prominent people: the High Priest, the Sanhedrin (Acts 23), Felix (Acts 24), Festus (Acts 25), and Herod Agrippa (Acts 26).

Before Festus in Acts 25:6-11, Paul invoked his right as a Roman citizen to appeal to Caesar and speak directly to the emperor. Every Roman citizen had this right, and Paul knew it. He obviously wanted to save this appeal for an opportune moment, if necessary. The apostle's subsequent journey to Rome had been previously prophesied to him on the road to Damascus by Jesus Himself (Acts 23:11).

After Festus asked Paul if he would be willing to go to Jerusalem to be judged, he knew the time had come. He was not only cognizant of this prophesy but had been informed that the Jews would attempt to ambush and kill him on the way. How else could the Lord have gotten His gospel to the courts of the most powerful man on Earth? The apostle had just made a critical opportunity to share the gospel.

When Paul arrived in Rome, once again, he proclaimed the gospel with anyone who would listen. Every situation became a potential evangelistic encounter. He anticipated an opportunity in every negative situation. God could and did work anywhere Paul found himself.

Paul wrote to the church at Philippi that the good news of Christ was advancing in this desperate situation.

> Now I desire to have you know, brothers, that the things which happened to me have turned out rather to the progress of the Good News; so that it became evident to the whole palace guard, and to all the rest, that my bonds are in Christ.
> Philippians 1:12-13

In Philippians 1:12-13, Paul wrote to the Philippians that many guards had heard the gospel and believed. Later, he closes his letter with a greeting from the household of Caesar (Philippians 4:22). So, Christians must also take the many opportunities the Lord may bring to proclaim the plan.

How can believers make or take these many opportunities when they arrive? First, they should pray and then watch for open doors. Paul requested that the Colossians pray that God would open up a door for the Word in Colossians 4:3. Second, they must be alert and aware of circumstances that suddenly arise where the gospel can be proclaimed. These have been mentioned earlier in the examples of Peter. Third, the apostles expected God at any time to place them into situations in which they could make or take an opportunity. They were not caught off guard. Jesus told them that they would be His witnesses (Acts 1:8), and they expected God to work. Christians should expect and experience the same.

Fourth, evangelism was a way of life. Paul declared to the Corinthians that he did all things for the sake of the good news so he could become a fellow-partaker of the gospel (1 Corinthians 9:23). As the saints were persecuted in the city of Jerusalem, they fled. Everywhere these saints traveled, they preached the gospel (Acts 8:4).

SHARING THE GOSPEL: THE DOCTRINE OF EVANGELISM

Key Concept: Christians should be alert, aware, and prepared for various opportunities to share the good news brought by the Spirit.

A Manifestation of Spiritual Gifts

When believers are sharing the gospel, they need spiritual power to see souls saved which comes from the Holy Spirit. The Holy Spirit works through His Word and prayer, but He also empowers His people through supernatural spiritual gifts. As Christians develop personal evangelistic strategies and make or take the numerous opportunities to share the gospel, they should and must be ministering in the area of their spiritual gifts. The main biblical passages discussing gifts of the Spirit are 1 Corinthians 12-14, Romans 12:4-8, 1 Peter 4:10-11, and Ephesians 4:11-16. This is often left out.

Every single Christian is given a spiritual gift in order to minister to the Body of Christ (the church). These spiritual gifts are supernatural abilities which should be employed in both bringing people into Christ's church (evangelism) and ministering to them (edification). Believers should consider using their gifts both inside and outside the church.

At salvation, individual believers are given at least one of the spiritual gifts for the common good. This would include saving and maturing. These gifts may or may not be tied to one's ability or personality. Gifts are given to every believer by the Spirit according to God's divine will.

Paul indicates that these gifts are manifestations of God's Holy Spirit.

> Now there are various kinds of gifts, but the same Spirit. There are various kinds of service,

and the same Lord. There are various kinds of workings, but the same God, who works all things in all. But to each one [saint] is given the manifestation of the Spirit for the profit of all.
1 Corinthians 12:4-7

In 1 Corinthians 12:4-7, Paul asserts that there are a variety of gifts used in a wide variety of ministries having a variety of effects. Yet, they are all manifestations of the Holy Spirit. When the saints are exercising their different gifts, everyone is viewing the Holy Spirit at work.

Sometimes, similarly gifted people may develop a gospel ministry together. At other times, a ministry may demand a variety of gifts to function. If the saints are ministering the gospel to older folks in a retirement center, they will need Christians with the gifts of mercy, service, or helps. If the church desires to feed those in need and share the gospel, they will need the gifts of leadership and administration to organize the event, the gifts of service to feed those in need, the gift of giving to provide the food and other expenses, and the gifts of teaching or exhortation to share the gospel with the crowd all together. Identifying the spiritual gifts of all the members of a local church is essential for developing evangelistic ministries needed to reach the unsaved.

How can the saints determine their spiritual gifts? Within the life of Spirit-filled righteousness, believers should begin examining their spiritual capabilities as they explore their use in a variety of ministries. These saints should consider their competency in expressing the gifts (Acts 6:1-6; 18:24-25) and the kinds of fruit that are produced (2 Corinthians 3:1-3; Romans 1:13). Their gifts should align with the desires, concerns, and burdens of their own hearts (Romans 10:1; 1 Corinthians 9:16). Their specific gifts should be confirmed by the saints who have similar giftedness (1 Corinthians 14:29), spiritual and biblical wisdom (Proverbs 1:5; 15:22), and those who are in authority (1 Peter 5:1-5; Hebrews 13:17).

Key Concept: Christians should carefully determine their spiritual gifts and then utilize them in sharing the gospel.

A Contact with the Unsaved

One must their spend time with unbelievers to share the good news. Jesus interacted quite often with unbelievers and treated them with compassion (Matthew 9:35-38) and love (Mark 10:21-22). The Lord ate with them (Luke 5:29), had discussions with them (Matthew 9:3-6), taught them (Mark 4:1-2), met their personal needs (Luke 17:12-14), attended their weddings (John 2:1-4) and funerals (Matthew 9:23-26), and even served them (Matthew 15:32). He spent time with them on a regular basis and they desired the same. This does not mean the Lord was ever "bound together" with them (1 Corinthians 6:14). Christ spent time with them to preach the kingdom, but none were his close friends. The closest an unbeliever ever came to Jesus was Judas who pretended to believe. Christians should spend their time with unbelievers to share the gospel and with other believers for fellowship.

Matthew, who was a scorned tax-gatherer, invited many of his friends and acquaintances to his house for a meal and to hear the Lord Jesus.

> It happened as he sat in the house, behold, many tax collectors and sinners came and sat down with Jesus and his disciples. When the Pharisees saw it, they said to his disciples, "Why does your teacher eat with tax collectors and sinners?" When Jesus heard it, he said to them,

"Those who are healthy have no need for a physician, but those who are sick do."
Matthew 9:10-12

In Matthew 9:10-12, the Lord went to share the gospel with them. The Pharisees rebuked Him for eating with sinners and Jesus responded. He told them that the righteous do not need Him, but sinners do. Jesus dined with a man named Zacchaeus, a sinner, in Luke 19:10. Once again, He was rebuked, but Jesus told them that He had come to seek and save the lost. Christians have to seek and save the lost.

Those who do not know and love the Lord Jesus Christ have to be sought out. Most will never come to a church to hear the pastor preach the gospel. Christians will have to depart from their churches and venture out into the world.

In Matthew 4:23, the apostle describes Jesus preaching the gospel all throughout Galilee. He went where they lived! Throughout the book of Acts, Paul traveled to numerous regions where the unsaved lived to share the gospel with them. He found unbelievers in the many different marketplaces buying, selling, and socializing. Paul entered into the midst of them and began to share the Word. What better place to go? This was where the unbelievers were frequently gathered. This was where life was being lived.

Christians must seek the unsaved in their neighborhoods, clubs, associations, and other organizations to which they belong and share the gospel. Christians may inadvertently become isolated from the unsaved world as they spend more and more time with family members and church friends. They lose the opportunity of sharing the good news because they no longer know any unsaved people. The saints must maintain or develop new relationships with unbelievers in order to share the gospel with them.

SHARING THE GOSPEL: THE DOCTRINE OF EVANGELISM

Key Concept: Christians should have contact with the unsaved regularly to proclaim the plan to them.

An Individually Tailored Presentation

In the New Testament, the same essential saving elements are found in every presentation of the gospel. Yet, they were all very different. One will not find in the Scriptures any two gospel presentations which were exactly the same. In John 3:1-5, Nicodemus, an important teacher in Israel, came to Jesus to speak with Him. Jesus presented the gospel as being born again with both water and the Spirit. Jesus expected Nicodemus to know the passage he was referring to (Ezekiel 36:25-27). In this passage, God says He will cleanse His holy people with water and the Spirit to give them a new heart.

In John 4:6-10, Jesus was sitting at a well and proclaimed the gospel to a Samaritan woman who had come to draw some water. Christ described Himself as having living water (the gospel) which sprang into eternal life. The Samaritan woman was poor and ignorant of the Scriptures. He was sitting in front of a well. She had come to draw water. This became the perfect opportunity to utilize the situation to His advantage. He simply began to speak of a different kind of water that He could offer her.

Peter had a different situation occur. In Acts 2:14-16, Peter began his presentation with what was happening at that very moment.

> But Peter, standing up with the eleven, lifted up his voice, and spoke out to them, "You men of Judea, and all you who dwell at Jerusalem, let this be known to you and listen to my words. For these aren't drunken as you suppose seeing

it is only the third hour of the day. But this is what has been spoken through...Joel."

Acts 2:14-16

There was a loud noise like a wind, and they were speaking in various languages that they did not know. This was the fulfillment of a prophecy by the Holy Spirit. His listeners, who had gathered, were devout Jews who had come to celebrate the feast of Pentecost. They would have known the prophecy.

In Acts 3:12, Peter preached the gospel beginning with the power and name of Jesus. He had been put to death and rose again, and it was His power that healed the lame man. The one who was now walking. There had been only a very short time since Christ's crucifixion. They would have been very familiar with the death of Christ. In Acts 8:26-35, Philip met an Ethiopian eunuch who was reading from Isaiah, and then Philip began his presentation in that passage. The eunuch was a God-fearing Gentile; he was familiar with prophecy.

In Acts 13:15-23, Paul entered a synagogue on the Sabbath in Pisidian Antioch and spoke from the Old Testament and its prophecies in the scrolls in front of him. He proclaimed God's deliverance of Israel from Egypt, in the wilderness, in Canaan through the times of the judges, all throughout the entire era of the kings, and through the promised Messiah. In Nazareth, the Lord also read from the Holy Scriptures, and He proclaimed that He was the fulfillment of the many prophecies of the Old Testament (Luke 4:21). In both cases, His audience would have been devout Jews who understood all these things.

In Acts 14:8-15, Paul arrives in Lystra and heals a crippled man. A crowd gathered and declared them to be gods to which Paul preached the gospel using creation as a starting point. Paul was speaking to polytheistic heathens on the street, so he began with creation. In Acts 17:23-34 Paul enters Athens and notices the statue dedicated to an unknown god among many statutes of false deities. He then proclaimed to the people that he had come to reveal to them the identity of this unknown god. Paul realized that these intellectuals did not want to offend any god they may have forgotten and began his presentation there. In Acts 22:1-6, when Paul was arrested in Jerusalem for supposedly bringing a Gentile into the temple, Paul stood before a crowd of Jews and began with his personal testimony and how he came to Christ as a Jew in their language, which was Hebrew.

The good news is best proclaimed in response to a given situation and given context utilizing the essential elements of the gospel message. The presentation was weaved around the preacher, the one who was to hear it, and the situation in which they found themselves. Then, the essential gospel message was proclaimed. This does not mean that Christians do not have the right to simply begin with heralding their message of salvation as an ancient messenger would have done with a proclamation from a king. This is how ancient leaders communicated their people.

> *Key Concept: Christians should weave their gospel presentations around specific situations in which they encounter unbelievers.*

A Lack of Hindrance to the Gospel

Paul was extremely sensitive to people. He did not want to offend them so they would refuse to listen to the gospel. In 1 Corinthians 8-10, Paul discusses Christian liberty. Then in 1 Corinthians 10:32-33, Paul summarizes his teaching on this important aspect of Christian living.

> Give no occasions for stumbling, either to Jews, or to Greeks, or to the assembly of God; even as I also, please all men in all things, not seeking my own profit, but the profit of the many, that they may be saved.
>
> 1 Corinthians 10:32-33

Christians are to give no opportunity for stumbling to Jews, Greeks (unbelievers), or the church (believers). He desired to please all men in all things, seeking the profit of the many, not his own that the many may be saved.

In 1 Corinthians 9:12, the apostle declares that he could have asked for remuneration from them for his preaching, but he didn't. He did not want to cause a hindrance to the gospel. The context for these passages concerns Christian liberty. It is in the area of Christian liberty that believers do not want to offend those who will be hearing the gospel. The believer should be more than willing to give up whatever liberty he may have to share the gospel.

> *Key Concept: Christians should never offend the unsaved in the area of Christian liberty in their proclamation of the plan.*

Not a Lack of Offense

This hindrance has nothing to do with the offense of the good news. A gospel of sin and judgment will offend. A Son of God who dies and rises from the dead will offend. In 1 Peter 2:8, Peter declares that Christ is a stone that people will stumble over, and He is a rock that will offend them. In 1 Corinthians 1:23, Paul declared that the continual preaching of the crucifixion and person of Jesus Christ was a stumbling block to Jews and foolishness to Gentiles. When Christians preach the good news, it will offend some but to those who are being saved, it is the power of God (verse 18). Therefore, they should not water down the gospel.

> *Key Concept: The hindrance has nothing to do with the offense of the gospel because it does offend.*

Not an Issue of Holiness

This offense has nothing to do with personal holiness. Christians are not to compromise their holiness in order to keep the gospel from offending someone. They cannot sin in order to fit in. They cannot participate in evil, so the good news is then welcomed by unbelievers. Paul describes his behavior among the unsaved and the saved as being pure, holy, and with godly sincerity. His conscience testified of this, and it resulted in a real confidence (2 Corinthians 1:12). The Greek word translated by the English word "holiness" refers to being "separate from" or "wholly different" in our thoughts, words, and actions (righteous).

Paul never in any way compromised his holiness to share the gospel with the Jews and Gentiles. In fact, he went out of his way to make sure no one could accuse him of any kind of wrongdoing or evil. Christians cannot compromise their righteousness to adhere to some sinful custom or cultural activity. Righteousness should never be compromised. Jesus was accused of being a drunkard and a glutton, but these were lies. Jesus associated with the lost in order to share the good news with them (Matthew 11:19), but He did not sin with them. Christ merely associated with them.

> *Key Concept: The hindrance has nothing to do with the holiness of believers because personal holiness is never compromised.*

Not a Problem of Doctrine

This hindrance has nothing to do with sound doctrine. A group of false teachers had unknowingly crept into Galatia and demanded that all Gentile believers become God-fearing Jews first, then believers. All these false teachers promoted circumcision, legalism, and ritual among the Christians. In Galatians 2:4-5, Paul stands against these false teachers who wanted to bring them into bondage.

In Acts 15, at the end of his first missionary journey, Paul settled into Antioch, and these same kinds of teachers came into their congregation. So, Paul stood against them. In verse 2, Luke states, "Therefore when Paul and Barnabas had no small discord and discussion with them." Paul did not just say, "Let's all get along." He was unwilling to compromise in any way. This forced the church in Antioch to send them to the apostles in Jerusalem to resolve the issue. When it comes to truth, Christians cannot compromise in order to prevent an offense of the gospel. Yes, there are doctrines that appear intolerant and narrow to unbelievers but ignoring them will not take the offense away. It will only postpone it.

> *Key Concept: The hindrance has nothing to do with compromising doctrine because sound doctrine is never to be compromised.*

A Removal of Christian Liberty

Finally, the hindrance to which Paul is speaking does not involve the offense of the gospel, personal holiness, or sound doctrine. Instead, it involves the area of Christian liberty. Paul defined Christian liberty in 1 Corinthians 8:8-9, when he discussed the eating of meat that had been sacrificed to idols and then sold in the marketplace. In verses 4-7, Paul disclosed that there were some who lacked knowledge and would never eat any meat sacrificed to idols because they thought it defiled them. He explains that there was really no defilement due to the idol being nothing. Then in verses 8-9, he makes an important general statement when he asserts that eating any particular food did not commend Christians to their God. Their relationship to the Lord is not better or worse for it. Caution should be taken because this liberty might be a stumbling block to the weak. Christian liberty involves things that are basically spiritually neutral. They will not spiritually help believers, nor will they actually hinder believers, such as food.

One more important thought. Christians may not show "solidarity" to another religion by engaging in one of their idolatrous practices. In 1 Corinthians 10:14, Paul commands the saints to flee from idolatry. John utters almost the exact same exhortation in 1 John 5:21. Here, he indicates that they should guard themselves from idolatry. In fact, idolatry is listed as one of the deeds of the flesh (sins) in Galatians 5:20. Believers cannot participate in false religious rituals because these are from the doctrines of demons (1 Timothy 4:1). They would be a part of demonic worship.

Paul continued this critical thought in Romans 14:23. He exhorted the Romans not to eat any food if they had doubts. This eating would not come from faith. What does not come from faith is sin for them. According to 1 Corinthians 2:9-12, if Christians know that something within their Christian liberty is seen as a sin to another person, they should not do it. This encourages that weaker person to sin.

Another area of Christian liberty involves the rights saints have that could be set aside so the spread of the gospel is not hindered. The example Paul used in 1 Corinthians 9, was his right to earn a living from his proclaiming of the gospel. Many false teachers were preaching among the churches for the purpose of peddling God's Word and attempting to gain money from the gospel (2 Corinthians 2:17). Paul refused to be accused of this sinful behavior, so Paul worked with his own hands to support himself. In verses 13-15, he set aside that right. Now there would be no offense and no hindrance.

Another area of the believer's liberty involves man-made customs, manners, and social etiquette. Christians are not bound by these practices. In Philippians 3:20, Paul says, "For our citizenship is in heaven, from where we also wait for a Savior, the Lord Jesus Christ." We are free from all these Earthly things. Nevertheless, in Romans 12:17, Paul discloses that Christians are to respect what is right in the sight of all men. Men deem certain things as respectable, and they are to respect those things for the sake of the gospel.

In 1 Corinthians 9:19-22, Paul summarized his personal evangelistic strategy in this important area.

> For though I was free from all, I brought myself under bondage to all, that I might gain the more. To the Jews I became a Jew, that I might gain Jews; to those who are under the law, as under the law, that I might gain those who are under the law; to those who are with-out law, as without law (not being without law toward God, but under law toward Christ), that I might win those who are without law. To the weak I became as weak, that I might gain the weak. I have become all things to all men, that I may by all means save some.
> 1 Corinthians 9:19-22

He told the church at Corinth that though he was free from everything, he brought himself under bondage to win some for Christ. To the Jews, he gave up rights or took on customs that they respected. Then, he did the same for the Gentiles. To the weak, he became weak not eating certain food. He became all things to all men, so some would be won to the gospel. Then he describes the utter self-control that was needed to accomplish this by comparing the Christian life to a race.

In 1 Corinthians 10:32-33, Paul told his readers he did not want to offend or give an opportunity for their stumbling. Paul, the apostle, meant he would not offend others with spiritually neutral objects given significance by them. This also included rights that he had which others had abused or practices and customs meaningful to others.

Once again, becoming "all things to all men" will never involve the offense of the gospel, the holiness of Christians, or the true doctrines of the faith. Christians are to be careful that in their lives in the community, they do not bring some hindrance to the gospel. Christians are not to offend those who are unsaved or saved in their Christian liberty. They must be careful because they do not know whether someone in the community that they may have offended was to be brought to Christ through them.

Key Concept: Christians should try not to offend the unsaved or saved in their Christian liberty.

A Love Relationship in Christ

Christians are to portray Christ to the world by the way they interact with each other. The Lord has placed Christians into a very unique relationship with each other. Saints are called into one flock (John 10:1-15), one vine (John 15:1-10), one kingdom (Colossians 1:13), one body (1 Corinthians 12:1-27), one household and family (Ephesians 2:19), one bride betrothed to one groom (Ephesians 5:22-32), and one temple

(Ephesians 2:20-22). Regardless of their ethnicities, backgrounds, social status, and gender, they are called into one body by the Spirit. Paul declares in 1 Corinthians 12:13 that all Christians are baptized into and made to drink of one Spirit. How believers interact with one another is to be a testimony to the world. They demonstrate that Christ is alive and is at work among them. This unity can only be achieved supernaturally, and the world knows it.

In the New Testament, this important corporate witness of the early church involved the amazing fellowship that Christians were having with one another. One simply has to trace these two words with a concordance and will see the importance of these "one another" commands. Besides these commands, it involved teaching, prayer, and communion. In Acts 2, Peter standing with the others from the upper room preached a powerful sermon and about 3,000 came to Christ. What did they do after this?

In Acts 2:42-46, Luke described this amazing interaction just mentioned.

> They continued steadfastly in the apostles' teaching and fellowship, in the breaking of bread, and prayer. Fear came on every soul, and...wonders and signs were done through the apostles. All who believed were together and had all things in common. They sold their possessions and goods, and distributed them to all, according as anyone had need. Day by day, continuing steadfastly with one accord in the temple, and breaking bread at home, they took their food with gladness and singleness of heart.
> Acts 2:42-46

It involved fellowship, the breaking of bread (communion), prayer, and devotion to the teaching given by the apostles.

SHARING THE GOSPEL: THE DOCTRINE OF EVANGELISM

Every day they were meeting in the temple and each other's homes with joy and sincerity. They took care of any person having need. This was all done in public view. This had a great impact on the city. In verse 47, Luke concludes that the saints had favor with everyone, and the Lord Jesus increased their number daily.

This is seen again in Acts 4:32-36. Peter had completed his second sermon and about 5,000 were saved. This brought the size of the church to over 10,000 counting the woman and children who were saved. This great assembly of people was of one heart and soul. They met the needs of each other through the mutual sharing of things in common.

In Acts 5:1-10, Ananias and Sapphira fell dead from God's hand because the two of them had deceived the church. Yet, more importantly, they had lied to God about the profits of the land they sold for an offering. This had quite an impact on the community around them. In verses 11-16, Luke recounts that some people were too afraid to join, but others were coming to Jesus Christ. Great fear came upon everyone who heard, but all the people honored them. These actions among the saints were having a huge impact.

The gospel, which Christians preach, may cause some to call them foolish (1 Corinthians 1:23), others to claim they are mad (Acts 26:24), some to criticize and revile them for the gospel's sake (Matthew 5:11), but the unsaved world cannot criticize the fellowship believers can have together in love, sacrifice, sharing, and unity. They must do nothing else but stand in awe and respond with honor.

The world longs for what Christians are able to produce in Christ. This can only be produced through the power of the Holy Spirit. In fact, Paul lists the fruits of the Holy Spirit in Galatians 5:22-23 and most have to do with interaction with others: love, joy, peace, patience, kindness, goodness, faith, gentleness, and self-control. The evil deeds of the flesh in Galatians 5:19-21 have to do with the believer's interaction with others: adultery, sexual immorality and uncleanness, lustfulness, idolatry, sorcery (or drugs), hatred, strife, being jealous, all outbursts of anger, rivalries, divisions, heresies, being envious, murders, drunkenness, and orgies. Which of these will be a testimony to the world?

Both Jesus and Paul portray Christians as lights to the world that should shine brightly (Matthew 5:15, Philippians 2:15). As a body of believers, the saved must portray their light in the fruits of the Spirit toward one another. The early church struggled with this as Christians do today. James accused his readers of frequent fighting and arguing among themselves due to the lusts of their flesh and friendship with the world (James 4:1-6). Paul accused the saints in Corinth of having far too many divisive and contentious groups. These different groups were organized according to the teachers that they followed: Paul, Peter, Apollos, and Jesus Christ (1 Corinthians 1:10-12). They were not displaying the fruits of the Spirit for all to see. Jesus sums up this concept in John 13 in the upper room at the last supper in His parting words.

In Luke 22:24-30, the author discloses that there grew a dispute among the apostles as to who was the greatest. This dispute demonstrated the lack of a servant attitude and love. Jesus began the supper by washing the apostles' feet and then gave them a new commandment. They were to love one another as Christ had loved them. By this, the world would know that they were His disciples.

Christians are to be a part of a local congregation. How they interact with each other will testify of the authenticity of their relationship to Christ. This love should have a huge impact but so may the strife and divisions. The church will be a witness for good or bad depending on their interactions with each other.

> *Key Concept: Christians are to proclaim the gospel out of a love relationship with Christ involving sharing, sacrifice, and real unity with others in the church.*

Chapter 10

Positive Reactions

When people consider the positive reactions, others could make to Christ and His gospel, many think of the moment of salvation. Yet, the Scriptures teach and describe a variety of reactions before and after salvation. Before salvation, some may immediately believe in the gospel when they first hear, but others may need additional time. After salvation, some might respond with great joy but others in all seriousness. Many reactions are possible.

Yet, the actual response or reaction to Christ's gospel that saves people is specific and clear. There are several precise and non-negotiable responses which must occur at salvation to be truly saved. This in no way undermines the powerful and essential work of the Holy Spirit. In fact, it was His idea since He wrote the Scriptures which present it.

In Ephesians 2:4-10, Paul explains that the mercy of God was shown forth toward Christians not only giving them the grace to be saved but the very faith needed to be saved. It is all God's work. Yet, when God is at work in people's lives, they will respond in one or more of these positive ways to be saved. This next section describes different reactions, before, during, and after salvation.

The many authors of the New Testament paint one scene after another of people from every tribe, nation, and tongue responding to the gospel message positively in a multiplicity of ways. Each scene portrays the work of the Holy Spirit as He calls men unto Himself. The positive reaction at the exact moment of salvation is specific and explicit in the Scriptures.

SHARING THE GOSPEL: THE DOCTRINE OF EVANGELISM

Key Concept: Though people may react in various ways before and after salvation, there is an essential response they must make to be saved.

The Positive Reactions to the Gospel Before Belief

The process of becoming a Christian does not necessarily occur in a moment of time at the first presentation. Often, it is a pilgrimage to salvation. Salvation itself does occur in a moment of time, but it also may be the result of a series of steps someone might take in their journey to the cross. The disciples struggled for a long time in their pilgrimage to full belief in Christ. In Matthew 8:27, after Jesus had calmed a turbulent sea, the disciples responded by questioning each other. They wanted to know what kind of a man the wind and seas could obey. They had seen many miracles, heard much teaching, and yet still questioned. In Matthew 14:33, Christ's doubting disciples saw Him walk on the water and pull a doubting, disturbed Peter from the deep. Yet, they declared in amazement that Jesus truly was the Son of God! It was finally beginning to dawn on them that Jesus was the Messiah and divine.

Even after the resurrection, Thomas would not believe. He stipulated that he would not believe unless he saw the resurrected Christ and touched the wounds with his own hands. This was a bold assertion considering that after him most would never see them and believe.

> Then he [Jesus] said to Thomas, "Reach here your finger, and see my hands. Reach here your hand and put it into my side. Do not be unbelieving but believing." Thomas answered him, "My Lord and my God!"
>
> John 20:27-28

In John 20:24-28, when Thomas did meet Christ, he declared that Christ was his Lord and God! Finally, Thomas fully believed. When the disciples of the Lord received the Great Commission from the risen Jesus, Matthew disclosed that some of the eleven still doubted (Matthew 28:16-20). In Acts 1:3, Jesus spent forty days fully convincing the apostles of His resurrection, deity, and mission.

In Acts 8, the Ethiopian eunuch had been a God-fearing Gentile for some time before he was saved on the road from Jerusalem to Gaza. In Acts 10, Cornelius had been a devout God-fearing Gentile for some time before he had a divine vision to send for Peter to hear the gospel. In Thessalonica, it took over three Sabbath's of preaching before many believed (Acts 17:2-3). In Acts 17:10-12, it took many days of Scripture examination before many of the Bereans in that city would come to Christ.

As has been seen, the Holy Spirit convicts the world of sin, righteousness, and judgment (John 16:8). This may take time as He opens up the eyes of the blind (2 Corinthians 4:4) and plants the seed of the gospel in the hearts of the unsaved (1 Corinthians 1:3-7). The point is clear, some may come to Jesus Christ immediately after a presentation of the good news, but others may not. Christians should understand the variety of positive responses people make as they journey to the cross. They should not be discouraged if the unsaved do not initially come to Jesus Christ.

Yet, Christians must also acknowledge that people may have initial positive reactions to the gospel, but never come to saving faith. This becomes confusing to believers. They see these positive reactions and cannot understand how they could fall away. In Matthew 13:20-22, Jesus describes seeds that fall on the rocky places and others which fall among the thorns. Both of these seeds represent people who may make positive reactions to the good news initially but simply walk away. They may have tasted of the things of the kingdom of God but did not fully receive it into their hearts and minds (Hebrews 6:4-5).

One will fall away because the seed isn't firmly rooted, and persecution uproots it. The other will fall away because the worry of the world or the deceitfulness of riches chokes the Word in their hearts. In 1 John 2:19, the apostle John explains that they left the body of Christ because they never were really a part of the His church. Why? So, it could be demonstrated that they were not true believers.

> *Key Concept: Some might respond positively to the gospel, but not immediately come to Christ or not at all.*

A Deep Conviction

Some might respond with a deep conviction. In Luke 3:1-17, John the Baptist came preaching repentance for sin as he prepared the way for the coming of the Lord. The people responded with a deep conviction of their own sin. This led them to an important inquiry. They asked John what should be done differently as they prepared for the coming of the Messiah.

> Now when they heard this, they were cut to the heart, and said to Peter and the rest of the apostles, "Brothers, what shall we do?"
> Acts 2:37

In Acts 2:37, Peter proclaimed the resurrection of the Lord Jesus Christ, and the crowd demanded to know how they might be saved. Luke described their hearts as having been pierced. This was a deep conviction on their parts. Yet, Peter continues to preach with many other words and kept on exhorting them for some time to be saved (verse 40). They might have been convicted of their sins, but Peter felt they needed to hear more before they believed.

Conviction is not enough. They must understand the good news and believe which may require additional explanation. Some people may want or need to hear much more than the essential good news to believe. Yet, others may need some additional time to seriously think through what was said. Christians should view this as a positive response and give unbelievers all the information or time they might need to understand and believe.

> *Key Concept: Some might respond positively to the gospel by experiencing a deep conviction of sin but require more explanation or time to believe.*

A True Ignorance

Some might respond with true ignorance. There are some people who don't necessarily have a hardened heart toward God but are simply awaiting God's message about His Son. They simply do not know enough about the coming of the Messiah and His gospel. In Romans 1:20, Paul asserts that God the Father has revealed Himself clearly through His creation. Everyone begins life knowing that there is a God through the natural world that He created.

In Romans 2:14-16, the author remarks that every person has another witness to the knowledge of God besides just creation. Inside all human beings is His law (conscience) constantly convicting them of sin and indicating a coming judgment. To come to Christ, men must respond to creation

SHARING THE GOSPEL: THE DOCTRINE OF EVANGELISM

and to their conscience. They must recognize there is a God, honor Him, thank Him, and sorrow over their sin (Romans 1:21). Then in God's timetable, the gospel will be delivered to them.

Between the time of the responding and the presentation of the gospel, they may experience true ignorance as they are on their journey toward Christ. This is a positive reaction in their preparation to be saved. Paul claims he experienced this true ignorance. In Acts 22:3-10, Paul speaks to the Jews in Jerusalem of his previous zeal for God. Paul explains that he genuinely thought he was serving the true God in his faith by persecuting all the Christians. He was genuine and ignorant. The ignorance had led unfortunately to a great and powerful persecution at his hands.

In 1 Timothy 1:12, Paul discusses the abundant mercy of God in calling him to salvation.

> And I thank him who enabled me, Christ Jesus our Lord, because he counted me faithful, appointing me to service; although I was before a blasphemer, a persecutor, and insolent [spite]. However, I obtained mercy, because I did it ignorantly in unbelief.
> 1 Timothy 1:12-13

Though he was previously a blasphemer, a persecutor, and insolent, he did it ignorantly in unbelief. He did not know or understand the true gospel. He was not like the Pharisees who had fully understood the gospel and rejected it. Instead, the true knowledge of the good news did not come until he encountered the Lord Jesus Christ on the road to Damascus (Acts 9). When Saul finally heard the gospel, he immediately believed. This was the very moment that Saul's eyes were opened, and he was saved the penalty of his sins.

In Acts 19:1-7, Paul traveled to Ephesus and met several disciples of John the Baptist. These men had heard about the coming Messiah. Yet, they had not been present when John baptized the Lord Jesus as the Lamb of God. They were truly ignorant. When they heard the good news from Paul, they immediately believed. Christians may meet some who are ready but ignorant. Their genuine ignorance is a positive response to the gospel. They are on the right path, and they simply need real saving knowledge. This will require a fuller picture of Jesus than others who may have grown up with His teachings.

Still others, who may have false understandings of Jesus, will need correction concerning who Jesus really is. As Paul thought He was truly serving God, there may be those in the cults who are on a journey to the cross. These ignorant souls may require much correction of their misunderstandings of Christ to be saved.

> *Key Concept: Some might respond positively to the gospel by responding to creation and conscience but may need information concerning the good news of Jesus Christ.*

A Searching Heart

Some people might respond to the good news with hearts that are searching for the truth, and they want to continue that search with you. This is distinct from the last point, though may be connected. These kinds of people may not only be genuinely ignorant but also are searching for the truth. Paul was not searching because he thought he had found the truth. This person is honestly and truly seeking an authentic relationship with true God but needs someone to lead them to Him through His gospel.

SHARING THE GOSPEL: THE DOCTRINE OF EVANGELISM

Sergius Paulus, who resided on the island of Paphos, sent for Paul to hear the Word of God. When the apostle arrived on the island during his initial missionary journey, Elymas, the magician, thwarted his attempts. Elymas was strongly opposed to the proconsul hearing the gospel of Jesus Christ (Acts 13:6-7). Sometimes, unbelievers will come to Christians seeking answers for their hopelessness and despair.

This is evidenced in the story of the God-fearing Gentile Cornelius, who was searching for the truth.

> Now there was a certain man in Caesarea, Cornelius by name, a centurion of what was called the Italian Regiment, a devout man, and one who feared God with all his house, who gave gifts for the needy generously to the people, and always prayed to God.
>
> Acts 10:1-2

In Acts 10:1-2, the writer Luke indicates that this man was someone who was seeking after God, serving Him, and praying to Him. This centurion of the Italian Cohort had not even heard about Jesus Christ. In verses 3-5, God addresses him through an angel in a vision and directs him to send for Peter. Peter did not search for him, he found Peter. This took some time because Peter was not ready to preach the good news to the Gentiles. God had to prepare Peter through a vision. When Peter arrived, Cornelius fell down before him (Acts 10:24-33). This is a searching heart.

In Acts 28:30-31, Paul had been chained in Rome waiting to stand before Caesar. Luke testified that Paul preached the good news of the kingdom to all who came to him. The true seekers who came would have received Christ. There will be those who will come into the lives of Christians searching for God. This should be seen as a positive response.

Key Concept: Some might respond positively to the gospel by searching for the truth but may desire more time to find a person to share it.

An Honest Confusion

Some might respond with honest confusion. There may be those who may not accept Christ right away because they may be honestly confused. This was the exact predicament of the Ethiopian eunuch. As has been seen, this official was a God-fearing Gentile reading a portion of Isaiah traveling on the road from Jerusalem to Gaza. Unfortunately, the man could not understand the passage he was reading.

> Philip opened his mouth, and beginning from this Scripture, preached to him Jesus. As they went on the way, they came to some water, and the eunuch said, "Behold, here is water. What is keeping me from being baptized?"
> Acts 8:35-36

In Acts 8:35-36, the Spirit of God supernaturally transported Philip to that road in order for him to explain the passage and bring Him to Christ. His heart was right, but his mind was confused.

Even the disciples spent much of their earlier time with Jesus honestly ignorant, not always understanding His many teachings and actions. One example is found in John 6:48-69. When Jesus told His followers that they must eat his body and drink His blood to be saved, Peter did not comprehend what he meant. This was an analogy of a full relationship with Him to be saved. Many fell away, but Peter refused to leave. Why? He knew Jesus spoke the words of eternal life. Though he was ignorant of what the Lord meant, he knew with more time and explanation he would eventually come to understand. When Christians share the gospel, it might take some more time for the Spirit to open the minds of the unsaved (John 15:26; Acts 16:14). The saints must be patient as God works in the lives of those to whom they share. This may take a small or large amount of time.

> *Key Concept: Some might respond positively to the gospel by being honestly confused but may desire more clarification.*

A Continued Persuasion

Some may respond by requiring a more persuasion. This persuasion might include more biblical explanations and proofs, not the persuasion of a sales pitch. Some unbelievers will honestly listen to a presentation of the gospel but need some additional facts or proofs from the Scripture.

In Acts 17:1-2, when Paul arrived in Thessalonica, he had to reason with these citizens for three Sabbaths, before they began to commit themselves to the Savior.

> Now when they…passed through Amphipolis and Apollonia…came to [city of] Thessalonica, where there was a Jewish synagogue. Paul, as was his custom, went into them, and for three Sabbath days reasoned with them from the scriptures.
> Acts 17:1-2

Paul was asking the Gentiles among them to give up the idol worship that the entire population believed their whole lives (1 Thessalonians 1:9). He was asking the Jews among them to believe that Jesus was their long-awaited Jewish Messiah.

This would require the Jews to believe that Jesus had not blasphemed, though He was murdered for it. Instead, He actually was the Son of God (Acts 17:4-5). Once saved, they fervently spread this good news throughout the regions of Macedonia and Achaia (1 Thessalonians 1:6-7). Christians might have to take much more time to biblically convince some in order to bring them to Jesus Christ. They should see this as a positive response.

> *Key Concept: Some might respond positively to the gospel by listening but need additional persuasion by providing facts or proofs from the Scripture.*

A Scriptural Consideration

Some might respond with a scriptural consideration. One, who is from a Judeo-Christian background, may desire to legitimately search the Scriptures for themselves. They will commit themselves to Christ after a careful examination. The unsaved citizens of Berea are an example of this scriptural consideration. After the apostle fled from Thessalonica, Paul entered the city of Berea and preached the gospel. This was a more noble-minded people, and they would not just listen and believe.

In Acts 17:10-11, Paul presented the gospel to the people, and they meticulously searched the Old Testament. They knew these books and desired to determine the veracity of Paul's claims through them.

> The brothers immediately sent Paul and Silas away by night to Berea. When they arrived, they went into the Jewish synagogue. Now these were more noble than those in Thessalonica, in that they received the word with all

> readiness of…mind examining the scriptures daily to see whether these things were so.
>
> Acts 17:10-11

The Bereans were awaiting the coming Messiah. Their hearts were open to God, but they demanded to see the proofs that demonstrated that Jesus was the Messiah. Notice, Luke calls them nobler for doing this in verse eleven. The result was the belief of many (verse 12).

When the Lord identified Himself as the Messiah to the woman at the well, she went and told many in the city. They all came out to meet Jesus for themselves, then they believed (John 4:39-42). Sometimes, it will be necessary to allow some people time to meet Jesus for themselves in the Scripture. A very positive response to the good news is to question the Scriptures, study them, and ponder these spiritual things.

> *Key Concept: Some might respond positively to the gospel by verifying the truth of its claims which will require more time to study the Scripture.*

An Open Mind

Some may respond with open minds. There may be those who are willing to listen to the gospel because they have an open mind. They might not have settled on one particular belief system or religion and are willing to discuss religious things. In Acts 17:16-21, Paul met a group of these people in Athens. The Areopagus (a religious council) screened every new teaching to determine whether or not it was from their gods.

In Acts 17:33-34, Paul finished preaching the gospel. Some mocked him but others wanted to hear more.

> Thus, Paul went out from among them. But certain men joined with him, and believed, among whom also was Dionysius the Areopagite, and a woman named Damaris, and others with them.
>
> Acts 17:33-34

These people including Dionysius and Damaris came to the Lord. They obviously were more open-minded and returned for a second hearing.

Another example might be King Herod Agrippa, who heard Paul's defense in Acts 26. This man was open-minded enough to not rely on the testimony of Festus but to hear Paul himself (Acts 26:28). Though Festus thought Paul was out of his mind, Agrippa determined that Paul was about to persuade Him. Agrippa was listening without interruption.

In Acts 16, Paul entered the city of Philippi and found no synagogue. When Paul heard there was a place of prayer down by the river, he went to share the gospel to whomever he encountered. One of these people was a woman named Lydia. When Paul proclaimed the good news to all these Jewish women, Lydia did not storm off. Instead, she heard the gospel with an open mind. As Lydia was listening, the Lord opened her heart to receive the Word (Acts 16:14).

In Acts 18, when Paul had been sharing the gospel in the synagogue in Corinth, many resisted him. So, Paul went to the house of Titius Justus, a worshiper of God, who resided next door to that synagogue and preached there for some time. Many had open minds enough to come and hear him preach. As a result, Crispus, the official of the synagogue, and all in his household with many Corinthians believed. As Christians share the gospel, they will encounter unbelievers with open minds and are willing to listen to the truth. This should be seen as a positive step in the direction of belief in the good news and all it involves.

> *Key Concept: Some might respond positively to the gospel by listening to the good news because they have an open mind.*

A Fearful Awakening

Some might respond with a fearful spiritual awakening. There may be those who encounter a fearful situation or serious crisis from the Lord in their preparation to accept the gospel. Something frightens them and they begin to open up to God. Occasionally, the Father will have to do something dramatic and eventful in people's lives to turn them to Him.

This is what happened in the life of the jailer in Philippi. In Acts 16, Paul removed a demon from a servant girl and destroyed her fortune telling abilities. After they lost their business, her masters had Paul and Silas beaten and thrown into the local jail. Yet, Paul and Silas were just singing and praying which the prisoners and their jailer must have heard. Suddenly an Earthquake occurred causing the jailer to think the prisoners had escaped. The Philippian jailer would have been killed for allowing this to happen, so he decided to take his own life.

Paul cried out for the jailer to stop because everyone had remained. No one had escaped. The jailer fell at Paul's feet in fear and trembling begging him to be saved.

> He called for lights and sprang in, and, fell down trembling before Paul and Silas, and brought them out and said, "Sirs, what must I do to be saved?" They said, "Believe in the Lord

Jesus Christ, and you will be saved, you and your household."

Acts 16:29-31

In Acts 16:29-31, Paul brought him and all of his household to Christ. It required an Earthquake to prepare that man for salvation. God may use a fearful awakening to bring those who are called to His Beloved Son. In Luke 15, in the story of the prodigal son, the Lord brought a terrible famine in the land which brought fear and desperation. This finally drove the son back to his loving father. As he longed for the food the pigs were eating, the son had a spiritual awakening and realized that he needed his father.

Saul was diametrically opposed to the gospel. In Acts 8-9, he went about persecuting Christians everywhere they fled. Then on the road to Damascus, Paul encountered the risen Lord Jesus in a dramatic way. Paul witnessed a blazing light from heaven brighter than the sun, heard the voice of Christ speak to Him, and was struck with blindness for three days. This was a fearful conversion experience (Acts 9:3-9). Since God does not provide visions today, He may do something fearful to the unsaved to drive them to Him. At these times of crises, the Lord begins to spiritually awaken them because of fear which provides a great chance to share the gospel.

> *Key Concept: Some might respond positively to the gospel by seeking their salvation after experiencing a fearful circumstance brought into their lives.*

A Difficult Opposition

Some might respond with a struggle against opposition. There are people who recognize that there is a true God of creation and a real lawgiver from their conscience. They are moving in their spiritual journey toward the Lord but are opposed by someone. Satan has raised someone up to stop them from coming to Jesus Christ. This produces a difficult struggle. Some may have to deal with this opposition before they can come to Christ. This could be a friend taking up time or a spouse not allowing contact by the evangelist.

A clear example of this is found in Acts 13:6-8, when Paul traveled to Cyprus.

> Who was with the proconsul, Sergius Paulus, a man of understanding. This man summoned Barnabas and Saul, and sought to hear the word of God. But Elymas the sorcerer (for so is his name by interpretation) withstood them, seeking to turn aside the proconsul from the faith.
>
> Acts 13:7-8

Sergius Paulus, the proconsul of the island, sent for Paul, because this official wanted to hear the Word of Paul's God. Elymas, a sorcerer, who was an advisor in his court, opposed the apostle. Elymas did not want the proconsul to come to Christ. Finally, Paul struck him with blindness for a season. As Paul rebuked him, he called Elymas a son of the Devil. Paul knew who was behind his opposition. When Sergius saw this and heard Paul's gospel, he believed.

Christians should be aware that there might be people in their lives who may attempt to keep them from coming to Christ as they share the good news with them. These people might even be in their own family. Not everyone walks into the kingdom unopposed. Jesus warned his disciples of this in Matthew 10:33-34. He proclaimed that He would not bring peace but a sword between a man and his father, and a daughter and her mother, and among the members of their own household. Family members, children, friends, fellow students, or co-workers who oppose the unsaved may have to be dealt with first.

> *Key Concept: Some might respond positively to the gospel by struggling with the opposition of others and need time to overcome it.*

An Additional Presentation

Some might respond with a desire to hear the good news again. Sometimes people may need to hear the gospel more than once before they receive Jesus Christ. In Acts 19:8, Paul arrived in Ephesus and taught in the synagogue for three months reasoning from the Scriptures. Over and over again, the members of the Jewish synagogue were hearing Christ's gospel. He taught two years in the school of Tyrannus and many in the whole region came to hear about Christ. In Acts 19:18-20, Luke records that many were forsaking their magic practices in Ephesus and then burned all their demonic and wicked books of spells, etc. The Word of God was growing rapidly and prevailing against this evil. With their continual sharing of the gospel, many would have heard the gospel multiple times before coming to Christ.

Previously, in Acts 13:42-44, Luke records that the people of Antioch begged Paul to return the next Sabbath and speak to them again.

> So when the Jews went out of the synagogue, the Gentiles begged that these words might be preached to them the next Sabbath. Now when the synagogue broke up, many of the Jews and of the devout proselytes followed Paul and Barnabas; who, speaking to them, urged them

> to continue in the grace of God. The next Sabbath almost the whole city was gathered together to hear the word of God.
>
> Acts 13:42-44

The next Sabbath almost the entire city had arrived to hear what Paul had to say. The ones who had originally heard his words went and told others to come and hear also. In their sharing, the saints might be required to present the gospel to some more than once to win them to Christ. The person may almost be ready but need one more presentation.

> *Key Concept: Some might respond positively to the gospel by desiring to hear the gospel multiple times which may take additional time and effort.*

A Sudden Realization

Some might respond with a sudden realization that Christ is the Son of God, and they must be saved. God may work quickly when the good news is preached. Unbelievers may immediately and dramatically realize that Christ is indeed God, place their faith in Him, and never turn back. This is true concerning the conversion of the apostle Paul.

In 1 Timothy 1:13 and Acts 26:10, Paul delineates how he vehemently pursued Christians traveling everywhere they fled to persecute them even unto death. Then the incident on the road to Damascus occurred. Suddenly, the apostle was now pursuing people everywhere they went to win them to Christ (Acts 22:3-16). What a sudden realization he had!

In fact, so sudden was His conversion that he frightened the saints. In Acts 9:26, when Paul went to Jerusalem, many Christians were hesitant to associate with him.

> When Saul [Paul] had come to Jerusalem, he tried to join himself to the disciples; but they were all afraid of him [Paul], not believing that he was a disciple.
>
> Acts 9:26

They did not believe that this miracle could possibly happen. Christians should always be prepared for an unbeliever's sudden and dramatic conversion to the Lord Jesus Christ. This is an amazing sight!

Key Concept: Some might respond positively to the gospel by immediately and dramatically believing and receiving Jesus Christ.

The Positive Reactions to the Gospel at Belief

Just as there are specific and distinct elements of the message of salvation, there are equally precise reactions or responses that correspond to them. Many people today, even from the cults, will claim that they have "Jesus in their hearts" or that "Jesus is their personal Savior." Unfortunately, they are deceived. These terms are used frequently today. Yet, they obscure the real response one must make to be saved. It isn't as simple as just "believing in Jesus" or saying "Jesus is my Savior." True saving faith is more than an intellectual knowledge that "Jesus loves me." It is a belief and a trust that literally changes one's life. This "belief" requires an understanding of the true identity of Christ, His purpose for coming, His words and actions, and how to respond.

James argues this very point in James 2:19. The demons have the right knowledge about God. At least they shudder. They have some kind of response. He contrasts that with those who claim to believe in Christ but produce no fruits or good works. They act the same as they did before belief. In Luke 8:28, the demons rightly exclaimed that He was the Son of the Most High God! They rightly believed, but this belief is not enough. Belief must pour forth into a transformed life.

This same concept is displayed in Matthew 7:22-23. Jesus has just informed His disciples that numerous false prophets and deceitful teachers would arise after His ascension. These evil workers would claim a saving relationship with Him among His people and on judgment day. Yet, the Lord Jesus will send them away declaring that He never knew them. Many will have claimed to have prophesied in His name, cast out demons by His authority, and done miracles by His charge, yet the Lord will deny having any relationship with them. Whatever they may have said or done in His name was not from Him. They may have had the right intellectual belief, but that belief was not life changing!

Then Jesus points to the crux of the issue: they were living lawlessly. He indicates that these wolves in sheep's clothing could easily be identified by their insufficient fruit or their lack of transformed lives. The pretenders will be people of unrighteousness (no change), though they will appear to do great feats in His name. Their lives will not demonstrate a divine relationship. Why? Their beliefs are not life changing! This critical precept does not only apply to false prophets but anyone who claims the name of Jesus Christ. In verses 24-27, He broadens His claim by acknowledging two kinds of people. Some will hear His words and act upon them. These will build their houses upon rocks, and the storms of life will not wash them away. Others will hear but will not act upon His words. They will build their houses upon the sand, and the storms of life will wash them away.

This hearing and doing of Christ's Word involve hearing, believing, and acting upon those beliefs. In 1 John 3:10, John provides two criteria to determine if those who claim Christ are really saved. Real saints love the brethren and practice righteousness. These two actions do not produce salvation in one's life; they are merely the distinguishing marks of those who are saved. These true believers have transformed lives indicated by the love of their fellow Christians and righteous living. Believing in Jesus intellectually or knowing who He is will not be enough to produce these crucial signs of a true relationship with Christ.

Then, one might ask, "What about all the Bible passages that simply say believe? There are two reasons for this. First, the concept of "believe" utilized by the Lord has a much fuller meaning. It involves an understanding of Christ's true identity, His purpose for coming, His words and actions, and how one must respond. If one truly believes, one will respond appropriately. This is exactly what Jesus meant in Matthew 7:21, when He claimed that those who did the will of His Father, not those who cried, "Lord, Lord" would be saved. A complete understanding and belief in these things produce a godly response. Belief in Jesus is life changing.

Second, Jesus, the apostles, and the other inspired writers of the New Testament described the process of becoming a Christian by emphasizing one or another of the beliefs and actions one must take to be saved during or after salvation. This did not imply in any way that all of the components for saving faith was not necessary. They simply could not be spoken or recorded every time the gospel is mentioned.

Just one example should suffice. After Peter's sermon in Acts two, the crowd asked him how they might be saved. Peter responded that they needed to repent and be baptized. Here Peter is viewing saving faith from the initial action to the final reaction. They must repent to be saved and then respond to their saving faith through baptism.

SHARING THE GOSPEL: THE DOCTRINE OF EVANGELISM

It should be expected that the writers of Scripture could not possibly have recorded every word that was uttered in every presentation of the gospel. Often, they would have provided the most essential for their intended purpose for mentioning the incident. This is known by a comparison of the gospel accounts of a particular incident. Each writer will provide some similar details and some additional details, yet without contradiction.

Often, the writers indicated that they were not recording everything that was actually said. In fact, according to Acts 2:40, Peter testified and exhorted the crowd with many more words. These words Luke does not record, but they would have filled in the biblical portrait of a full saving response. John claims that if he had written every word and action of Jesus, the world couldn't hold the books that would contain them (John 21:25). The writers through the inspiration of the Holy Spirit revealed what the Father wanted revealed (John 14:26; 2 Peter 1:20-21).

Reading and understanding all the passages that relate to the gospel through the New Testament set forth a complete doctrine on the proclamation of God's plan of redemption. Christians do not understand all God's teaching on marriage by studying one passage of Scripture. They must take into account every passage that mentions or alludes to marriage to view the full portrait of this blessed institution. It is the same with the good news. Therefore, all of Scripture must be evaluated to receive a complete understanding.

The saving response described below embodies all of the teachings of the writers of the New Testament. These specific positive reactions or responses will spring forth into life eternal and the deeds that demonstrate that life. If one truly "believes in Jesus" then the following aspects of belief and saving responses will occur! How does one know? The Bible discusses all of these beliefs and responses in conjunction with salvation. All of these individual teachings must be collected and joined together to give someone a true picture of saving faith. As a result, all these truths become the keys to eternal life through the Savior and Lord, Jesus Christ.

The Seeking of His Kingdom

As Christians present God's plan of redemption and the offer of the kingdom of God and eternal life, the response of unbelievers will be a "seeking" of His kingdom. Essentially, this entails the acceptance of the offer. They will want to become a part of the kingdom. In Matthew 6:33, when the Lord was explaining to the people that in His kingdom they did not have to be concerned about clothing and food, He asserted that they should be seeking the kingdom instead.

> But seek first God's Kingdom [participation], and his righteousness; and all these things will be given to you as well.
> Matthew 6:33

This "seeking" is how people truly respond to the offer of the kingdom of God. This is why Jesus told them that if they seek His kingdom, they will find it (Matthew 7:7; Luke 11:9-10). In Luke 15:8, Jesus characterized true believers as those who sought His kingdom like one searching for a lost coin. She lit a lamp, cleaned the house, and diligently sought to find the coin.

The Greek word that is translated "seek" means "to crave, demand, strive after." These people will deeply desire to be in the kingdom and desperately want to live it out. This is why they repent of their sins and begin to seek His divine righteousness and holiness.

This is the initial step in the salvation process when the kingdom of God and eternal life is offered to them, and they desire to join. When a piece of fruit is ready to be picked, it will almost fall off into one's hand. In the same way, the saints who share will not have to argue the unsaved into the kingdom of God. They will "fall into one's hand" seeking it.

> *Key Concept: To be saved, unbelievers must seek and accept the offer of joining God's kingdom.*

The Repentance of Sin

One's response to the proclamation of sin and judgment is the repentance of sin. This results from a real understanding of the absolute holiness of God, His Son, and Spirit. Once the unsaved realize who Christ is, they will understand how unworthy and sinful they are. This was the response of the centurion when he requested Jesus to heal his servant. In Luke 7:1-10, he asked Jesus to heal him from afar because the centurion was not worthy to have Jesus come to his home. He was a sinner, and he knew it.

No person can be saved without full repentance, which demonstrates true belief. In 2 Timothy 2:24-26, Paul exhorts Timothy, his son in the faith, to gently correct those who are opposing him. Why? Perhaps, God will cause them to repent and lead them into the knowledge of the truth. In Matthew 3:2, John the Baptist declared people should repent because the kingdom of God was at hand. In Matthew 4:17, the apostle reveals that the ministry of the Lord was also the preaching of repentance and proclaiming that the kingdom of God had come. Repentance is an essential part of the saving response.

There are three aspects to this concept of "repentance" in the Scripture. As in the concept of "belief," "repentance" has a fuller meaning. It involves three aspects which are presented in various places by different writers in the New Testament. Repentance involves Christians admitting that they have sinned, sorrowing over their evil doing, and turning away from that sin toward righteousness.

The first is the admission of sin. People must admit that they have sinned. John discloses this important aspect as he deals with some in the church that had decided they had matured past sin. He begins in 1 John 1:8 and 10 by saying these people are liars and deceivers of themselves. In verse 9, he provides a characteristic of Christians. The saints confess their sins and find forgiveness. The Greek word translated "confess" literally means to say the same thing. Confession is "to say the same thing about sin" that God says.

When Jesus encountered a rich young ruler, he claimed to have kept the law from his youth up. Could that be true? No, he simply refused to admit his sin. Paul described this wretched condition in Romans 1:18; he was suppressing the truth in unrighteousness. Perhaps, so much so that he had convinced himself he was able to keep the whole law. So, Jesus told him to sell all he had which he refused to do. This manifested the real evil in his heart (greed), which was not displayed outwardly to the Lord (Mark 10:17-31; Matthew 19:16-30; Luke 18:18-30). He had to come to Christ admitting he was a sinner, which he refused to do. Instead, this ruler left Jesus with his self-righteousness intact but not saved.

The second is to mourn over sins. In the Beatitudes, Jesus says that a characteristic of those in the kingdom of God is mourning. This word speaks of mourning over the dead. In that passage, it has a spiritual application. The word implies mourning over sins and their consequence of spiritual death. When someone receives the Lord Jesus, they admit their sin and mourn, grieve, and sorrow over it.

SHARING THE GOSPEL: THE DOCTRINE OF EVANGELISM

In 1 Corinthians, Paul describes the sins and difficulties this church encountered because they had been prideful and rebellious. Paul was terribly hurt because the church had taken a stand against him. False prophets had risen up and found a leader in the church. This leader with most of the church stood against Paul and his ministry. So, he sent the difficult and confrontational letter of 1 Corinthians. When he visited, they did not respond well so he shortened his visit and departed. Later, Paul sent Titus to discover their final response to him and his many words of rebuke. When Titus returned, he brought good news of the church's repentance for standing against Paul.

In 2 Corinthians 7:9-10, Paul describes how much sorrow the church had over their sin.

> I now rejoice, not that you were made sorry, but that you were made sorry to repentance. For you were made sorry in a godly way, that you might suffer loss by us in nothing. For godly sorrow works repentance to salvation, which brings no regret. But the sorrow of the world works death.
>
> 2 Corinthians 7:9-10

This sorrow was a godly sorrow which produced repentance leading to salvation. This is the sorrow Christians have when they come to Christ. This is the sorrow Christians have when they live for Christ. The first leads to initial salvation and the other to final eternal salvation. This is the true sorrow over sin that eternally saves. This is the sorrow that produces real repentance.

This is the sorrow that was expressed by the woman who came to Jesus in Luke 7:37-39. This grieving woman washed His feet with her tears and wiped them with her hair. What sorrow over sin! The repentant woman kissed His feet and anointed them with expensive perfume. What humility and mourning over wrongdoing!

Also, in the Corinthian passage, Paul describes a sorrow that only leads to death. This sorrow is one that produces bitterness, despair, anger, and pride. This sorrow lashes out at the other person for hurting them, rebuking them, or even interrupting their sin. It vents at oneself in punishment and self-hatred. They will not plead forgiveness nor repent. Then they will despair of what they have done.

Third is the repentance of sins. Though this word is used with a fuller meaning in defining the entire concept, it also has a unique meaning of its own. The Greek word translated repent means to turn around in the other direction or change one's mind or behavior. One must turn around from sin and go in the opposite direction.

Luke records Peter's denial of knowing Christ in Luke 22:62 and how the apostle wept in great sorrow and remorse afterward. Later, Luke records in Acts chapter two, three, and other passages the many sermons that Peter preached in great boldness for Christ. Peter demonstrated that he had turned in the opposite direction from that sin. Of course, the Holy Spirit will provide the strength needed to accomplish this supernatural feat (Acts 2:4; Romans 8:13).

Contrast that with Judas. In Matthew 27:3-9, he would not repent before the Lord Jesus, nor would he humble himself before Jesus. Judas refused to request any forgiveness, thus removing the guilt and sorrow. Instead, he killed himself to alleviate them from his life. This is the sorrow unto death.

At times, the saints may not want to offend their unsaved acquaintances, neighbors, and friends so they will leave out this important saving step in their presentations. Instead, they will replace it with the hurt or sorrow these unbelievers may feel over their unmet needs, trials, or difficulties. They offer Jesus as the great healer, who will save them from their unfulfilled lives.

This is not the gospel. This will not allow those hearing the message to view Jesus Christ as the righteous judge and Holy One. The Lord will save them from their punishment for unrighteousness and bring them safely to an eternal, supernatural life, not a comfortable, temporal life. People must be confronted about their sins to see their desperate need for salvation in Jesus Christ. Their saving response will be the admission of their wrongs, sorrow over their sin, and a turning toward righteousness.

> *Key Concept: To be saved, unbelievers must repent by admitting, mourning, and turning from sin.*

The Belief in Christ as God

One's response to the proclamation of Christ as God must be belief in Christ's deity. No one can be saved unless that person believes Jesus Christ is God, one with the Father as His Son (John 8:58-59; 10:30). In 1 John 2, the author John is dealing with those who call themselves Christians but don't believe in the deity of Jesus, only His humanity. In verse 22, John calls them liars. If they do not confess the Son, they do not confess the Father.

In 1 John 3:23, the apostle John explains to his readers that God's most important and essential commandment is to believe in the name of His Only Son, Jesus Christ. When people believe in His Son, they are becoming obedient to the commands of the God of the universe.

> This is his commandment, that we...believe in the name of his Son, Jesus Christ, and love one another, even as he commanded.
>
> 1 John 3:23

Finally, in chapter 5, verses 9-13, John explains that God has testified concerning His Son, Jesus Christ. If one does not believe in the Son, he calls God a liar and does not have eternal life. This doctrine of the deity of Christ must be fully believed. This full belief issues forth in all the other aspects.

The classic passage which verifies this important truth in John 3:16 where Jesus declares that God loved the world so much that He gave His only begotten Son, so that everyone who believes in Him should not perish but will have eternal life. John finishes his proclamation of the good news in his book by declaring Jesus had performed many other signs that were not written in the gospel, but the ones that were written were to prove Jesus is the Christ, the Son of God (John 20:30-31). Eternal life comes from believing that Christ is the Son. This is the "belief" Jesus is referring to when he declared over and over that one must "believe in Him" to be saved. It is important to note that the cults do not believe in the full divinity of Christ; instead, they believe He was an angel, a created god, or someone less than fully divine. The saints must include this truth in their presentations of the gospel which will lead to belief in His deity.

> *Key Concept: To be saved, unbelievers must believe that Christ is the Son of God, one with the Father.*

The Reception of Christ as Savior

One's response to the proclamation of Jesus Christ as only Savior of the world is to receive Him as Savior. The unsaved

SHARING THE GOSPEL: THE DOCTRINE OF EVANGELISM

must believe that Christ died on the cross to pay the penalty for their sins and accept His saving grace by receiving Him. Jesus was crucified between two thieves. One of the thieves came to realize who Jesus was. Hanging on a cross that thief asked Christ to be His Savior. In Luke 23:42, he cried out to Jesus asking Him to remember him when He came into His kingdom. Jesus assured him that on that very day he would be in paradise. This dying thief and robber in the very last moments of his Earthly life received Christ that day.

In 2 Timothy 1:10, Paul declares to Timothy that the one who has abolished death and brought life and immortality through the gospel was "our Savior Jesus Christ." Notice, he uses the possessive pronoun "our" to refer to the Lord being ours. That is a relationship word. The same phrase can be found in 2 Peter 1:1. In that passage, Peter refers to Jesus as "our God and Savior." The acceptance of His saving work is implied in the term "our Savior." This is why in recent years Christians speak of "accepting Christ as Savior."

John clarifies this concept using the term "received." The proper biblical term for one's relationship with Jesus Christ is "received." Christians should be identifying themselves as having "received Jesus Christ as Savior and Lord." This is found in the opening words of the beloved disciple in the good news he wrote concerning the deity of Jesus.

> But as many as received him, to them he gave the right to become God's children, to those who believe in his name.
> John 1:12

The Greek word translated "receive" simply means "to take." It refers to taking with the hand, laying hold of any person or thing in order to use it, to make it one's own, or to give a person access to oneself in a face-to-face relationship.

In John 6:21, this key term was used physically when John described the disciples allowing Christ to enter their boat. They saw the Lord Jesus walking upon the water and were frightened because they thought He was a ghost. When He had convinced them otherwise, they received Jesus into the boat. When He entered, they were immediately at the shore. The Greek word is used spiritually of receiving Christ into people's lives and allowing Him to do His work through His Spirit. As they received Him into the boat, unbelievers are to receive Him into their lives.

In John 19:27, while on the cross, Jesus asked John to care for His mother. John records that she was received into his household from that day forward. Mary became a part of his family. She entered into an intimate, familial relationship with him. In the same way, when Christ is received by one, he enters into a familial relationship (children of God) with Him.

In John 20:22, when the Lord foretold the coming of His Spirit to the disciples, He portrayed it as "receiving" the Holy Spirit. When the Holy Spirit comes into the life of believers at salvation, He is literally received into their bodies (1 John 2:27). They become temples of the Holy Spirit (1 Corinthians 3:16; 6:19). Christ in His Spirit becomes the most important person in their lives and changes them (2 Corinthians 5:17).

This also means trusting Christ for one's eternal salvation as the absolute, only way to heaven. One must believe that Christ is the only way to heaven to be truly saved. This is a core belief. It was Jesus who stated in John 14:6, "I am the way, the truth, and the life. No one comes to the Father, except through me." Then in Acts 4:12, Peter said, "There is salvation in none other, for neither is there any other name under heaven, that is given among men, by which we must be saved!" If some say that they have received Jesus Christ but believe He is not the "only way" to heaven, they have received the wrong Jesus.

The Corinthians were questioning the resurrection of the dead. In 1 Corinthians 15:12-21, Paul claims that they were rejecting the very foundation of the Christian faith. If there is no resurrection, Jesus Christ was not raised. Without Him, believers have no real faith, so they are dead in their sins. Yet, Jesus has been raised and so shall they. Christians trust in Him and Him alone for their resurrection from the dead. What an affirmation from Paul that every Christian has.

When Christ is proclaimed as the only Savior, unbelievers must come to Him, recognize His saving work on the cross for them, acknowledge that He is the only way, and receive Him as the Savior accepting His free gift of eternal life.

Key Concept: To be saved, unbelievers must receive Christ as the only Savior of the world.

The Submission to Christ as Lord

One's response to the proclamation of Christ as Lord is the recognition of His Lordship producing in the Christian the appropriate response: submission and obedience to Him as Master. This is not complete and absolute obedience, for this is impossible in this life. In Romans 8:22, Paul describes the groaning that all Christians have within themselves for redemption. In the redemption of their bodies, Christians will find true and absolute submission and obedience. It will not be fully experienced in this life.

The flesh, which is contained in what Paul called the body of death, battles the believer's new man day by day (Romans 7; Ephesians 4:22-23). It is instead, the desire and striving after submission and obedience that is found in Romans 12:1-2. True Christians strive after presenting their bodies every single day as living sacrifices, holy, and acceptable to God in service to Him. They endeavor to not be conformed to this world but be transformed by the renewing of their minds and be pleasing to God. This results in what John calls practicing righteousness in his first letter (1 John 2:29). This is referred to as "obeying Christ" or "doing good deeds."

In 1 John 3:5-10, he goes further by stating that one who is born of God, does not continually commit sin. The verb is in the present tense signaling continuous action in present time. One who commits sins (continuous action in present time) is of the Devil. The key concept is continuous action as a pattern of life. Christians sin as individual acts but do not practice sin. They may have difficulty obeying their Lord on some occasions, but as a pattern of life obedience is present.

True Christians recognize that Jesus Christ is their Lord. This will pour forth into obedience to His commandments. In Matthew 16:24, Jesus indicated to His disciples that they needed to deny themselves, take up their crosses, and follow Him, if they wanted to come after Him. When Paul recounts his personal testimony in Acts 22:6-10, he was struck down and asked, "What shall I do, Lord?" This was the recognition that Jesus Christ, to whom he was speaking, was Lord and demanded obedience from that moment onward. When we receive Christ, the submission and intent to obey pours forth into salvation. If that submission and intent is real, then the fruit of obedience and good works will demonstrate our true faith. Faith will be shown by works (James 2:14).

In Acts 16, Paul and Silas were singing and praising God in prison. A powerful Earthquake occurred, and the jailer thought everyone had escaped. Since the jailer would have been killed for this, he prepared to commit suicide.

> And brought them out and said, "Sirs, what must I do to be saved?" They said, "Believe in the Lord Jesus Christ, and you will be saved, you and your household."
>
> Acts 16:30-31

Paul cried out that all were still there. Awestruck, the jailer asked how he might be saved. Paul's response in verse 31 was clear; he needed to believe in the Lord Jesus Christ. The jailer must believe in the Master Jesus Christ. This implies submission and obedience. In Romans 10:9, Paul told the Romans that if they confessed with their mouths that Jesus is Lord and believed in their hearts that He had risen from the dead they would be saved. His Lordship is essential. It must never be omitted from presentations. Obedience is required from the first days of following Christ.

Some would like to separate the Lordship of Christ from His saving work. This is impossible. Can one be saved and produce no fruits? Some want this to be because a loved one they know claimed to know Jesus but never lived for Him. Unfortunately, there is not one example of this in the New Testament. The thief on the cross never had an opportunity to live for Christ. Yet, in the moments the thief did have, he declared that Jesus was sinless and rebuked the other thief for taunting Him! This was the only good work he could do, and he did it. Jesus Christ as the Lord demands submission and obedience issuing forth in good works, even on a cross. Those saved on their death bed will experience the same, even if only for moments or hours. Anyone who has truly repented of sin, turned the other way, and now has the opportunity to live for Christ will produce fruits. Why? They understand that He is the Lord!

In Matthew 20:1-16, the Lord told a parable about day laborers who were hired to work in the field at different times of the day, and each received the same wage. Every one of them, including the ones hired just before the day was over, worked in the field. This was a picture of salvation. All produced works, once hired, some more, some less. The full understanding of who Jesus is issues forth in submission and obedience to Him as Lord. Now, how does this work? Once people encounter the deity, majesty, glory, power, and authority of the Lord Jesus Christ and believe, they fall on their face in obedience to Him.

> *Key Concept: To be saved, unbelievers must submit to Christ as Lord and strive to obey Him.*

The Affirmation of Christ's Resurrection

One's response to the defense of the deity of Jesus Christ is the firm belief that He is the Son of God from the miracles, fulfilled prophecies, and His resurrection from the dead. The biblical response to this is an affirmation of the resurrection.

> That if you will confess with your mouth that Jesus is Lord, and believe in your heart that God raised him from the dead, you will be saved.
> Romans 10:9

In Romans 10:9, Paul said if one confesses that Jesus is Lord with His mouth and believes He rose from the dead in his heart, he will be saved. In 1 Corinthians 15, Paul gives the essence of the gospel which is Christ died, was buried, and rose again according to the Scriptures (verses 3-4).

In John 20:24-30, Thomas, His disciple, refused to believe in the resurrection of Christ until he witnessed the wounds on His hands and put his finger in His side. Eight days later, Jesus appeared and allowed Thomas to verify this miracle with His own senses. Immediately, he declared that Jesus was "my Lord and my God." Notice the possessive pronoun. He was declaring his own salvation from the recognition of Christ's resurrection which proved His deity. Jesus Christ, the Lord, was God and now He was his God and his Lord based on those wounds which he saw.

Then Jesus paints a portrait of believers in the future, who will never witness the wounds. These beloved saints will be blessed because though they will not have seen, yet they will believe in His resurrection. This describes all those who have come to Christ after His ascension, except Paul. In their gospel presentations, the saints should include the defenses of Christ's deity and ask for affirmations of His resurrection to demonstrate their newfound belief in His deity.

> *Key Concept: To be saved, unbelievers must affirm that Christ rose from the dead.*

The Relationship to Christ in Love

One's response to the proclamation of a relationship with Christ is to love Him. The word love used of Christ in the Greek in its most basic understanding is to value or to prize. It does not convey the feelings implied by the English word. Feelings may be part of it but does not compose the central aspect. The key is this valuing and prizing of someone or something which issues forth in a variety of loving words and actions. It also has to do with the right understanding of the person or object loved.

John delineates these critical fundamental elements when he describes exactly how to love the brethren in 1 John 3:18. He asserts that they are to love in deed and in truth as well as in their words and language. To love someone must by its nature be expressed. Those expressions are found in both verbal and physical actions with loving language and deeds according to the truth. The truth here refers to the Scripture. Loving someone is always according to God's Word. We must love Jesus according to His commands.

Those who receive Jesus as Savior and Lord believe that He is the God of the universe, has died for them, forgiven their sins, submitted to Him as Lord, and love Him for it. They then spend their lives learning about Him through His Word, talking to Him through prayer, and loving Him through obedience and good deeds. They love Him the way the Bible tells them to love Him. The way He desires to be loved. This love then grows and grows.

In John 14:15, Jesus declares that if someone loves Him, he will keep His commandments. Then in verse 24, the Lord pronounced that someone who does not love Him does not keep His commandments. Obedience flows out of love.

> Jesus answered him, "If a man loves me, he will keep my word. My Father will love him, and we will come to him, and make our home with him."
>
> John 14:23

Then, Jesus makes an amazing statement that if someone loves Him, the Father will love them. Also, if one loves the Son, then one loves His Father, the true God. In John 17:26, Christ professes that the love that a Christian has for Him (Jesus) is in reality the love of the Father for Jesus in them. When He was asked which commandment was the greatest, Jesus said that it was to love the Lord with all one's heart, mind, soul, strength, and understanding. True believers also love the Son in the same way. This is a love relationship.

SHARING THE GOSPEL: THE DOCTRINE OF EVANGELISM

Over and over, the writers of the New Testament describe Christians as those who love Jesus Christ. In Ephesians 6:24, Paul closes his letter with a blessing of grace that addresses all his believing readers as those who love the Lord Jesus Christ. In 1 Corinthians 16:22, Paul concludes his letter by pronouncing a curse on all who will not love the Lord Jesus Christ. Here, he is speaking generally of all unbelievers but also alluding to the false prophets that were disrupting the Corinthian church and were standing against him. They will spend an eternity in hell without God.

In James 1:12, the half-brother of Jesus promises a reward to all the Christians who persevere under trial. He addresses them as "those who love Him." Later in chapter 2, verse 5, the head of the Jerusalem church contrasts the poor of this world with the rich. He discloses a promise to the poor who are believers. The Lord promises that those who love Him will be rich in faith and heirs of the kingdom. Once again, he addresses believers as the ones who love the Lord.

In 1 Peter 1:8, Peter complements his readers concerning their love for Christ. He characterizes them as those who are filled with joy. Why? Though they have not seen Him, they love Him! He portrays true believers as those who believe in Jesus Christ as God and love their Lord. This was a lesson that the apostle learned the hard way! When Jesus restored Peter to ministry after his denial, Jesus questioned his love for Him (John 21:16-17). Why? Love for Christ is the core of one's salvation.

This love for Christ will be in direct opposition to the love of the world. When an unbeliever repents, he forsakes the love of the world and replaces it with a love for Christ. The world would be the society of unbelievers with everything that is evil within it. John describes it in 1 John 2:15-16. The world is comprised of the lust of the eyes, the flesh, and pride of living. This would be whatever the eyes and flesh passionately desire and whatever causes an unbeliever to boast concerning the way in which he or she lives.

In James 4:1-10, James stands against all those who seek their own pleasure above God among his readers. This led to fighting and quarreling among themselves. He exclaims that friendship with the world is enmity against their God. These seekers of pleasure wanted all that the world offered, and James identifies them as spiritual adulterers. He uses the Old Testament concept of Israel's idolatry as adulterating their love relationship with God (Ezekiel 16:15-19, 30; Hosea 1:2). Their love of the world and its pleasures was the same kind of adultery. Christians view the Hebrew people as sinning in a way they would never do; yet, often do the same thing.

This adulterous love can take a variety of forms: the love of men's approval (John 12:43), the love of money (1 Timothy 6:10), the love of self (2 Timothy 3:2), the love of pleasure (2 Timothy 3:4), the love of this present world (2 Timothy 4:10), the love of the wages of unrighteousness (2 Peter 2:15), and the love of preeminence (3 John 1:9).

Why? Why must one turn from loving this world and to loving God instead? The answer comes from the parable of the seed thrown among the thorns in Matthew 13:22. The love of the world (the deceitfulness of riches and its worries) choke the Word and they fall away, never allowing the seed of faith to take root. Jesus clarifies this struggle between two loves when He speaks of those serving two masters in Matthew 6:24. Either they will love one and hate the other or be devoted to one or despise the other. People cannot love God and love money (the essence of the world system). They are naturally and supernaturally opposed to each other. This does not mean that true believers will not struggle with the flesh. They will, but they will also regularly win the battle.

In Romans 7:18-20, the apostle claims he desires good, but sometimes does evil. He battles his flesh (sin principle in the body) within his mind. In Galatians 5:17, Paul indicates that the Spirit in Christians will oppose the flesh in them so they will not do what they want. Here lies the key point. A true believer will desire to be righteous through the Spirit in Him, but his body will desire to be evil. As the daily battles are fought, the believer will regularly choose good, but the unbeliever will choose evil.

As one can see, this love for Him is deeper than human love. There are those who may have the feeling of love for Christ, which is stirred anew with penetrating music, funny and appealing sermons, colorful lighting, a dramatic stage, being around others who feel the same feelings, attending a huge service, and be enveloped with surround sound, yet not be saved. Feelings are not enough. If people only have the feelings of love for Christ, they will discover that those feelings fade. Then, they will be off to the next feeling of love in another religion. All human feelings go up and down, but true faith and real love remain for a lifetime.

> *Key Concept: To be saved, unbelievers must enter into a love relationship with Christ.*

The Dependence on Faith Alone

To be saved, unbelievers must believe that faith alone will save them. They must trust in Christ's saving work on the cross alone rather than the accumulation of good works or personal righteousness.

In Roman 3:28, Paul declares that Christians are justified by faith apart from the works of the Law. In Romans 5:1, Paul asserts that believers are justified by faith alone.

> Being therefore justified by faith, we have peace with God through our Lord Jesus Christ.
>
> Romans 5:1

When false teachers fooled the Galatians into thinking that the Gentiles must first be circumcised, Paul explained to them that the works of the law could not justify but only hearing by faith (Galatians 2:16). Men can only be justified (declared righteous) by faith in what Christ did for them on the cross. This true faith is pure and real. It is placed in Jesus Christ alone not one's own righteousness.

In Ephesians 2:8, Paul clearly explains that salvation is a result of faith, not works. Why? So, no man can boast before God. No one will ever be able to claim that he worked his way into heaven. Instead, as has been seen, good works pour forth from a life of faith. In Ephesians 2:10, Paul continues his discussion by indicating that once faith comes Christians are to walk in good works. In Colossians 1:10, Paul prays that the church would walk in a worthy manner, pleasing God in everything, and producing fruit in every good work. In 2 Timothy 6:18, Paul encourages Timothy to instruct the saints, who are well-to-do, to become rich in good works. Righteous works flow supernaturally from true faith, they do not save.

> *Key Concept: To be saved, unbelievers must believe that faith alone in Christ's work on the cross will bring eternal life.*

The Response of Water Baptism

In Matthew 28:18-20, the risen Lord Jesus commanded His followers to make disciples by going, baptizing, and teaching. This is a marvelous framework for our evangelism and edification. First, they were to go out into all the world. Then they were to share the gospel (evangelism) and baptize those who were saved. Then they were to take those new converts and make them into full disciples.

This was also the pattern of Jesus Christ and the apostles in their proclamation of the gospel. In John 3:22, the apostle John records that Jesus was in the land of Judea baptizing. Obviously, this occurred after the preaching of the kingdom which is always described by the gospel writers as Christ's message of redemption (Matthew 4:17; Mark 1:15; Luke 8:1). They believed then were baptized. In actuality, Jesus was doing the preaching of the kingdom, but His disciples were baptizing the new believers (John 4:2).

In Acts 2:41, after the people received Peter's word (the gospel), they were baptized.

> Then those who gladly received his word were baptized. There were added that day about three thousand souls.
> Acts 2:41

They first received Jesus Christ (John 1:12), and then were baptized. This would have been a momentous undertaking because at least three thousand people were saved that day. Yet, they baptized all of them. Why? Baptism after salvation was God's desired pattern. Christ went about proclaiming the kingdom, and all who received Him were baptized.

In Acts 8:12-13, Luke records that after the citizens of Samaria believed in the good news of the kingdom and Jesus Christ preached by Philip, they were being baptized. The apostle Paul evangelized the lost with this same paradigm. In Acts 16:15, Lydia and her household believed and were baptized. Then a few verses later in Acts 16:33, the jailer and his household believed and were baptized. In Acts 18:8, Luke described the salvation of Crispus, his household, and many others. Paul proclaimed the Word, they believed, and were baptized. Baptism was immediately after salvation.

Baptism came immediately after salvation. It was always a baptism of true believers. No babies were ever baptized. Baptism was invariably by full immersion in physical water. Baptism was never seen as something one does in the church many years later because they finally are living for Jesus. Baptism was always performed in front of unbelievers as a testimony of faith to them, not exclusively before believers.

> *Key Concept: Once saved, new believers should be baptized immediately before the saved and unsaved as a testimony to them.*

The Positive Reactions to the Gospel After Belief

Salvation is the critically important moment of a person's physical life upon this Earth. It is dramatic and life-altering in every possible way. In Ephesians 2:1-5, Paul declared that all unbelievers are dead in their trespasses and sins. In this condition, they follow after the prince of the power of the air, are sons of disobedience, live in the passions of the flesh, carry out the desires of the body, and are by nature children of wrath!

They have no spiritual life in them. When they receive Christ, they become fully alive in Jesus Christ! They reject the Devil, no longer follow after the passions and lusts of the flesh and are by nature children of blessing as sons and daughters of the Lord God. Everything is different. These new believers were spiritually dead but now are spiritually and supernaturally alive. What a momentous event!

In 2 Corinthians 5:17, Paul describes a new creation.

> Therefore, if anyone is in Christ, he is a new creation. The old things have passed away. Behold, all things have become new.
> 2 Corinthians 5:17

The word "new" in the Greek language means brand-new of a different kind. Christians become a new creation in Jesus. This is such a truly powerful event that it may elicit a variety of positive responses. The Christian, who shares the gospel, needs to be prepared for the kinds of positive responses after salvation that a person may have. All new Christians will react in some positive way to their new belief in Christ. Some people will react more intensely than others. The New Testament provides many examples of these wonderful and exciting reactions. As those who shared with them, we can enjoy their rejoicing in Christ as they begin to live new lives.

> *Key Concept: After becoming Christians, some may experience a variety of positive reactions.*

A Tremendous Sense of Blessing

When some become new Christians, they may become filled with an overwhelming sense of blessing. The mercy and grace of God issuing forth in the forgiveness of all their sins and wickedness becomes almost too much to bear. They suddenly feel a sense of wonder and become awestruck by God's patience and love for them. His mercy astounds them.

The apostle describes this sense of blessing to Timothy in 1 Timothy. He jubilantly expresses to his son in the faith the incredible blessing of the grace, mercy, and patience that God had showed toward him at salvation.

> However, for this cause I obtained mercy, that in me first, Jesus Christ might display all his patience, for an example of those who were going to believe in him for eternal life. Now to the King eternal, immortal, invisible, to God who alone is wise, be honor and glory forever and ever.
>
> 1 Timothy 1:16-17

Then, as if overwhelmed by it all, Paul breaks into a great doxology of praise concerning God's blessing upon him and cries out for the Lord God's honor and glory forever and ever. In Galatians 4:12-15, the apostle dealt with a group of churches who had been deceived by many false prophets attempting to bring them back under the bondage of the law to save them. Paul reminded them of the tremendous good fortune and blessings they felt when the weight of the law was lifted from their spiritual shoulders.

> *Key Concept: After becoming Christians, some may experience a great sense of blessing.*

A Great Feeling of Joy

When some become new Christians, they may experience a flood of joy when they receive Jesus Christ. In Acts 8:8, when Philip preached the good news in Samaria and healed many people, Luke wrote that there was rejoicing in the city. So many people were healed and being saved that the city was absolutely jubilant. In verses 38-39, after the Ethiopian eunuch heard the gospel and came to Christ, Luke described him as traveling down the road rejoicing.

When Paul brought the good news into the household of the Philippian jailer and they believed, the home was full of rejoicing (Acts 16:30-34). Once again, the entire household was filled with joy. His household had entered into the kingdom of God and eternal life. Is this not something that is worth rejoicing over? What could possibly fill one's heart with happiness, genuine happiness, than this?

The Thessalonians had experienced this same kind of joy and gladness upon their salvation.

> You became imitators of us, and of the Lord, having received the word in much affliction, with joy of the Holy Spirit, so that you became an example to all who believe in Macedonia and in Achaia.
>
> 1 Thessalonians 1:6-7

In 1 Thessalonians 1:6-7, Paul described how the believers in the city had found Christ in the midst of intense persecution and still had great joy. Some Christians might experience the opening of the floodgates of happiness when they receive Jesus Christ as their new Savior and Lord. As they mature in Christ, this new believer's joy will be replaced with a deeper and more abiding one.

Key Concept: After becoming Christians, some may experience a great feeling of joy.

An Overwhelming Desire to Evangelize

When some people become new Christians, they might immediately begin to share the good news with their friends and acquaintances. They now have something amazing that has happened to them and want to share it with the world all the time. This is precisely what occurred in the opening seven chapters of Acts. The saints were declaring the good news of

Jesus everywhere they traveled to everyone they encountered. Christ was adding to their number daily.

Then persecution instigated by Saul broke out. Would the Christians be silenced and go into hiding? No, they would not. Instead, wherever they scattered, they shared.

> Therefore, those who were scattered abroad went around preaching the word.
> Acts 8:4

In Acts 8:4, when the persecution broke out due to Stephen's preaching and Saul's rise, the Christians were scattered and kept sharing the gospel. They had all recently come to Jesus Christ. When Paul was saved, he went out to share the good news immediately. This frightened the church because they had never seen such a transformation (Acts 9:26). In the rest of Luke's historical account in Acts, Paul essentially shared the good news everywhere he traveled. As people receive the gospel and trust in Christ, some may desire to respond immediately by sharing the good news everywhere they go to everyone they meet. This may frighten some people who might not be used to this kind of boldness in the church. Yet, the Holy Spirit will produce this exuberance in some.

> *Key Concept: After becoming Christians, some may experience a great desire to immediately share the good news.*

A Wonderful Willingness to Suffer

When some become new Christians, they might become extremely enraptured and captivated by Christ. Their minds might be so completely set on Him that they are willing to pay any price for Him at the very next moment. This is what the

Thessalonians experienced. In 1 Thessalonians 1:6-7, Paul praises his readers for receiving the Word in much affliction with the joy of the Holy Spirit. What examples!

In Hebrews 10:32-33, the author acknowledged that his readers were drifting from the faith due to persecution. He reminds them of their past willingness to suffer.

> But remember the former days, in which, after you were enlightened, you endured a great struggle with sufferings; partly, being exposed to both reproaches and oppressions; and partly, becoming partakers with those who were treated so.
> Hebrews 10:32-33

He prompts them to really reflect upon their earlier days of salvation when they were willing to suffer for the name of Christ. When they first came to Christ, they were willing to be mocked and laughed at publicly, to lose their property, and even be thrown in jail. Why? They had a better eternal possession which could never be taken away. Though Jesus said that suffering for His name will be the experience of all Christians, some receive it in a violent form than others. In any form, some who come to Christ will welcome it with joy and open arms.

> *Key Concept: After becoming Christians, some may experience a great sense of joy amid persecution.*

A Strong Devotion to the Proclaimer

When some become new Christians, they may become so grateful, they may develop a strong devotion to the one who proclaimed Christ to them. This is recorded throughout the

New Testament. Besides His disciples, Jesus had a group of women he healed from many infirmities who followed Him and supported Him financially. In Luke 8:3, it states, "And certain women who had been healed of evil spirits and infirmities: Mary who was called Magdalene, from whom seven demons had gone out; and Joanna, the wife of Chuzas, Herod's steward; Susanna; and many others; who served them from their possessions."

The apostle Paul had numerous churches and individuals devoted to him. These supported him and his ministry both prayerfully (Ephesians 6:18-20) and financially (Philippians 4:15). When he was taking a collection for needy saints, they supported gave sacrificially (1 Corinthians 16:1-5).

As has been seen previously, the Galatians received Paul as if he were an angel of God.

> That which was a temptation to you in my flesh, you didn't despise nor reject; but you received me as an angel of God, even as Christ Jesus. What was the blessing you enjoyed? For I testify to you that, if possible, you would have plucked out your eyes and given them to me.
> Galatians 4:14-15

They were so grateful that these saints were willing to pluck out their own eyes to help him (Galatians 4:14-15). This may have been a reference to his poor eyesight.

So, a Christian may experience a sense of gratefulness to the person who shared the gospel with him or her in a very powerful way. These feelings of thankfulness can bring a deep attachment to this person because the person took the time to bring them into the kingdom of God and eternal life.

This person brought into their lives all the blessings of God and they may want to be a part of this in others' lives.

> *Key Concept: After becoming Christians, some may experience a strong devotion to those who brought them the good news.*

An Immediate Participation in Ministry

When some become new Christians, they might want to begin to serve their Lord almost instantaneously. In Acts 16, Paul came into Philippi on his second missionary journey and apparently did not find a Jewish synagogue. He went down to the river which was a very common place for Jews and the God-fearing Gentiles to meet. In verses 13-15, Paul encountered Lydia who came to Jesus Christ. Immediately, she invited him into her home and the church was started there. Lydia had become immediately involved in ministry. After Paul and Silas were released from jail, they returned to the church in Lydia's home and departed (verse 40).

In Philippians 4:15-16, while Paul was in Rome awaiting trial, he received a generous gift from the Philippians.

> You yourselves also know, you Philippians, that in the beginning of the Good News, when I departed from Macedonia, no assembly shar-ed with me in the matter of giving and receiving but you only. For even in Thessalonica you sent once and again to my need.
> Philippians 4:15-16

He recounted their past support in his letter. New Christians might desire to become immediately involved in ministry.

Key Concept: After becoming Christians, some may experience a great desire to immediately participate in a ministry in the church.

A Removal of Things from the Old Life

When some become new Christians, these saints might have accumulated evil or demonic objects from their former lives and desire to immediately remove them. Their new life in Christ is now so incompatible with these "old life" objects, they must be removed soon afterward (2 Corinthians 5:17). This may involve different kinds of objects: Ouija boards, magical stones, tarot cards, crystal balls, magazines, sexual or drug paraphernalia, technology, alcohol, or drugs.

In Acts 19:18-19, Paul ministers in Ephesus bringing many people out of the magical arts (occult practices).

> Many also of those who had believed came, confessing, and declaring their deeds. Many of those who practiced magical arts brought their books together and burned them in the sight of all. They counted their price, and found it to be fifty thousand pieces of silver.
> Acts 19:18-19

Immediately, these newborn Christians collected their many books of magic and burned them. As people are brought to Christ, they may become so passionate about repentance that they will almost immediately destroy all objects from their old lives. Now, all would know Christ made them new.

Key Concept: After becoming Christians, some may experience a great desire to remove the evil objects of their old lives fully and completely.

A Dramatic Transformation

When some become new Christians, these might change dramatically in their outward behavior. Perhaps, one day they were involved in drugs, illicit sex, alcoholism, or other sins. The next day without any apparent struggle, these sins were gone from their lives.

As Paul experienced a dramatic change (1 Timothy 1:13-15), so did the church at Thessalonica. The apostle had been in the city for a few weeks, and they already had a working faith, laboring love, and enduring hope. Their example was made known in the region (1 Thessalonians 1:2-3).

The Colossians had a similar sensational transformation.

> Because of the hope which is laid up for you in the Heavens, of which you heard before in the word of the truth of the Good News, which has come to you; even as it is in all the world and is bearing fruit and growing, as it does in you also, since the day you heard and knew the grace of God in truth.
>
> Colossians 1:5-6

From the day these new saints heard the good news of Jesus, they too demonstrated faith, love, and abounding fruit. All of it was constantly increasing for everyone to see.

Sometimes, people become Christians and make startling and dramatic changes in their lives through the Holy Spirit. This does not always happen to every Christian, but it does to some of them.

> *Key Concept: After becoming Christians, some may experience dramatic changes in their lives.*

Chapter 11

The Negative Reactions

As the New Testament and Christian experience depicts, not everyone responds positively to the gospel. In Acts 2:41 and Acts 4:4, after Peter's two great sermons, it is noted by Luke that several thousand came to Christ. Yet, there were many thousands who would have been in Jerusalem at the time who did not respond to the gospel positively. In Acts 6, Luke chronicles in detail the preaching of Stephen. He describes many positive reactions to the gospel to the point that even many priests were coming to Christ (verse 7). Yet, Stephen himself was arrested and dragged before the Jewish Sanhedrin and eventually stoned for his faith (Acts 7:58).

Believers should continually remember what Jesus Christ said about the road to eternal life. It is narrow and very few find it (Matthew 7:13).

> Enter in by the narrow gate; for wide is the gate and broad is the way that leads to destruction, and many are those who enter in by it. How narrow is the gate, and restricted is the way that leads to life! Few are those who find it.
> Matthew 7:13-14

This means that Christians will encounter more people who will respond negatively to the good news, than positively. There may even be disturbingly violent negative reactions. These negative responses are recorded all throughout the New Testament. The final and most severe of those negative reactions by people will occur when the beast in Revelation (possessed by the dragon) kills a multitude of souls because they proclaimed the Word of God (Revelation 6:9; 17:6). The saints must realize that sharing the gospel may bring many negative reactions. Some reactions may be mild and others very severe. Some of the negative responses to the gospel found in the Scriptures may never be encountered in some countries due to their religiously tolerant laws. Yet, around the world Christians have experienced many of the ones that are found in Scripture.

> Key Concept: Unbelievers will have a variety of negative reactions which will range from mild to severe toward Christians who proclaim the gospel.

A Physical Retribution

When Christians proclaim a gospel of sin and judgment coupled with a Savior who is the only way to heaven, there will be negative reactions. Most will not accept this gospel. Some will desire to respond physically and violently to the message. In Acts 5, Christ's apostles were arrested for their preaching of the good news. They were brought before the Jewish Sanhedrin and ordered not to preach. In verses 29-32, Peter declared to these leaders that they must obey God, not men. Peter then preached the gospel to them. They became angry and wanted to see them dead. In Acts 7:54-60, when Stephen preached to this very same council, they became so enraged that they stoned Stephen to death. This is physical retribution at its worst.

Violence came to others also. In Matthew 14:1-10, John the Baptist was beheaded for his righteous rebuke of Herod. The king and his brother's wife, Herodias, married each other after divorcing both of their spouses. This was against the God's law. The daughter of Herodias danced before King Herod the Tetrarch at a great banquet and in a drunken daze Herod offered her up to half of his kingdom. When the daughter inquired of her mother Herodias what she might request, she told her to ask for John's head on a platter. In Acts 12:2, Luke records that Herod Agrippa I, put James, the brother of John, one of the twelve, to death with the sword because the people were pleased by it. So, he arrested Peter intending to do the same thing, but an angel rescued Him.

In 2 Corinthians 11:24-27, Paul described to the church at Corinth the numerous persecutions he experienced. These included receiving forty stripes five times and being beaten with rods three times. Often, he was cold, naked, hungry, and thirsty. He suffered shipwreck three different times and spent a night and day in the ocean. In 2 Corinthians 6:4-8, he described the hardships, beatings, riots, and prison time that he endured among other vicious negative responses.

Paul summarized his persecutions in 2 Corinthians 4:11.

> For we who live are always delivered to death for Jesus' sake, that the life also of Jesus may be revealed in our mortal flesh.
> 2 Corinthians 4:11

He was being handed over to death daily as they attempted to murder him for Christ's sake. He expressed to them that his persecutions resulted because they hated the Christ he was preaching. Since they could no longer lay their hands on the Lord, they would instead kill His emissaries. This only proved that Christ was still alive as they preached Him and suffered for His name's sake. Christians around the world are experiencing extreme violence daily as they proclaim the gospel and face death for their Savior and Lord.

SHARING THE GOSPEL: THE DOCTRINE OF EVANGELISM

Key Concept: Some unbelievers may respond to the gospel by becoming physically violent, even to the point of murder.

A Personal Accusation

Often, Christians will not be persecuted in a physical way as they share the gospel; instead, they might be personally attacked. This might involve slander, libel, personal lies, and insulting Christians by calling them a variety of derogatory names. Since unbelievers cannot make an accusation against Christ, they will instead focus on His followers.

In Acts 6:11-15, Stephen was accused by the Sanhedrin of speaking blasphemies against Moses and God. In Acts 16:20-21, after Paul cast out the demon in a fortune telling slave girl, her masters lost all of their income. They brought Paul before the magistrates and charged him with stirring up strife in the entire city and presenting anti-Roman customs to observe. All were lies.

In Acts 17:18, they dismissed Paul as an idle babbler. When Paul preached the gospel to Festus, in Acts 26:24, he was accused of being crazy with all of his learning finally driving him insane. In Galatians 1:10, false prophets had crept into the church and were charging Paul with being a man-pleaser. In 2 Corinthians 2:17, still others of their kind, indicted Paul as a man who only preached for the money he could receive. In 2 Corinthians 10:10, some others even attacked his personal appearance calling him strong in his letters but weak in appearance and speech.

This was not that unusual because Jesus Christ was also charged with being mad, crazy, and insane (Mark 3:20-21). In John 7:2-5, the brothers of Jesus had not yet believed in Him and insisted that the Lord leave them and go into the region of Judea. The brothers sarcastically chided him for wanting to be known so openly. The Jew's Feast of Booths was about to occur, so they challenged Jesus to perform His works there. This way everyone would know who He was.

Often, the Lord Jesus ate among the unsaved to share the gospel with them. As a result, in Luke 7:34 some accused Jesus of being a drunkard and a glutton.

> The Son of Man has come eating and drinking, and you say, "Behold, a gluttonous man, and a drunkard; a friend of tax collectors and sinners."
>
> Luke 7:34

In John 1:14, Nathanael's initial reaction to Philip concerning Jesus was to question Christ's birth town and its reputation. He inquired as to whether anything good could come out of Nazareth. The people of Nazareth accused Jesus Christ of being just a carpenter (John 6:41). Believers who share the gospel must be prepared for personal accusations. Some unbelievers may react by attacking them personally as well as attacking the message.

> Key Concept: Some unbelievers may respond to the gospel by making personal accusations, even to the point of slander and libel.

An Outright Rejection

Some unbelievers might not react negatively to Christians physically, nor accuse them personally, but might simply reject the gospel totally. In Acts 17:32, when Paul preached the gospel, the historian Luke records one group's reaction. He wrote that they were sneering at and mocking everything he said. This essentially is outright rejection.

> When Paul arrived in Corinth, he entered the synagogue to proclaim the good news as was his custom. Many did not react in a positive way, but instead with outright rejection. But when some were hardened and disobedient, speaking evil of the Way before the multitude he [Paul] departed from them, and separated the disciples, reasoning daily in the school of Tyrannus.
>
> Acts 19:9

In Acts 19:9, Paul proclaimed the good news at Corinth and Luke writes that some of the citizens had become hardened in their hearts, disobedient, and spoke evil of the Way (the name for Christians). In Acts 28:17-24, Paul arrived in Rome and many of the Jews came to see what he had to say. Luke records that some citizens believed, and some did not. The evangelistic ministry of all believers will be filled with some who will believe, but others who will reject the gospel.

> *Key Concept: Some unbelievers may respond to the gospel by rejecting it simply and totally.*

A Total Indifference

Some unbelievers may hear the good news and just won't care. It is not that they reject the gospel outright; instead, they have absolutely no interest in Christ. In fact, in many religiously tolerant countries, this may be the main reaction. They are indifferent to the gospel. They are not for or against Jesus. They are not interested in who He is or what He did. They literally could care less about Him and His cross.

In Acts 13:44, Paul and Barnabas traveled to the city of Antioch of Pisidia. Paul preached a powerful sermon in the synagogue, and many asked him to come back and preach again on the next Sabbath. This time, Luke records, nearly the whole town came out to hear him. Notice, not everyone came, some were indifferent. Once Paul preached again, not all came to Christ. Some were saved, some were indifferent, and some were jealous and stirred up a crowd against them. Oftentimes, Christians often focus on the ones who respond or reject the gospel; yet there are others who may not care.

In Acts 18:14-16, Paul was dragged before the proconsul of Achaia and accused of instigating people to worship God contrary to the law.

> But when Paul was about to open his mouth, Gallia said to the Jews, "If indeed it were a of wrong or of wicked crime, you Jews, it would be reasonable that I should bear with you; but if they are questions about words and names and your own law, look to it your-selves. For I don't want to be a judge of these matters." He drove them from the judgment seat.
>
> Acts 18:14-15

Gallio's response was to drive them from his judgment seat. He was not at all interested in listening to things as trivial as religious vocabulary, customs, and laws. He was apathetic. Those evil people responded to the proconsul's indifference by beating the leader of the Jewish synagogue, Sosthenes, in the presence of this important man. Still, this Roman leader was unaffected. Some people might hear the gospel and be completely indifferent to Jesus and His good news.

> *Key Concept: Some unbelievers may respond to the gospel by being apathetic and indifferent.*

A Blind Confusion

Some people, no matter how simply a Christian explains the gospel to them, no matter how much time is taken, will not be able to understand it. No amount of explanation will aid in their comprehension. Christians might assume that some additional information is all that is necessary to bring them to Christ when they are actually blinded by their own hardened hearts, not ignorant understanding.

This is one of the reactions referred to by Jesus Christ in His parable concerning the various seeds that were sowed. In Matthew 13:3, Jesus describes a farmer who had thrown seeds by the side of the road, and it was devoured by the birds. This is the one who hears but does not understand.

> When anyone hears the word of the Kingdom, and doesn't understand it, the evil one comes, and snatches away that which has been sown in his heart. This [seed] is what was sown by the roadside.
> Matthew 13:19

In verse 19, Jesus explained that some hear the Word and don't understand it. Immediately, the Devil intercedes and snatches the seed away from them.

How does this happen? Is it fair for the Lord to hold some accountable if they do not understand? Yes. The reason is explained by Paul, the apostle, himself. In Romans 1:18-23, Paul paints a clear portrait of how this ignorance proceeds from man's original knowledge of God. All people clearly see the nature, attributes, and power of God in His creation. Then, they begin suppressing the truth in their sinfulness. They desire to sin, do not want judgment, and reject the true God. Rather than honor Him as God or give thanks to Him, they become futile in their thinking and their foolish hearts are darkened. Though they claim to be wise, they turn into fools. As fools, they create a variety of their own images of gods. The knowledge of the true God is lost to them.

In Ephesians 4:17-18, Paul identifies the unbeliever as one who is futile in his mind, darkened in his understanding, and alienated from the life of God because of the ignorance in him. Why? It is due to the person's hardness of heart and the giving of himself over to sensuality and impurity among other evils. The hardness of heart causes the ignorance and lack of understanding. They create their own confusion.

In 2 Corinthians 4:4, Paul writes that the god of this world has blinded the mind of the unbelieving so they cannot see the light of the gospel. Once man has rejected this creation knowledge, Satan blinds them further. This is the state of the natural man. In 1 Corinthians 2:14, Paul asserts that a natural man does not accept the things of God due to his inability to understand them. The truth of God is utterly foolish to him. Some unbelievers will simply not understand the good news due to their hardened hearts.

Key Concept: Some unbelievers may respond to the gospel by being confused in their hardened hearts.

A Vain and Prideful Investigation

There are those who take great delight in philosophical, metaphysical, and theological discussions. There are those, who will listen to the gospel, discuss the concepts, and even investigate Christianity but only as an intellectual exercise. They endeavor in their pride to have an intellectual debate concerning Christianity and the Bible. They usually want to begin with the dinosaurs or whether Cain had to marry his sister to obtain his wife. These unbelievers want to find the controversy or supposed errors in the Bible and go head-to-head with a believer. It is wasteful and useless because the discussion goes nowhere. These people are not truly seeking wisdom but only to hear themselves talk. In 1 Corinthians 1:18-25, the apostle contrasts the wisdom of the world with the foolishness of God. The world in their wisdom could not find God, but He could only be found in the folly of what Christians preach. To the unsaved who are perishing it is foolishness, but to those being saved it is the power of God. These vain and prideful wise men investigate and research, discuss and pontificate but will never find God. God can only be found in the humble good news with a truly seeking heart.

An example of such a group is found in Acts 17. Luke records that Paul entered Athens and was provoked in his spirit by all the idols that he observed. Athens was one of the ancient philosophical, intellectual, and cultural centers of the world. They desired to represent virtually every god that could possibly exist in the universe. In case they missed one, they had an idol whose inscription read, "To the unknown God." In verses 18-20, Paul encountered several of the Epicurean and Stoic philosophers of the city. Paul began to proclaim the gospel. Luke records that they were conversing with Paul. The vain and prideful intellectual pursuit had begun.

In verse 18, some criticized him, and others thought Paul was proclaiming some kind of a strange deity, but they all wanted to understand this new teaching. They needed to know more about his gospel. So, they brought Paul to the Areopagus, which was a sort of philosophical, theological, religious court to discern whether new teachings were from the gods. One might think that they were completely open and interested in understanding a stranger's new teachings.

In fact, they were not. The truth was not the important issue; it was the discussion.

> In Acts 17:21, Luke adds that these Athenians were very well known for spending much of their time in nothing else but hearing and discussing new ideas. They loved this! Now all the Athenians and the strangers living there spent their time in nothing else, but either to tell or to hear some new thing.
> Acts 17:21

They loved to pontificate (with all their so-called wisdom) the many ideas that were new and different. The intellectual exercise involved was what stimulated them in their pride.

Timothy had to deal with these pseudo-intellectuals. Paul describes men like these in 1 Timothy 1:6-7 as ones who have turned aside to fruitless discussion. These people wanted to be teachers of the law. They made confident assertions about matters they knew nothing about. In 1 Timothy 6:3-5, Paul describes them as teaching a different doctrine. They did not consent to sound words but were conceited and really knew nothing. They were all obsessed with disputes, word battles, and arguments. They actually assumed this would result in greater godliness.

These people appeared as seriously committed Christians with intellectual integrity. They also presented themselves as people who were seeking real answers concerning the truth, but it was all a facade. These false believers simply enjoyed discussions of philosophical, metaphysical, and theological issues. They wanted to know about Christ, discuss spiritual concepts, and talk and talk about Christianity. They pursued this for vain and prideful intellectual pleasure but not for knowledge. This consumed much time with no results.

The apostle then warned his son in the faith in chapter 6, verses 20-21, to avoid all of this worldly, empty chatter and opposing arguments of false knowledge. Timothy was to guard and protect the truth of God that had been entrusted to him. This guarding did not involve endless arguments.

A Christian may attempt to discuss the gospel with these vain and prideful investigators, but the conversation will go around and around. This will culminate in the Christian's endless frustration but in their immense delight. These "free thinkers" investigate Christianity like they investigate every philosophical, metaphysical, or theological system. They do it to feel superior about themselves. Pride is the motivating factor.

> *Key Concept: Some unbelievers may respond to the gospel by discussing it as an intellectual exercise but not be real seekers of the truth.*

A Feigned Interest

There might be some people who will feign interest in the presentation of the gospel because they want something from the presenter. They may be seeking a handout, support in their political campaign, or even a romantic date from an unsuspecting Christian. They will play the part of someone pursuing the truth but have ulterior motives driving them.

Two infamous people in Scripture illustrate this particular negative reaction. In Luke 23, the Lord is on His way to the cross. Christ appeared before the judgment seats of Annas, Caiaphas, and the Sanhedrin. Unfortunately for them, none had the power to condemn someone to death. This had to be done by Pilate, the Roman governor. Pilate examined Him and found no guilt worthy of death or even imprisonment.

Then Pilate discovered Jesus was from Galilee. Since Herod Antipas was in Jerusalem at the time, Pilate sent Jesus to him. Herod had jurisdiction over Galileans.

The ruler of the Jews was ecstatic. He had always desired to see one of the miracles of Jesus. He sat before Jesus and heard His case pretending to seek justice. The chief priests and scribes stood by vehemently accusing the Lord, but He said nothing. The Messiah did not speak, nor did He offer a sign or miracle to Herod. So, Herod put his pretense aside and allowed his soldiers to mock, mistreat, and dress Jesus up in the regal robe of a king and then return Him to Pilate.

A second example occurred when Paul stood before Felix, the Roman Procurator of Judea, in similar circumstances. In Acts 24:24, Paul preached the gospel to Felix. When Paul spoke of the judgment to come, Felix became so frightened that he sent Paul away.

> Meanwhile, he also hoped that money would be given to him by Paul, that he might release him. Therefore also he sent for him more often, and talked with him.
>
> Acts 24:26

In Acts 24:26, Luke, the historian, records the real motives of Felix. He was hoping to be bribed by Paul, so he often called for Paul to discuss his case with him. Felix feigned interest hoping to be bribed, but it didn't work.

An unbeliever might simulate interest in the gospel due to something they might desire from a Christian, such as approval, advice, praise, or perhaps a friendship or possibly romantic relationship. Since Christians cannot look into the heart to discern motives, they must rely upon God to expose the other's ulterior motives. God exposed the deeper motives of Simon the magician in Acts 8:13-24, when he tried to buy the power of the Holy Spirit from Peter and John.

> *Key Concept: Some unbelievers may respond to the gospel by feigning interest with a desire to receive something from the presenter.*

A Personal Admiration

As Christians proclaim the gospel, there might be some who listen out of admiration for the speaker. They are not really listening to the good news but are wrapped up in the speaking ability and skills of the messenger. They enjoy the way or manner in which the speaker talks or acts.

Herod the Tetrarch is the perfect example of this personal admiration. Mark records the horrific event of the reluctant beheading of John the Baptist by Herod in his gospel.

> For Herod feared John, knowing that he was a righteous and holy man, and kept him safe. When he heard him, he did many things, and he heard him gladly.
>
> Mark 6:20

In Mark 6:20, Herod considered John to be a righteous and holy man and feared him but also used to hear him gladly. This indicates Herod really enjoyed listening to John. There is no indication that John's words had any impact on Herod.

Herod did not release John, nor repent and was baptized by John but just enjoyed his rhetorical skills. He enjoyed John's many presentations. In Mark 6:21-28, Herod made an impulsive oath to give the dancing daughter of Herodias up to half the kingdom; instead, she asked for John's head on a platter. So, Herod decided to execute John the Baptist to preserve his reputation.

In Acts 4, when Peter and John gave a defense before the Sanhedrin, Luke indicated that these leaders marveled at the confidence of these two men since they were uneducated and untrained. The Jewish leaders admired their boldness and rhetorical skills but not their message. It offended them terribly, but their great courage and eloquence inspired them. These two apostles had a great presentation, but their gospel was rejected.

This occurred frequently with many of the prophets of the Old Testament. The people admired the messenger but not the message. In Ezekiel 33:30-33, God spoke to the prophet Ezekiel and described how His own people treated him. He compared Ezekiel to a woman singing a sensual song. They liked his voice and how his message was delivered. They "liked him as a person" but never listened and obeyed his message.

People may admire the Christian and listen over and over to the gospel message but never accept it as the truth. An evangelist or pastor who speaks the truth may be drawing huge crowds, but many may not become Christians because they enjoy the message but refuse to deal with their sin.

> *Key Concept: Some unbelievers may respond to the gospel by admiring the messenger's rhetorical skills but never come to the knowledge of the truth.*

A Religious Acceptance

Some people may respond to the gospel with a religious acceptance. They may see Christians as religiously similar in some way to them even though they will never believe their message. They will accept them as religiously related. They are willing to listen but will never believe. They are willing to associate with Christians but will not accept their message as authoritative truth. They have no problem with agreeing to disagree because they are all religiously connected.

This can be observed in one reaction of the philosophers in Athens to Paul.

> Some of the Epicurean and Stoic philosophers also were conversing with him. Some said, "What does this babbler want to say?" Others said, "He seems to be advocating foreign deities," because he preached Jesus and the resurrection.
>
> Acts 17:18

In Acts 17:18, some thought Paul was proclaiming strange deities. The word "foreign" connotes "strange or unusual." He was proclaiming gods and deities of which they were not familiar. The statue of the unknown god in town allowed for the possibility of many additional divine beings that had not been honored. Perhaps, his God was among the unknown (Acts 17:23). Their theology allowed for some co-existence.

Many Jews and Romans saw Christianity as nothing more than a sect of Judaism (Acts 18:12-14). The Pharisees were much stricter adherents to the law, but the Sadducees were more liberal in their understanding. They did not believe in the resurrection or angels. The Zealots believed that politics and the law went hand in hand. So now there arose another Jewish group who were followers of Jesus. In these early days, the Christians gathered in the temple (Acts 3:1) and the synagogues (James 2:2) which added to the misconception. Public officials, such as, Pilate (Luke 23:4) and Gallio (Acts

18:14-15) viewed Jesus Christ and His followers as part of the Jewish religion. These officials placed them in exactly the same theological, philosophical, and religious group. If these people had decided to associate with one group, then they would associate with the other.

There might be people in the lives of Christians who may view themselves as a part of Christianity. They may accept some of the Christian truths but not every one of them. This has happened with some of the cults who desperately desire to be seen under the "cloak" of Christianity. Yet, they have a different Jesus and a false gospel. Sometimes, people will claim to be spiritual but not religious and are able to coexist with Christians without much furor. Perhaps, unbelievers enter the church but are never confronted about their lack of belief. All the believers assume they are saved. They become a part because the church makes them feel good or "centers" them. The people are so friendly that they want to stay.

Key Concept: Some unbelievers may respond to the gospel by accepting it from a religious perspective but never come to the knowledge of the truth.

A Sympathetic Support

There might be those who will identify with a Christian's serious commitment, sympathize with his plight, and even support his cause but not become true Christians. There are humanitarian people who will join hands with true believers in their good works toward man but not come to Christ as Savior and Lord.

In Acts 27, Luke describes a man such as this. His name is Julius. Paul was on his way to Rome to stand trial. Julius was the centurion in charge. In verses 1-3, he treats Paul with great consideration by allowing him to visit his friends and receive their care. Julius was a kind humanitarian who was concerned about the needs of Paul.

> Later, the ship encountered a terrible storm and rammed into a barrier reef near an island. Since it meant death for the soldiers if any prisoner escaped, the crew decided to kill all the prisoners on board the ship. How could this be since it had been predicted that he would travel to Rome? In God's providence, God intervened through an unlikely unbeliever. The soldiers' counsel was to kill the prisoners, so that none of them would swim out and escape. But the centurion, desiring to save Paul, stopped them from their purpose, and commanded that those who could swim should throw themselves overboard first to go toward the land.
> Acts 27:42-43

In Acts 27:42-43, Julius stopped them from bringing harm to Paul though Julius was not a Christian. He did not accept Paul's gospel but simply lent Paul sympathetic support.

As with Julius, Pilate had sympathetic support for Jesus. In the gospel accounts, He tried to release Him by sending him to Herod. He tried to exonerate Christ by beating Him. Perhaps, this would satisfy their jealousy. The governor even gave the Jewish leaders the option of providing clemency for Jesus, rather than Barabbas. Unlike Jesus, this evil man was a criminal who had committed heinous crimes against Jews. Nothing worked against these persistent Jewish leaders who desired Jesus of Nazareth dead. Unfortunately, the governor could not take the political pressure and succumbed to their demands (Matthew 27:24).

There might be those who listen to the presentation of the gospel and desire to provide sympathetic support. They may empathize with their humanitarian goals, agree with their holy lifestyle, adhere to some of their values, even admire their courage to speak, but they don't believe in their gospel. Their association is strictly philanthropic. They might have corresponding goals, comparable charitable activities, and similar altruistic aspirations but only on a human level.

Key Concept: Some unbelievers may respond to the gospel by identifying with the humane efforts of the messengers, even assisting them but never come to the knowledge of the truth.

A Fearful Resistance

There might be some who will become so fearful of what Christians say that they will rebuff these evangelists. When Christians share the condemnation and judgment for sin in their gospel presentations, these people may become utterly terrified and want nothing to do with them. In Romans 2:15, Paul describes God's law within the heart of every man that continually accuses him of sin and the resultant judgment that will follow. In Romans 1:18, Paul explains that this is constantly being suppressed. A gospel message may loosen sin's grip and the fear of judgment may flood their hearts.

This occurred with Felix, when Paul presented the gospel.

> As he [Paul] reasoned about righteousness, self-control, and the judgment to come, Felix was terrified, and answered, "Go your way for this time, and when it is convenient for me, I will summon you."
>
> Acts 24:25

In Acts 24:25, Paul shared the good news with this Roman procurator. He spoke of righteousness, self-control, and then judgment. Felix was so terrified that he sent Paul away.

Often, Christians are afraid to alienate the unsaved, so they leave sin and judgment out of their gospel presentation. When this occurs, how can unbelievers repent in order to be saved? It does not allow for this critical response. No one enters into the kingdom of God without repentance. The saints should allow people to become afraid because this ought to drive them to repentance. Though the unsaved may reject this at first, they might repent later. This is the Lord's way (1 Corinthians 14:24). In fear, they will seek to find the only deliverance from their horrifying future at the cross of the crucified and then risen Savior. This is the Holy Spirit's work.

Key Concept: Some unbelievers may respond to the gospel by being terrified of judgment yet reject Jesus Christ and never come to know the truth.

An Impassioned Hate

When Christians present the gospel, some might respond by passionately hating Christ's messengers and His message. This hate may be expressed in a wide variety of ways from verbal to physical persecution. The hate may be deep-seated, intense, and arousing a fury in some.

In Luke 4:29, Jesus spoke in the synagogue of Nazareth among his own family and friends, neighbors and fellow citizens. When He was finished, they were so enraged that they attempted to cease Him and throw Him off the edge of a cliff outside the city. In Acts 14:19, the Jews of Antioch and Iconium came into Lystra and stirred up the crowds against

Paul. Since their feelings were so intense, they stoned him, dragged his body out of the city, and left it to rot.

In Acts 7:54-60, the leaders of Israel were cut to the quick by Stephen's words, so they covered their ears, gnashed their teeth, shouted with one voice, and seized him. They were in such a frenzy that these distinguished religious officials of Israel stoned and murdered him in cold blood.

Again and again, Jesus refers to these types of incidences. He repeatedly announced to His disciples that people would hate them on account of Him. Jesus warned His followers that hating Him would mean hating them (Luke 6:22).

> You will be hated by all men for my name's sake, but he who endures to the end will be saved.
> Matthew 10:22

In Matthew 10:22, Jesus sent His disciples out into the world to preach His gospel. He warned them to be aware that all men will loathe them because of His name. They would have to endure until the end.

In John 15:18-19, Jesus explains the reason that the world despises them. Unbelievers will hate them because they hate Christ! The saved are no longer a part of the world system. This system will not love and embrace them but hate and persecute them.

Christians who want to be embraced by the pop culture will be sorely disappointed. Christ and His true gospel, not the one dressed up in a pretty package without sin, will be hated by the world system; therefore, so will His followers. Saints might experience a passionate hate from unbelievers when the good news of Jesus is shared with them.

Key Concept: Some unbelievers may respond to the gospel by hating the messenger because they detest the name of Christ.

A Relentless Pursuit

Another negative reaction by unbelievers could be the relentless pursuit of the messengers. They become incensed by the message and follow all those who are evangelizing everywhere they go. These pursuers then agitate the other listeners until they are stirred into a frenzy. They continue until finally they lash out at those sharing the gospel.

In Acts 13:14-52, Paul preached in Pisidian Antioch, and many came to Christ. When almost the entire city came out to hear him, the Jews became jealous. So, they stirred up some of the leading men and prominent women of the city against Paul. This animosity toward Paul and his fellow companions led the persecutors to throw them out of the entire region.

In Acts 14:1-7, Paul traveled to Iconium in Galatia and preached the gospel in the synagogue to the Jews. Some believed, but others did not. These others stirred up the Gentiles against Paul in the city. The entire city became divided between these two groups. When this antagonistic group decided to stone Paul, he and his companions fled.

In verses 8-19, Paul arrived in Lystra and healed a man. The people thought he and Barnabas were gods, but Paul denied it and preached a strong gospel. As a result, the Jews from Antioch and Lystra relentlessly pursued Paul to this city and incited the citizens against him. These antagonistic people stoned the apostle Paul, dragged him out of the city, and left him lying on the ground as dead or to die.

This happened twice again. In Acts 17:1-9, Luke records that Paul preached in the city of Thessalonica, angered the Jews, a mob formed, and he fled to Berea.

> But when the Jews of Thessalonica had knowledge that the word of God was proclaimed by Paul at Berea also, they came there likewise, agitating the multitudes.
> Acts 17:13

In Acts 17:13, Paul shared the gospel with the Bereans while they were searching the Scriptures for answers. As this was occurring, the Jews who lived in Thessalonica had heard that Paul had now entered the city of Berea. Immediately, they pursued him, stirred up the crowds, and Paul had to flee.

By Acts 23:12-14, the intensity of some Jews had grown to such a level, a plot was hatched to ambush and assassinate him. Paul had finished preaching to the Jewish council in Jerusalem, who responded with antagonism and outrage. The Romans perceived that things were quickly getting out of hand, so they seized Paul. While in their custody, these assassins approached the council requesting that they send for Paul. On his way, they planned to murder him.

When the nephew of Paul discovered this, he informed the centurion in charge. This centurion believed Paul was in terrible danger, so the officer sent Paul to Caesarea at night. He was accompanied by two hundred soldiers and seventy horsemen with two hundred spearmen. The assassins were in a relentless pursuit, and Paul would be heavily guarded.

Some Christians might not experience the terror of this kind of hostile pursuit but must be aware of its possibility. All the saints should remember that Peter compared Satan to a hungry, growling and roaring lion, who is prowling about seeking someone (a Christian) to devour (1 Peter 5:8). He does not have to bother with us himself, he has demons and the spiritually blind to serve him. They will pursue God's people for him.

> *Key Concept: Some unbelievers may respond to the gospel by relentlessly pursuing the messenger in order to stir up others against him.*

An Associative Persecution

When Christians proclaim the gospel, sometimes people may attempt to persecute family, friends, acquaintances, or anyone in some way associated with them. For some reason, they cannot persecute the actual messengers, so they oppress those who have been associating with them. This might be difficult for the believer to handle, since it involves others.

In Acts 17, Paul's preaching again incensed some of the Jews in Thessalonica. The Jews then recruited some wicked men from the marketplace to assist them. This angry mob went to the house of Jason, where they perceived Paul was staying, to seize him.

> When they didn't find them, they dragged Jason and certain brothers before the rulers of the city.
> Acts 17:6

In Acts 17:6, when the mob discovered Paul had left, they grabbed Jason and some other Christians and dragged them before the city's governing authority. Since they could not persecute Paul, they determined to persecute the ones they thought were harboring and supporting him in evangelism. Jason and other Christians had to bear Paul's persecution.

In Acts 19, Paul's conversions in Ephesus angered the businessmen who were earning their living from the idol worship of Artemis. These evil entrepreneurs began losing money. So, the angry artisans, idolaters, and businessmen began to enrage the Ephesians over the defaming of Artemis. The crowds were thrown into such agitation and confusion that they grabbed the traveling companions of Paul, Gaius and Aristarchus, and rushed with them into the theater for a confrontation. It seems that Gaius and Aristarchus would be a great way to attract Paul, if he was hiding. Perhaps, these two supporters of Paul could become the crowd's objects of wrath if he did not appear. Regardless, Paul's companions were persecuted due to their association with Paul.

Sharing the gospel is a rewarding experience but might also be a dangerous one for the witnessing Christian and his family, acquaintances, and associates. In John 15:20, Jesus warned His disciples that a student is not above his teacher. If they persecuted Him, they would persecute them. As has been previously seen, they may also persecute other people associated with them.

> *Key Concept: Some unbelievers may respond to the gospel by persecuting those who are associated with the messenger because they cannot persecute the messenger directly.*

A Political Opportunism

Some will respond negatively to the gospel, even to the point of persecution, as a political opportunity to advance themselves or their agenda in some way. These unbelievers might not be particularly angry or hateful of Christians but could see the personal and political advantage of rejecting them. The torment or mistreatment of the saved may win them some kind of political victory or allow some important political influence over others.

In Acts 12:1-4, King Herod Agrippa martyred James, the apostle and brother of John. When he saw that it pleased the Jews, he imprisoned Peter also. In Acts 24:27, Paul stood on trial before Felix, the Roman governor. Felix left Paul in prison in Caesarea for two years and then turned him over to his successor Festus because he wanted to gain favor with the Jews. If he had released Paul, the Jews would have been angered. Felix did not want to lose any political support.

Festus saw the same opportunity. In Acts 25:1-8, the Jews begged him to put Paul on trial. Festus met with both parties and heard the Jew's accusations and Paul's defense. Like his predecessor, He also wanted to gain favor with the Jews.

> But Festus, desiring to gain favor with the Jews, answered Paul and said, "Are you willing to go up to Jerusalem, and be judged by me there concerning these things?"
>
> Acts 25:9

In Acts 25:9, Festus asked Paul if the apostle would return to Jerusalem to stand trial before the Jewish council. Realizing Festus was attempting to appease these Jews, Paul exercised his Roman right and appealed to Caesar.

Once again, persecution was for his political ends. Some are motivated by the gain of political advantage. When they meet evangelizing believers, they may persecute them for a political victory. Political influence is a powerful motivator.

> *Key Concept: Some unbelievers may respond to the gospel by persecuting the messenger who brought it because it gives them a political advantage.*

A Merchant Reprisal

Some people might not react directly to the gospel itself but respond to what the gospel has done in someone's life. In this case, someone's financial gain has been curtailed. When certain unbelievers come to Christ, they may have incurred some sinful and wicked financial debts or obligations they can no longer meet. They might be involved in an industry that falls short of God's standard for righteousness and must quit. Therefore, businesspeople or merchants, with whom they work, may retaliate against the persons who instigated these changes in their lives.

One example may be a drug dealer who comes to Christ. The suppliers of the drug dealer might become enraged that their partner is no longer available to deal. Their businesses will be affected, and their income will decline. Or perhaps, a gang member turns his life over to the Lord and quits the gang. This person may hold an important position in their financial endeavors or have critical information concerning their illegal dealings. This may result in targeting not only the dealer but the person who turned him to the light.

A prostitute might find the Lord and turn away from her handler. He might find this situation utterly unacceptable in his dark world of perversion. He may search out the one who impacted her to obtain revenge for his financial losses. Some may have a network of others who are financially invested in their mutual sins.

When they turn to Christ, the network might retaliate. These perpetrators of sinful and illegal gain could desire to exact retribution upon those who share the gospel. There may be the reprisal of the merchants involved. Though this is often considered a better topic for the movies, Christians must be aware of this real-life possibility.

This principle springs directly from the experience of the apostle Paul mentioned before in other contexts.

> But when her masters saw that the hope of their gain was gone, they seized Paul and Silas, and dragged them into the marketplace before the rulers.
>
> Acts 16:19

In Acts 16:16-24, Paul arrived in Philippi and preached the gospel. A demon possessed slave girl followed them around proclaiming that they were servants of the Most High God. After many days, Paul became annoyed and cast the spirit of divination out of her body. Most likely, Paul did not want her fortune telling to be associated with his ministry. Once the demon was gone, her magical skills ceased.

It is assumed that she came to Christ and was a part of the early church at Philippi. When her masters found out that their financial asset was gone, they dragged Paul before the city magistrates. The city officials proceeded to beat him and throw him into prison. These evil merchants wanted revenge upon Paul because their income from their wicked gain was gone. Money can motivate men to commit some evil deeds.

This same kind of persecution happened in Ephesus. In Acts 19:23-41, Paul preached the gospel, and many came to Christ. They forsook their idolatrous worship of Artemis to such an extent that merchants were losing business. These business owners from many trades banded together to exact retribution upon Paul. After stirring their fellow idolaters up into a hysterical frenzy, the apostle could have been killed. Fortunately, the Christians would not let Paul even enter the theater to make a defense so an official of the city convinced the crowd to disperse from their disorderly gathering. After this, Paul left for the region of Macedonia.

Christians should understand that some unbelievers may have evil financial relationships. When they come to Christ, these evil connections might not appreciate the loss of their financial income as these new believers turn their lives fully over to Christ. Merchant's reprisals upon the messenger may result from this new life.

Key Concept: Some unbelievers may respond to the gospel by persecuting the messenger because they had lost some financial interest when an associate received Christ.

A Religious Animosity

When one begins to share the gospel, those who hear may not be coming to Christ out of a religious vacuum. They may have important religious connections that will be disrupted or severed. As the saints draw people from the ranks of false religions, other members may retaliate. The religious fervor they may feel for their beliefs could suddenly be directed in anger and retribution toward the messengers of the gospel. They will not want their devout adherents turning away from their sacred religion. Consider the different persecutors of Jesus in the New Testament. Many were religious people who were very zealous.

Who was it that really persecuted the Lord? The religious council, the Sanhedrin, persecuted Him because Christ was drawing many people away from their influence. It was the religious leaders of the Jews that hounded him and accused him of breaking Mosaic Law every opportunity they could. It was these religious zealots, who plotted His death and badgered the Romans into crucifying Him. In Luke 6:6-11, when the Lord Jesus entered the synagogue on the Sabbath, He encountered a man with a withered hand. The Pharisees

SHARING THE GOSPEL: THE DOCTRINE OF EVANGELISM

and scribes watched Him intently. Would Jesus heal on the Sabbath and defy their religious beliefs and customs? He healed the man, their rage grew, and they began plotting against Him.

These same officials led the mob that came to arrest Jesus.

> Immediately, while he [the Lord Jesus] was still speaking, Judas, one of the twelve, came- and with him a multitude with swords and clubs, from the chief priests, the scribes, and the elders.
>
> Mark 14:43

In Mark 14:43, the Lord was betrayed and arrested by the chief priests, scribes, and elders. These religious examples of righteous living were accompanied by many temple guards and Roman soldiers with a group of common people and unsavory characters. Yet, these Jews were in charge! They were the driving force behind the religious fervor of Christ's persecution and ultimate murder.

Before Annas, a Jewish religious official, Jesus was struck in the face (John 18:22). Before the high priest Caiaphas, they blind-folded Jesus and beat him with their fists. The soldiers demanded He prophecy and kept slapping Him. In Matthew 27:4-7, it was the Sanhedrin who condemned Jesus to death and led him to Pilate to stand trial. They did not have the power to execute anyone according to Roman law or His life would have ended there. This group of religious leaders, who ought to be the example of piety, righteousness, and love, then badgered and taunted Pilate into crucifying the innocent Jesus. They chose to release an insurrectionist and murderer into society to continue his malicious actions upon innocent citizens. They chose to condemn someone who was the epitome of love, compassion, and righteousness.

As has been seen over and over, the apostles and disciples received exactly the same treatment. Christians must know that sharing the gospel might upset the strongly religious in their families, among their friends, and neighbors. It might instigate retaliation from members of their religious group, church, or institution. Christians may face retribution from religious employees or managers within their work force or fellow colleagues within their profession. As has been noted, usually their persecution is even more intense because the persecutors think that they are truly and fully serving their god(s) when they criticize or harm Christians.

> *Key Concept: Some unbelievers may respond to the gospel by persecuting the messenger because they had lost a religious member of their family, friends, neighborhood, or church.*

A False Brethren Interference

As Christians become active in evangelism, Satan might send some false brethren to interfere with their evangelistic efforts. Often, Christians do not consider the possibility that so-called Christians from their own church or organization could obstruct their evangelistic efforts. Yet, this could easily happen from tares, he could sow among the wheat, within their own Christian group (Matthew 13:25). No one imagines opposition from their own members, but it happens.

In Galatians 2:4, Paul describes some false teachers who followed him into the area of Galatia. There, they attempted to bring the brethren, who had been freed by the gospel, back into the bondage of their Jewish customs. Their efforts disrupted Paul's evangelism ministry. These disrupters were even able to persuade Peter to stop eating with the Gentiles. As a result, Paul had to confront Peter (Galatians 2:11-14).

> This was because of the false brothers secretly brought in, who stole in to spy out our liberty which we have in Christ Jesus, that they might bring us into bondage.
>
> Galatians 2:4

Again, in 2 Corinthians 11:13-15, Satan sent several false brethren into the Corinthian church to continually disrupt Paul's ministry. As one can see, the attack of these false brethren might occur on numerous fronts. These tares might question an evangelist's internal motives (1 Thessalonians 2:3-5, Colossians 1:10), evangelistic methods (2 Corinthians 11:7), personal call (2 Corinthians 11:5, 23), or their doctrinal beliefs (Galatians 1:6-11). This can cause havoc to the ministry and testimony of Christians. It can even ruin their reputation and example in the church and community.

In Acts 20:28-30, Paul cautioned the Ephesian elders to beware of savage wolves that would arise from among them and would draw the flock away. Notice, these wolves will be leaders among them. They may be full-time false ministers thwarting the efforts of the true ones in order to discredit them.

Often, they might discredit them by simply declaring that the true minister's evangelistic methods are outdated, his gospel not hip enough, or his presentation not geared to the right audience. Though this may sound resourceful, it makes human wisdom, pragmatism, and marketing strategies the determiner of what methods are correct. Sometimes, they may even take the Bible out of context and quote Scripture to justify their claims. Beware of their interference.

> *Key Concept: Some false brethren in a church may respond to the gospel by questioning the doctrine, methods, or motives of the messenger.*

A Christian Misunderstanding

As believers share the good news, they may receive many negative reactions from those, who do not understand their ministry, inside the church. Not only could these real saints be opposed by false brethren among them but true believers who may be ignorant of biblical truth. Understanding the vast knowledge contained within the Scripture is a daunting task. Often, Christians choose to rely upon others for truth, rather than dig for it themselves in the Bible. This creates in them a susceptibility to error. These saints may read a book, listen to a sermon, or contemplate the subject themselves, and think they know all about a biblical topic. When others depart from this limited knowledge, they shun them.

This is exactly what happened in the early church. In Acts 10, Peter had just brought Cornelius and the members of his household to Christ in Caesarea. This display of God's great mercy upon a Gentile provided fuel for a challenge to Peter's methods.

> When Peter had come up to Jerusalem, those who were of the circumcision contended with him, saying, "You [Peter] went...to uncircumcised men, and ate with them!"
>
> Acts 11:2-3

In Acts 11:1-3, Peter arrived in Jerusalem and some in the church immediately began to question him concerning his regular eating with the Gentiles which was a Jewish custom that was forbidden. In verses 4-18, Peter defended himself by explaining that the gospel was to be given to the Gentiles. When the apostle completed his first missionary journey and arrived in the church at Antioch, Paul and Barnabas shared the great things God had done through them (Acts 14:26-27). This included winning many Gentiles to the faith and planting numerous churches. In Acts 15:1-3, some men traveled from Judea claiming that the Gentiles had to be circumcised to be saved. This caused such a problem that it provoked a calling of the Jerusalem council. The apostles as well as the whole church would have to become involved. Some of the Christians did not understand what God was now doing and opposed their methods.

As was seen previously, Paul spent a large amount of his time defending his ministry to the saints. In Galatia, it was so hostile that Paul had to ask them who had bewitched them. This not only occurs because Satan comes as an angel of light through his emissaries and attempts to lead the brethren astray (2 Corinthians 11:13-20). It also comes from the immaturity of Christians. On numerous occasions, the apostle had to admonish, teach, exhort, and encourage the church at Corinth on so many issues because were still spiritual babies (1 Corinthians 3:1-3). He complained that they still needed spiritual milk when they should be eating meat. These babies gave him the most trouble.

Unfortunately, Christians should understand that within their own churches or ministries, they may find opposition. There may be those who attempt to thwart their sharing of the gospel in some way due to ignorance of the Scriptures. It is important to note that everything Christians do, including the sharing of the gospel, must be judged by the Scriptures. Paul exhorts the church to examine everything carefully (1 Thessalonians 5:18). John demands that believers test the spirits (Holy Spirit or demons) behind the teaching of others (1 John 4:4). The Scriptures alone validate all ministries.

> *Key Concept: Some true brethren in a church may respond to the gospel by questioning the motives, methods, or doctrine of a messenger due to biblical ignorance or demon deceit.*

A Satanic Opposition

Why would the devil bother harassing Christians who are making an impact for Christ? When someone begins to bring souls into the kingdom, he may experience great opposition from this serpent of old. While Job was living righteously for God, this deceiver took notice of him and questioned his real motivation (Job 1:9). Christians should expect Satan to take notice of them when they begin to share the gospel. The Devil's attention will turn toward those who are rescuing his unbelievers from the domain of darkness and transferring them to God's kingdom of light (Colossians 1:13).

This opposition is found from the very outset of Christ's ministry. Jesus told those who opposed Him that they were of their father, the Devil, in John 8:44. When Peter attempted to stop Christ from his journey to the cross, the Lord replied with a rebuke to Satan. Why? Peter had believed one of the Devil's lies (Matthew 16:22).

Later, the Lord Jesus revealed something astonishing to this disciple. Satan had demanded permission to sift him like wheat and implied it had been granted by God. When he had turned back to the Lord (from the denial), Peter was to strengthen his brothers (Luke 22:31). Peter would have been reminded of this prophecy while he was weeping in deep grief over his denial of the Lord. Peter was sure he could stand against anyone to protect the Lord.

In 1 Thessalonians 2:18, Paul described the opposition he was experiencing from the Devil in his evangelistic ministry. This crafty, cunning fallen angel was attacking him.

> Because we wanted to come to you - indeed, I, Paul, once and again - but Satan hindered us.
> 1 Thessalonians 2:18

The word translated "hindered" in the Greek means "to cut into, to impede one's course by cutting off his way." This old serpent was cutting off Paul's way so he could not share the gospel. He was thwarting Paul's efforts.

Christians should realize that Satan may become active in their lives, as they become active in evangelism. As has been seen, this evil angelic being is still subject to the sovereignty of an all-powerful God. Christians can take solace in the fact that God is always in control. Those who will be saved will be saved in spite of Satan's attacks.

> *Key Concept: Satan will respond by opposing the messenger in a variety of ways to hinder the true advance of the gospel.*

Chapter 12

The Proper Response

It is important to understand that the majority of people will react negatively to the gospel. If the road is narrow that proceeds to life, most people will not follow it. Instead, they will respond with one or more of the negative reactions that were previously mentioned. For every person who comes to Christ, many others will not. Though all men are called, few are chosen (Matthew 14:22).

Why do many people negatively react to the gospel? Why do they persecute Christians? Why would they reject eternal life? The answers to these critical questions are found in the sinful nature of man. People are born with a propensity to commit sin (Romans 7:14-23; Romans 5:12,19; Ephesians 2:2). They are spiritually dead (Ephesians 2:1-5; Colossians 2:13-14; Romans 5:15; 6:4-7), hardened in their hearts (Romans 2:5; Acts 7:51; Ephesians 4:18-19), ignorant of spiritual things (1 Corinthians 1:18, 23; 2:14; Romans 1:21-22), prideful (Mark 7:21-22; Romans 1:30; 1 Corinthians 1:18-21), controlled by their lustful desires (Romans 1:26-32; 6:17-18; Ephesians 2:3), and blinded by Satan (2 Corinthians 4:4; Colossians 1:13; 1 John 2:11). They continually refuse to give up their beloved sin to humble themselves before Jesus Christ (Romans 1:18-32). With this desperate condition of unbelievers, what else should the saints expect from them but negative reactions leading to persecution?

How should all Christians respond? James and John, the apostles, thought Christians should respond with wrath. In Luke 9, the Lord sent messengers into a Samaritan village to make advanced preparations to lodge there. The messengers returned with a rejection from the villagers. They would not accommodate Him because He was travelling to Jerusalem. The Samaritans hated the Jews and their temple. Theirs had been destroyed a long time ago and they were jealous of the magnificent Herodian temple of the Jews.

> When his disciples, James and John, saw this, they said, "Lord, do you want us to command fire to come down from the sky, and destroy them, just as Elijah did?"
> Luke 9:54

In Luke 9:54, when James and John witnessed this refusal on the part of the Samaritans, they were livid. The two brothers immediately asked if they could command fire to come from heaven and consume these inconsiderate people. The Lord rebuked them. He had not come to destroy men's lives but to save them.

Christians are to respond to these negative reactions in a manner that save the lives of men, not destroy them. God has carefully articulated the various responses Christians are to have through His Son and the apostles. As will be seen, the following responses will be actions reflecting His person (character), purposes, and power.

> *Key Concept: When unbelievers react negatively to the good news, the saints should demonstrate God's person, purposes, and power in their responses.*

The Proper Response Explained

The response of Christians to their persecutors is the same as the reaction of believers to their enemies. Essentially, the two comprise the same group. Enemies persecute Christians and those who persecute Christians are their enemies. The Lord Jesus taught that God's people are to love, bless, do good to, pray for, not resist, and forgive their enemies. This critical discussion will explain how these responses were the true intent of God's law but were circumvented by God's nation Israel. The reasons for these supernatural responses lie in the person, purpose, and power of God that must be displayed in His people for the unsaved to see.

The True Intent of the Law

One of the purposes of the instruction of the Lord was to present God's true intent behind the divine law to Israel. God's offspring completely misunderstood His intent in the law because they had over time reinterpreted and added so many additional mandates to His righteous commandments. Then, they attempted daily to meticulously obey these man-made decrees or ordinances. This produced in them a false sense of righteousness. Their intent and motives could be evil as long as their outward actions appeared devout. He intended to correct this false notion by properly interpreting the law from God's point of view which had been lost. This required preaching God's true commandments and then to properly interpret them. The original intent behind the Lord God's ordinances had to be restored.

In Matthew 5:38-45 and Luke 6:27-36, Jesus challenges two of the decrees. One decree was "Take an eye for and eye, and a tooth for a tooth." Another of the decrees was "Love your neighbor and hate your enemies." All of the first saying and the first part of the second saying came directly from the Old Testament. The second part of the second saying was added essentially through human logic. In the first saying, the Jews misinterpreted God's law and His intent behind the law. In the second, the Jews added a part, He did not intend.

SHARING THE GOSPEL: THE DOCTRINE OF EVANGELISM

Once properly interpreted by Jesus, God's people were given the appropriate reactions they should take when any persecution comes their way. In them, Jesus describes the relationship that believers in Christ should maintain amid their persecutors, enemies, and unbelievers in general.

The concept of "an eye for an eye" comes from three Old Testament passages: Exodus 21:23, Leviticus 24:19-20, and Deuteronomy 19:21. These were judicial laws set up for the nation of Israel to govern its people. They were not moral precepts for individuals to follow in their relationships and dealings with others. The context of each of these passages involves dispensing justice by society. The moral precepts involved dispensing love by individuals.

The concept of "love your neighbor" is also found in the Old Testament but without the second part. This second part was added later by the Jewish religious leaders.

> You shall not take vengeance, nor bear any grudge against the children of your people; but you shall love your neighbor as yourself. I am Yahweh.
>
> Leviticus 19:18

God commands believers to not act in vengeance; instead, they should love their neighbors. These religious scholars disregarded the first portion and added instead "hate your enemies" as the logical conclusion. This allowed them to hate any person who was against them. This authorized them to hate in God's name.

> *Key Concept: When unbelievers react negatively to the good news, the saints should follow the personal precepts of love and not the governmental and legal precepts of justice as their primary motivation.*

The True Demonstration of God's Person

To love, bless, do good to, pray for, meet the needs of, and forgive someone's enemies are difficult tasks, something opposite to how the world would respond. Just before Jesus uttered these commandments in Matthew 5:19-20, He made a powerful statement to the Jewish people. He declared that unless their righteousness exceeded the Scribes and the Pharisees, they could not inherit the kingdom of heaven. God's standards are higher than man's, in fact higher than the highest of his man-made standards. Jesus explained in Matthew 5:45 and Luke 6:31-35 the five critical reasons why Christians need to take the higher path of righteousness, even towards enemies.

First, Jesus explained to believers that loving their enemies constantly demonstrates that they are children of God. In Matthew 5:45, He asserts believers do these things that they may be children of their heavenly Father. Second, loving enemies is a quality or characteristic of God Himself. Jesus goes on to present in the same verse that God makes the sun rise and rain fall to bless all people both the just and unjust.

Third, saints should be holier than unbelievers. The word "holy" means "separate" or "wholly different." In verses 46-47, the Lord Jesus explains that even the tax-gatherers (a hated, heathen group) love people who love them and greet their friends. When Christians do this, they don't in any way distinguish themselves from unbelievers. When they love those who do not love them, then that is wholly different.

> If you lend [money] to those from whom you hope to receive, what credit is that to you? Even sinners [unbelievers] lend to sinners, to receive back as much.
>
> Luke 6:34

In Luke 6:34, Jesus extends this doing good even to lending. Even sinners lend to those who they know will return the money. The love of Christians for enemies requires love at a supernatural level.

Fourth, a believer's reward for loving his enemies will be great. Jesus implies in Matthew 5:46 that there is not much reward in Christians loving those who love them. In Luke 6:35, He says that if the saints love their enemies, do good to them, and lend expecting nothing in return, then great will be their reward. Fifth, the children of God are to imitate their Father. In Matthew 5:48, Jesus says they are to be perfect as their Father is perfect and in Luke 6:36, believers should be merciful as their Father is merciful.

Even before these incredible words, Jesus explains that God's children are to be salt and shining lights in the world (Matthew 5:13-16). From these five reasons and elsewhere, it can be fully seen that shining lights and savory salt manifest God's person, purpose, and power to the world. Christians exhibit His person in that these are His characteristics, not man's. They portray His purpose since men can see clearly that He exists and loves all men. Since the unsaved will see His person, purpose, and power in their Christian lives, they will know that these believers are from the true God. This prepares them to hear His saving message.

These lights must continually shine even in the face of persecution and enemy attack. This salt must continually remain tasty even in the midst of mistreatment and enemy opposition. When Christians are tormented, harassed, and violently assailed, they are not to respond with revenge and retaliation, which is a human approach. Instead, they are to react in love, blessing, good works, prayer, meeting needs (not resisting), and forgiveness. In this, God is manifested, the good news can be presented, and God's power to save lives will be unleashed. Unbelievers will be able to identify Christians as the ones who have the true God in their lives.

To love, bless, do good to, pray for, not resist, and forgive one's enemies are characteristics of God's person. In Exodus 34:6-7, Moses was allowed to see the backside of God's glory. As God passed by, He proclaimed that He was gracious, merciful, forgiving, slow to anger, and full of kindness and truth. These attributes comprise His character. Even though men are in total rebellion to Him, God's character does not change. Whether men are enemies or children of God, they will experience all of His attributes though not always in the same way.

In Romans 1:19-20, Paul declared that God's deity, power, and attributes are clearly seen through his creation. In Acts 14:17, Paul proclaims that God's creation also displays to the world His grace and mercy since the rains from the heavens brings fruitful seasons, which satisfies their hearts with food and with gladness. His blessing upon them in creation will prepare them for the gospel.

Christians are growing more and more into the image of Christ. Their thinking, speaking, feeling, and behaving are becoming more and more like Jesus. Paul discloses to the Corinthians that believers are beholding the glory of the Lord in a mirror and being transformed into the same image of Christ from glory to glory (2 Corinthians 3:18). As they grow in Christ, they are being transformed into His image.

John has a similar thought regarding a believer's behavior as he lives for Christ.

> He who says he remains in him ought himself also to walk just like he walked.
> 1 John 2:6

SHARING THE GOSPEL: THE DOCTRINE OF EVANGELISM

In 1 John 2:6, John tells his readers that if Christians abide in Him, they ought to walk as He walked. True believers will obey this command (John 14:15,23). They will walk as their Savior and Lord walked. They will demonstrate God's holy character and person and behave like Him.

When His children come to share the good news, then unbelievers will know them. Christians will behave like the God they know from His creation and blessing. Even if they persecute them, the character of God's grace, mercy, love, and blessing will manifest itself through the words and actions of His children. Again, they will know that those who proclaim the gospel of salvation are truly from God.

To accomplish this, God reveals His judgment upon sin through His creation from outside man (Romans 1:18-20) and the conscience from within man (Romans 2:14-16). Men reject the knowledge of God because they suppress the truth in their wickedness (Romans 1:18). Instead of honoring or thanking God for His grace, man created his own gods to worship and venerate (Romans 1:21-23). God's response was the abandonment of man to every sexual sin (Romans 1:24, 26, 28). In this, His wrath is revealed. When men see this, they know wrath and judgment are coming.

When God's children come to present their message of judgment and Christ's deliverance, these sinful unbelievers will know them. Christians will be like their Father, who these unsaved know from His creation and blessing. Even if they persecute God's children, His grace, mercy, love, and blessing will come through their words and actions. Again, they will know that their message of judgment and salvation is truly from God. When they see hate and scorn in the eyes of those who share the gospel, they will not recognize them. Why? They cannot see the God that they have come to know from His creation. This is so important.

God's eternal power is exhibited throughout His creation and, more importantly, is clearly seen (Romans 1:20). Notice, Paul describes His power as eternal. It is divine power that has no limit. It extends from eternity past to eternity future. It comes from a Greek root word that means "perpetually, incessantly, or invariably." The root is translated "always" or "constantly." This power of God will always and forever be powerful. It will never cease!

The book of Romans is all about eternal judgment and salvation. This requires eternal power to eternally save or eternally condemn. Unbelievers clearly observe this power in creation, and they know it is eternal. Therefore, when they understand that their judgment is coming, they also know that God has the ability to make their condemnation eternal. Why? His power is eternal. They also understand that if they honor and thank God, He possesses the ability to make that salvation eternal because His power is eternal. When God's children proclaim the message of judgment and salvation, these unbelievers will know them. Christians will be like their Father, who they know from His creation and blessing. Even if they persecute the Lord's children, His grace, mercy, love, and blessing will shine through all their words and actions. These unsaved ones will know Christians have the gospel with the eternal power to save because they will see it displayed in their lives under persecution.

Key Concept: When unbelievers react negatively to the good news, the saints should manifest in word and deed the character of the God who sent them.

The Proper Response Described

For Christians to display God's divine character to their enemies in love, blessing, good works, prayer, and meeting their needs (not resisting them), it may require a battle with the supernatural forces of evil. Why? These responses are diametrically opposed to how human beings, society, or the Devil naturally think or feel toward enemies.

This battle will be against the flesh (James 1:14-15), the world (1 John 2:15-17), and the Devil (2 Corinthians 2:11). The flesh enjoys its natural impulses to hate, curse, and retaliate against enemies. Society has a long history of hate, cursing, and retaliating against national, cultural, racial, familial, and individual enemies. The Serpent has invested thousands of years of hating, cursing, and retaliating against God, His angels, and His people upon the Earth. This battle may require great effort and take some time to find victory (Mark 14:38; Romans 7:23; 1 Cor. 9:25-26; Hebrews 12:4).

For believers to stand against these antagonists, they will need supernatural strength. This strength must come from the Holy Spirit as Christians rely on His power (Galatians 5:16-24; Ephesians 6:10-22; 1 Peter 5:6-10). This is not only the childlike dependence of trust in God (the way a small child trusts in his dad for protection) it will require growing up in all aspects of Him (Ephesians 4:14-15; 1 Corinthians 13:11; 1 John 2:12-14).

As Christians grow up in Christ, the power necessary to battle these spiritual adversaries will be released (2 Peter 1:3-4; Philippians 2:12-13; 1 Thessalonians 1:5). First, the saints need to grow in the word (1 Peter 2:2; 1 Thessalonians 2:13; Ephesians 4:11-12). Second, believers need to pray with other believers for strength (Ephesians 6:18-19; Philippians 1:19; Matthew 26:41). Third, the saints need to be building up and edifying one another in fellowship together (Romans 14:19; 15:14; 1 Corinthians 14:12). This is so important. Those who are strong in these certain areas can encourage and provide examples for those who are struggling.

Fourth, those who love the Lord must be living a life of obedience (1 Corinthians 3:1-3; Romans 6:19; Galatians 5:7) constantly submitting themselves to their Master (Romans 12:1-2; James 4:7; Ephesians 6:6). Fifth, His people must put on the armor of light (Romans 13:12; Ephesians 6:11; 1 John 1:7). Sixth, Christians must resist all these adversaries (2 Corinthians 7:1; James 4:7; 1 Peter 5:9).

> *Key Concept: When unbelievers react negatively to the good news, the saints may have to do battle with the flesh, world, and Devil for a time, which will require supernatural strength to bring victory.*

The Leaving of Vengeance to God

In Matthew 5:44 and Luke 6:27, Jesus states that the saints are to love their enemies. In Romans 13:1-4, Paul states that it is the responsibility of governing authorities to be avengers of God. Christians are to show love to their enemies, but the government is to prosecute those enemies for harming them, violating their rights, and breaking the law. One is personal and the other is judicial. The personal precepts involve love. The judicial precepts involve justice.

Saints do not avenge, nor bear any grudge but love their neighbors as themselves. Vengeance comes from God and through the government. This is a critical distinction. This does not in any way imply that people should not or cannot defend themselves against harm. Of course, they may and should, but this topic is for another book.

This concept of loving enemies and leaving the vengeance to God is not only seen in the Old Testament in Leviticus 19:18 but also in the New Testament. In Romans 12:19, Paul quotes Moses in Deuteronomy 32:35 and fully reiterates the importance of not taking vengeance upon others but letting God do His judicial work.

> Don't seek revenge yourselves, beloved, but give place to God's wrath. For it is written, "Vengeance belongs to me; I will repay, says the Lord."
>
> Romans 12:19

In this passage, Paul clearly explains that vengeance belongs to God. That is His responsibility. In 2 Thessalonians 1:3-10, Paul praises the Thessalonians for their patient endurance of the suffering of persecution, which is a sign of the righteous judgment of God. He will repay their affliction.

When persecution comes, Christians should be concerned with spiritual matters first. How the saints treat unbelievers in the ways that have been discussed is critical. Christians may seek justice from their government and pray for justice (Psalm 94:1-7; Revelation 6:9-11). This does not imply that believers cannot defend themselves as the law allows.

> *Key Concept: When unbelievers react negatively to the good news, the saints should not take revenge, but rely instead, on God's retaliation through His direct hand or the government He has established.*

The Showing of Love to Persecutors

Jesus Christ explains in Matthew 5:44 and Luke 6:27 that Christians are to love their enemies, the ones who persecute them. The word "love" in this passage is not the concept of romantic love but something much deeper. The Greek word essentially means to value or prize someone or something. This word was utilized by Jesus and His disciples to speak of valuing to the point of sacrifice. The classic use of the word is found in John 3:16, where Jesus asserts that God so loved the world that He gave His Son. God so valued the world that He gave, even though it was hostile to Him. Like our God, Christians are to love the world that they also give, even though it is hostile to them. Sacrificial giving is crucial in demonstrating this love to the world and distinguishing the true people of God from the false people of God. This also distinguishes the true gospel from the false gospel.

This coincides with the great commandments that Jesus acknowledged in Luke 10:27. Men are to love God and love their neighbors as themselves. When a lawyer asked Him who was this neighbor, he referred to, Jesus told the story of the Good Samaritan in verses 30-36. This story indicated that his neighbor went beyond all races, genders, and creeds to anyone in need. Even enemies of saints may be in need and would obviously be their neighbor. In the story, the Jewish man, who was robbed and beaten, was aided by a Samaritan man. The Samaritans and Jews hated each other and were enemies. However, as God's people love themselves, they are to love their enemies.

This is found in the Old Testament as well. In Proverbs 11:12, Solomon declares that the despising of one's neighbor displays a lack of wisdom. Later in Proverbs 14:21, he calls it sin. In the New Testament, according to Jesus it is the second of the two great commandments (Matthew 22:36-40). Even Paul restates this command in his own way in the book of Romans. The loving of one's neighbor is an essential in the Christian life.

> Owe no one anything, except to love one another; for he who loves his neighbor has fulfilled the law.
>
> Romans 13:8

In Romans 13:8, Paul writes again that Christians are to owe nothing to anyone except to love one another. Believers are to have only one debt toward their neighbors. This debt is to love them. This love fulfilled the law. If one summed up all God's commandments toward others, it would be to love one's neighbor, whether they are enemies or not.

So much more could be said. A good concordance study of the word "love" would reveal much more. No matter what kind of negative reactions Christians may receive from the world, unbelievers are to be loved by those saints, especially ones who become their enemies. Jesus desires unbelievers to be valued, prized, and loved sacrificially as He did for us.

Key Concept: When unbelievers react negatively to the good news, the saints should demonstrate their love by sacrificially meeting their needs.

The Giving of a Blessing to Persecutors

Not only are Christians to love their enemies but are also to give a blessing to them. In the passages of Matthew 5:44 and Luke 6:28, believers are commanded to bless everyone who curses them. Providing a blessing was a very familiar concept in the Old Testament. A typical kind of blessing is found in Ruth 2:3-5 when Boaz went out into his own fields. When he found his reapers, he greeted them with, "May the Lord be with you!" Then they returned his blessing with a similar one, "May the Lord bless you!" This general blessing was extremely meaningful. This expressed the genuine and heartfelt desire that the other person would find safety and protection in God.

In Numbers 6:22-27, the Lord told Moses to have Aaron bless the people of Israel with the words the Lord gave him to speak. He was to request that the Lord bless them, keep them, make His face shine on them, be gracious to them, lift up His countenance on them, and give them peace. This was a manifold blessing as God poured out His grace upon them.

In Deuteronomy 7:13, God explained to Moses that if the Israelites kept His commandments, He would bless the fruit of their womb and multiply their offspring. God would pour out His grace upon them by blessing the fruit of the ground, multiplying all their grain, wine, oil, herds, and flocks. So, blessings can be general or very specific.

This is the kind of blessing Paul encourages Christians to give to their enemies and persecutors.

> Bless those who persecute you; bless, and don't curse.
>
> Romans 12:14

In Romans 12:14, he commands the church at Rome to bless those who persecute them and not curse them. The city of Rome was the seat of the Roman emperors. These despots were responsible for the persecution of saints using many horrific methods of terror. Martyrdom became a common way of life in many periods of this city's history; yet they were to bless these persecutors.

Paul endured many of these kinds of persecutions at the hand of the Jews and Gentiles. In 1 Corinthians 4:12, Paul describes his response to those who cursed him. He would give a blessing in return. He would wish God's grace upon those who railed against him. Though his words could have been unkind; instead, he blessed them. Believers who are persecuted should provide a blessing upon their persecutors or enemies, both in their hearts and from their mouths. Of course, God's ultimate blessing would be in their repentance.

SHARING THE GOSPEL: THE DOCTRINE OF EVANGELISM

> *Key Concept: When unbelievers react negatively to the good news, the saints should provide a verbal blessing from their hearts.*

The Doing of Good to Persecutors

Not only are all Christians to love and bless their enemies, but they are to do good to them. In Matthew 5:44 and Luke 6:27, all believers are commanded by the Lord Jesus to do good to those who hate them. When His followers are seeking to do good works for the glory of God, perhaps they should consider their enemies or persecutors. These could be the recipients of their righteous deeds and aspirations.

In Acts 14:8-18, both Paul and Barnabas entered Lystra and healed a man who had been lame from birth. Thinking they were gods (Hermes and Zeus), the people responded by worshiping and making sacrifices to them. Aghast by this inappropriate response, Paul and Barnabas tore their robes and declared to the crowd that they were mere men. Instead, they had come to proclaim the true God. It was time for the citizens of Lystra to turn toward the Lord God who had been testifying to these people throughout history. The true deity, whom they represented, had been sending rain from heaven and producing fruitful seasons to satisfy their hearts with food and gladness. In essence, His person, purpose, and power had been on display all along through His goodness. The point is that doing good to enemies is a characteristic of God. As a result, believers are to behave in the same manner as their Father.

In John 5:29, Jesus pronounced that those who did good deeds would proceed to a resurrection of life. Paul teaches the same concept in Romans 2:10, when he wrote that glory and honor and peace will be for everyone who does good.

> Even so, let your light shine before men; that they may see your good works…glorify your Father who is in Heaven.
>
> Matthew 5:16

In Matthew 5:16, Jesus indicated that His people should let their light shine before men, so that all will see His goodness in them and glorify God. The term "men" includes enemies.

In Ephesians 2:10, Paul views God's church as His divine workmanship, created in Christ Jesus for good works (good deeds). Then, Paul encourages his readers to walk in them. These good works must extend to persecutors, enemies, and unbelievers in general. In 2 Peter 2:18-20, the apostle Peter commands Christian slaves with unruly and mean masters to be submissive with all respect. The apostle argues that when these slaves, who believe in Jesus, suffer unjustly, yet submit and respect their masters, this finds favor with God. Would that not be a good work toward a persecutor or an enemy?

In Romans 15:1-3, Paul exhorts all believers to bear the weaknesses of those who are weak and not just seek their own pleasure. Then Paul provides a general principle. The saved are to please their neighbors (including enemies) for good and for their edification or building up. So, pleasing neighbors for their good is good works. In chapter 12, verse 21, Paul writes that Christians should overcome evil with good.

This includes the enemies and persecutors of Christians. Why? Enemies and persecutors desire to bring evil upon believers; this should be overcome with good works. In 1 Corinthians 10:24, he reiterates this command to the church in Corinth. Again, he writes that they are to seek the good of their neighbors (anyone in need). The implication is clear.

Therefore, a characteristic of all believers are good works. These are not just toward other Christians but all (including persecutors and enemies). In Galatians 6:10, Paul exhorted the Galatians to do good to all men, while they were given the opportunity, especially ones of the household of faith. So, the first priority of doing good is to other Christians and then to everyone.

What do good deeds entail? John explains that loving the brethren involves word, tongue, deed, and truth in 1 John 3:15. Would not good towards a neighbor involve both good words and good actions? This may seem humanly difficult to behave like this toward one's enemies, but it has always been the Lord God's way. If He had not sent His Son to offer salvation (good in word and tongue) and then die for men's sins (good in deed and truth), no one would ever have been saved. Wasn't mankind in rebellion and His enemy at the time? So, believers are to do good to those who oppose them because God did the same for them.

> *Key Concept: When unbelievers react negatively to the good news, all the saints should do good toward them in word, deed, and by meeting their pressing needs.*

The Offering of Prayer for Persecutors

Not only are all Christians to bless their enemies but pray for them. In Matthew 5:44 and Luke 6:28, Christians are told to pray for those who mistreat them and persecute them. Before Christians believe in our Lord, they are unbelievers, who are reacting negatively to the gospel. The Scriptures are replete with accounts of many formerly hostile unbelievers who eventually received Christ. These became illustrations of God's person, purpose, and power. Since He calls unsaved persecutors to His Son, the saints need to pray for them. An initial negative reaction may not predict a future rejection.

Nicodemus, the teacher of the Jews, began in John 3 with negative reactions to Jesus and His gospel. He is not spoken of again until John 19:39-42 when he brought the spices to anoint the dead body of the Lord Jesus. Sometime between his conversation with Jesus in John 3 and His anointing of the body of Jesus in John 19, Nicodemus became a Christian.

Before this, Nicodemus was an important member of the Sanhedrin. As a result, he must have participated in the variety of ways this Jewish council hounded, mocked, and discredited Jesus which ultimately led to the murder of the Lord Jesus. This teacher of Israel reacted negatively at first, later he believed. Perhaps, the Lord prayed for Nicodemus when He went off to pray though he was an enemy.

As has been noted, Paul was a vicious persecutor of the church. His negative reactions to the good news went to the furthest extremes against believers: tracking the newborn Christians, storming into their private homes, hauling off these innocent people, throwing these virtuous saints into prison, and eventually martyring them (Acts 8:1-3; 9:1-2). He began with negative reactions, lavishing in being both an enemy and persecutor of the church. Eventually, he came to Christ (Acts 9:5). Perhaps, those who were fleeing from Saul prayed for his salvation.

Paul and the other apostles witnessed many enemies and persecutors of Christians transformed into supporters and proclaimers of the gospel. In Acts 16, Paul was thrown into prison in Philippi. It can be reasonably assumed the jailer did not give him a warm reception, since he was ordered to put Paul and Silas into the stocks to secure them from escape. In verses 35-41, Paul did a good work in the jailer's life by saving him from killing himself. This gave Paul the opportunity to share the good news and he and his whole household came to the Savior. The jailer went from negative reactions to the gospel and being an enemy and persecutor to one of the original members of the newly founded church at Philippi. Perhaps, Paul and Silas were praying for the jailer even while their limbs were stretched out in the stocks.

In Acts 18:1-11, Paul was resisted, mocked, criticized, and eventually thrown out of the synagogue in Corinth. Would the leader of the synagogue be instrumental in this negative reaction? Yes. Yet, when Paul was instructing in the house next door, owned by Titius Justus, Crispus, the leader of the synagogue, received Jesus Christ as Lord and Savior with all of His household. Crispus was transformed from being a persecutor of the church to being a staunch advocate and proclaimer of Jesus Christ. In previous discussions of Paul's missionary journeys, it has been continually demonstrated that the hostile Jews and Gentiles, though they were enemies and persecutors of Christians, ultimately became believers. Could Paul have been praying for Crispus and these others?

When Paul was imprisoned in Rome for the first time in Acts 28:30-31, the Philippian church was concerned about him and needed much encouragement. In Philippians 1:12, he explained what God was doing in Rome. He asserted that there was a greater progress of the gospel. The Greek word he used which is translated "progress" refers to a pioneering work. It was used to describe the work of Roman soldiers when they had to cut through the thick habitation of an area. As a result, they would be able to build a decent road in order to transfer troops from one place to another.

God was building a road for the gospel into Rome. How was God accomplishing this? In verse 13, Paul reasons that the slumbering church in Rome had awakened because of his boldness. The saints in the capital city of the Roman Empire were now out boldly preaching Christ. The whole Praetorian

Guard had heard the gospel among many others who were coming to him. In Philippians 4:22, the letter closes with his final example of the pioneering work, when he sends a greeting from those who now believed from Caesar's own household. All of this was taking place right in the emperor's own city while Caesar Nero was a horrific persecutor of the church. Perhaps, the apostle was praying for these guards and household members while imprisoned.

Why are all these examples important? God can and does bring the persecutors and enemies of the gospel to Christ. No man or woman is beyond the reach of the all-powerful, almighty, sovereign God. Consequently, salvation should be the first thing on the lips of believers as they are praying for their enemies and persecutors.

In the previous chapter, the role of prayer in evangelism was discussed. It was discovered that prayer is an essential part of evangelism. Likewise, evangelism is an essential part of prayer because it can move the hand of God. Christians must be praying for the souls of their unsaved enemies and persecutors. They should petition the Lord to open doors in the midst of their enemies, ask for His wisdom in how they ought to speak, and boldness to speak it amid persecution. Saints are to request that the Word spread rapidly among all of these lost people. Believers should request God to bring many additional workers into the harvest so as many as has been appointed to eternal life may be saved.

There is another appeal Christians should make to their Lord. It is found in Paul's first letter to Timothy. It involves those who are the governing authorities in their land. These important rulers are capable of legislating, administering, and then enforcing their laws which could protect Christians from persecution. This was displayed so clearly in the rise of Constantine the Great, who brought peace to Christendom.

We see this today in many countries of the world as well.

In 1 Timothy 2:2, Paul urges young Timothy to pray for those who are in authority, so these would allow Christians to live peaceful and quiet lives in godliness and dignity.

> For kings and all who are in high places; that we may lead a tranquil and quiet life in all godliness and reverence.
> 1 Timothy 2:2

This is a prayer that petitions God to soften the hearts of the unsaved rulers so they will look kindly upon Christians and not seek to persecute them. This was a request that believers be allowed to share the good news, worship their Lord, and walk in His holiness unencumbered by the government.

Christians should regularly bring the unsaved to God in prayer, especially those who respond negatively to the good news. They are to plead for the salvation of their persecutors and their proclamation of the gospel to them. They should pray that the governing authorities will allow them to live in peace.

> *Key Concept: When unbelievers react negatively to the good news, the messengers should pray for their souls, the preaching of the good news, and for the authorities to allow them to live in peace.*

The Unwillingness to Resist Persecutors

In Matthew 5:39-41 and Luke 6:29-30, Jesus declared that his followers should not "resist their enemies." The Greek word translated "resist" means to oppose or stand against. A careful reading of the context demonstrates that it has to do with enemies in need. In Matthew 5:42, after providing three examples of not resisting enemies, Jesus presents the general guiding principle. His followers are to give to every person who asks or wants to borrow from them. They should not oppose them because they are enemies. When people need something the saints have, they should generously provide it for them, even if they are enemies or persecutors. Jesus is contrasting this to their concept of "take an eye for an eye and a tooth for a tooth." This would dictate when enemies ask, Christians should resist them or deprive them of what they need because they don't deserve it. This is not what God does. He provides for the needs of all mankind.

Therefore, the three examples the Lord provides has to do with someone who is in need. The first illustration involves the shaming and humiliating of believers who have offended their enemies. In Matthew 5:39 and Luke 6:29, this enemy of the believer slaps him on the right cheek. Being hit on the right cheek would indicate the believer was hit backhanded with the enemy's right hand. A straight slap would hit the left cheek. In ancient times, this slap was a challenge, a sign of humiliation to the offender by an offended person.

In the context, an unbeliever becomes offended while he is in need. The Christian has no obligation to give him what he desires even though he may think he deserves it. When the Christian refuses, he slaps him. The believer should let the enemy humiliate him. This is why Jesus said that His followers should just turn the other cheek. Let him humiliate the believer even more. Real Christians do not retaliate when humiliated. Yet, it would be better, if he had just provided it for him. Self-defense is not an issue here.

The second illustration involves an enemy who thinks a Christian possesses what he needs, so he sues the believer in court. In this example, the enemy needs the coat of the saint, so he sues the saint for it. Someone does not sue another unless he needs something that the other may possess. The enemy decides that he deserves it, and the law will support him. This enemy needs this Christian's undergarment, his tunic. In some way, he thinks it is his, so he decides to sue. Jesus says, just give him the undergarment. While a believer is at it, let him give him his cloak also.

The Christian is not to retaliate or get angry. This saint should relinquish and give up his most essential garment, the cloak. The "cloak" was not only the undergarment that every person wore, but it also could be used for a blanket at night for warmth, if one needed it. Christians should go out of their way to reconcile with these enemies in need of what they have.

The third illustration involved soldiers who were in need of help. These military men did not need objects from others but physical help. By law, soldiers could ask regular citizens to carry their pack for them for a distance. As an example, Simon the Cyrene was required to carry the cross of Jesus (Matthew 27:32). Roman soldiers were hated by the Jews and were considered enemies and persecutors. The implication was powerful. This hated Roman soldier asks a Jew to walk a mile with his pack. He is to take it two miles. So, when an enemy is in need of physical help, a believer should give him twice as much as he needs.

In Romans 12, Paul states that saints are to never repay evil for evil but to seek peace with men, if it is possible.

> Therefore "If your enemy is hungry, feed him. If he is thirsty, give him a drink; for in doing so, you will heap coals of fire on his head."
> Romans 12:20

In the next verse, Romans 12:20, believers are given another aspect to Christ's mandate to never seek vengeance. It is easy to withhold something an enemy needs out of vengeance. God will avenge, believers must feed their enemies. If they are cold, then give them a coat. These good deeds will heap hot coals upon their heads (a reference to humiliating them with good). Christians are to overcome evil with good.

The point of the Lord is extremely clear. His followers are nothing like their unbelieving counterparts. They will go out of their way and beyond their comfort to meet the needs of people. Does someone need something a believer has and tries to humiliate him to get it? There is no need to challenge him because he can have it. Does someone sue a believer because he needs something the believer might be wearing? He should not bother because he will give him two articles of clothing. Does someone need a believer to help him carry something some distance? There is no problem because he will carry it twice as far. Believers are not like other people even their enemies will be helped.

> *Key Concept: When unbelievers react negatively to the good news, the saints should not resist them, but meet their needs, even beyond what may be desired.*

The Willingness to Forgive Persecutors

Christians should forgive their persecutors and enemies. Though this concept is not seen in these Matthew and Luke passages which were mentioned earlier, nevertheless, it is an important consideration. There are several passages in the Bible that attest to the importance of this principle. In any discussion of how Christians should treat their enemies the examples of Jesus and Stephen must be examined.

In Luke 23:34, the Lord is hanging on the cross, dripping with blood from the crown of thorns and the nails in his hands and feet. In His excruciating pain from the tortures and violent beatings, agonizing in the slow dying process, humiliated from the mocking of the people, He cried to the Father to forgive these ignorant persecutors. The Romans, who were doing all the dirty work the Jews could not do, did not realize that they were really crucifying the ultimate King of Kings and Lord of Lords. The common Jews, who were standing around the cross throwing insults at the Lord, could not fully understand that their longed-for Messiah was hanging from that cursed tree.

The frightened disciples who were hiding from the mob could not comprehend that their great moment of victory in salvation had not been lost in that dying man. Instead, it was about to be completed when the price was paid, and Christ had risen from the dead. Even, many of the rulers, who were caught up in their self-righteous pride, could not perceive that the veil of the temple was about to be split into two. The lamb would be sacrificed, and the new eternal high priest would enter the Holy of Holies to represent them before the Father in heaven. In the midst of his deep anguish. Christ knowing all of this, looked down with great compassion, and cried out for the Father's forgiveness. Christians know through their study of the Scriptures that the prayer could only be fulfilled if these ignorant, hardhearted persecutors and enemies of the cross received the soon to be risen Son of God as Savior and Lord. Yet, implied in the merciful cry to His Father, is a God who became truly man, and as man forgave His persecutors, tormentors, and scoffers.

In Acts 7:54-59, Stephen preached before the Sanhedrin and indicted them for their sin and what they did to the Lord by killing their Messiah. They responded by rushing him, dragging him out of the city, and stoning him to death.
> He kneeled down, and cried with a loud voice, "Lord, don't hold this sin against them!" When he had said this, he fell asleep.

A BIBLICAL HANDBOOK

Acts 7:60

In his final words in Acts 7:60, Stephen took up Jesus Christ's compassionate mantle and begged God for their forgiveness. I am sure for the same reasons. Once again, true forgiveness from God must be obtained through and only through His Son. Once again, implicit in his compassionate words is his own forgiveness of these murderers.

The question then arises, "Does the Bible explicitly teach that Christians are to forgive their unbelieving enemies and persecutors?" Most Christians acknowledge that they must forgive their fellow saints (Ephesians 4:32; Colossians 3:13). Yet, most of these are not so sure of the specific teaching concerning the forgiveness of those who have not turned to Christ. Are believers to forgive? The answer proceeds from the mouth of the Lord Himself.

All Christians are compelled by their Lord and Savior to forgive anyone and everyone, believer or unbeliever, friend or foe, brother or acquaintance, and persecutor or supporter for any and all transgressions! This is a tall order. This is not human but a real supernatural phenomenon. In the gospels and epistles, it clearly states that saints are to forgive both other believers and unbelievers. Why? Saints are forgiven by God. Because they have experienced forgiveness, they must show forgiveness.

In Matthew 6:12, during the Sermon on the Mount, He declared that the prayers of God's people should end with "Forgive us our debts, as we also forgive our debtors." Also, in Mark 11:25, on His way to Jerusalem, Jesus explained to His disciples that whenever they stood praying, they should forgive, if they had anything against anyone. In Luke 11:4, when asked how to pray by His disciples, He delivered the

Lord's Prayer a second time saying, "Forgive us our sins, for we ourselves also forgive everyone who is indebted to us."

There is no distinction between believers and unbelievers. Jesus utilizes the words "debtors," "anyone," and "everyone." So, forgiveness is extended to all. He makes no distinction in the kinds of transgressions that ought to be forgiven. They must all be forgiven. Therefore, Christians must forgive their enemies and persecutors for what they do against them, no matter how bad the persecution.

One might ask the question, "What about justice?" It is for the Lord to determine when He will administer His justice in this life (Luke 13:1-4; Acts 12:23). Christians know that His justice will be administered at the great white throne. This is where every single transgression anyone has committed against believers will be judged. Their names and specific sins against them will be presented to the unsaved to be judged and punished (Revelation 20:11-15). Christians must understand, if any of their enemies or persecutors receives Jesus Christ, they too will be forgiven of all their sins, including the persecution. These enemies of the cross, if they repent and believe in Jesus as Savior and Lord, they will be forgiven, as those they persecuted were forgiven of all their sins. Paul was God's classic example (1 Timothy 1:15-17).

> *Key Concept: When unbelievers react negatively to the good news, the saints should forgive them as they are forgiven.*

Chapter 13

The Proper Presentation

The response in attitudes and actions that the saints are expected to have toward their enemies amid persecution has been discussed. These supernatural responses are to reflect God's person, purpose, and power. Now, the question arises, what should believers actually say to their persecutors? The concise answer is to preach the gospel again! Over and over, the disciples were persecuted and then brought before their persecutors to speak. These evangelizing Christians had to stand trial for their denial of certain religious beliefs, defend their message and actions, and explain the good news that they were preaching. How did they respond?

These heroic believers simply preached the gospel again. These courageous Christians could have become involved in discussing every detail of their beliefs verses the persecutors' beliefs. Instead, they simply continued to proclaim the basic message of salvation in Christ Jesus. These brave individuals focused on the sole message that Jesus Christ is their Savior and Lord.

Paul described this strategy as the apostle contrasted his method of proclamation with the different methods of those who were wise in the world.

> For I determined not to know anything among you, except Jesus Christ, and him crucified.
> 1 Corinthians 2:2

In 1 Corinthians 2:2, the apostle indicates that he preached the simple message of salvation. In context of this passage, Paul contends that those who were worldly wise depended on their excellent speaking skills, logical argumentation, and persuasive manipulation. He depended on the power of the Holy Spirit to change the hearts of men (1 Corinthians 2:1-5).

In Matthew 10:16, Jesus sent His disciples out to preach as sheep among wolves. He warned them about these men who would deliver them up and scourge them. Then, in Matthew 10:19-20, He told them not to be anxious concerning how or what they would say. In that hour, the Holy Spirit would guide them as they spoke. These words can certainly apply to any Christian who shares the good news and experiences persecution from enemies. Why shouldn't it?

In 1 Thessalonians 1:6-9, Paul recognizes the work of the Holy Spirit in the lives of the Thessalonians who not only received God's Word but proclaimed His Word in much affliction. The Holy Spirit guided Paul in his proclamation and their salvation. Now, He was guiding the church in their proclamation and the salvation of many in their region. God, through the Spirit of Christ, will superintend every aspect of the proclamation of His redemptive plan, as has been noted in the discussion of God's role in evangelism.

This does not preclude the Spirit providing principles that should be followed. As He guides His children, the Bible prescribes a pattern to follow or a structure to frame their presentations. The following principles will help Christians structure their thinking as the Spirit leads them in the development of their gospel response to their persecutors and enemies. Any believer, who expects to be persecuted, should learn these important principles.

> *Key Concept: When unbelievers react negatively to the gospel, Christians may be allowed to speak and should preach the gospel again as the Spirit leads.*

A Beginning with a Simple Declaration

In the Book of Acts, wherever the apostles and the other followers of Jesus traveled, whether they encountered Jews, Greeks, philosophers, men, women, slaves, or government officials, the gospel was simply declared. No matter how negative the reactions, how hardened their hearts appeared, or closed they seemed, they heard the gospel. In 2 Timothy 3:16, Paul indicates that one of the important ways in which the Scriptures can be utilized is for teaching. The preaching of the gospel is a part of that teaching.

In Acts 4:1-9, the apostles were in Jerusalem proclaiming the resurrection of Jesus (the gospel). The Sanhedrin arrested them and held them in custody until the next evening. They were brought before the high priests, rulers, and scribes and interrogated. They wanted to know in whose name or by what power enabled them to heal the lame and crippled man and speak to their people.

> Be it known to you all, and to all the people of Israel, that in the name of Jesus Christ of Nazareth, whom you [Jews] crucified, whom God raised from the dead, in him does this man stand here before you whole.
> Acts 4:10

In Acts 4:10, Peter began with the death and resurrection of Jesus Christ and proclaimed the gospel. This same gospel they had already heard from Jesus with the addition of the now risen Savior. They did not seek to argue or reason with them; instead, they proclaimed the good news again! When told to cease their preaching, the apostles refused and went out and preached the gospel again (v. 31). Though it may be difficult, continuing to proclaim the gospel in the midst of persecution is the biblical pattern.

SHARING THE GOSPEL: THE DOCTRINE OF EVANGELISM

In Acts 5:28-32, when Peter and John found themselves before the Sanhedrin, they proclaimed Christ. In Acts 6:8-15, Stephen was hauled before the same council because the Jews had been overcome by the Spirit and wisdom of his preaching. In Acts 7, when Stephen spoke to these hostile and angry religious men, he declared the good news of Jesus Christ. In the rest of Luke's account, Paul declared the gospel before the angry crowd of Jews (chapter 22), the Sanhedrin (chapter 23), Felix (chapter 24), Festus (chapter 25), King Herod Agrippa (chapter 26), and before the Emperor of Rome (Philippians 1).

All of these people responded negatively. They were cold, contentious, and hardened of heart, but all heard a simple declaration of the good news. The goal in every evangelistic encounter, whether persecution comes or not, is to share the gospel. When the persecution comes, Christians are to share the gospel again. Why? Salvation is the ultimate goal of the saints. No amount of argumentation, criticism, or persuasion will diminish their opposition. Their only responsibility is to share the gospel. God's responsibility is to open the heart and provide the faith to believe through His love, mercy, and grace. Is this not Paul's contention in Ephesians 2:4-10? God does the work once His Word is presented.

> *Key Concept: When unbelievers react negatively to the gospel, Christians should share the gospel in a simple declaration as the Spirit leads.*

An Ending with a Careful Admonition

In many of the presentations recorded in the gospels, after a negative reaction occurred, there was a careful admonition or warning. This admonishment was a caution that danger was ahead. There could be a warning of the judgment of sin and resultant condemnation in hell if they refused to believe. It would continue for all eternity.

In Acts 13:38-41, when Paul announced the gospel to the Jews in the synagogue in Pisidian Antioch, he ended with a careful warning. He knew that he had received a great deal of resistance in his missionary journey from the Jews, so he cautioned them not to become scoffers who perish. He did not want them to mock his gospel and Savior which would inevitably lead to their punishment for sin in the fires of hell. In 2 Timothy 3:16, Paul indicates that one of the important ways in which the Scriptures can be utilized is for rebuke. This careful admonition is a part of that rebuke.

In Acts 28:23-28, Paul was imprisoned in Rome and sent for the Jewish leaders. He desired to explain his chains and proclaim the gospel to them. Some believed in the gospel and others would not. To those who did not believe he admonished them from the prophet Isaiah. He asserted that these Jewish authorities would continue to hear but would not understand. The rulers would continue to see but would not perceive. Their hearts would become dull. If they closed their eyes and ears they would perish in their sins.

There might be times in which the Holy Spirit will lead a Christian to issue a warning of judgment if the unbeliever refuses to embrace Christ. Christians should not shy away from this warning. All throughout the Old Testament, God sent His prophets to issue severe warnings to people and many responded. A prime biblical example is the reluctant preaching of Jonah and how more than one hundred and twenty thousand Ninevites believed in the God of Israel.

> *Key Concept: When unbelievers react negatively to the gospel, Christians should share the gospel and end with a careful admonition as the Spirit leads.*

SHARING THE GOSPEL: THE DOCTRINE OF EVANGELISM

A Discussion with a Gentle Correction

Sometimes, as Christians proclaim the gospel again, there may be a need for a gentle correction. When one is sharing the good news, confusion, perplexity, or misunderstandings may occur, which needs correction, for the true gospel to be understood and believed. In 2 Timothy 3:16, Paul indicates that one of the important ways in which the Scriptures can be utilized is for correction. This discussion which includes a gentle correction is a part of that utilization. As Christians proclaim the gospel again, they might have to answer some questions, and clear up some misunderstandings, or discuss some differences.

This correction can be observed in several places in the book of Acts in the midst of sharing the gospel with those who are antagonistic. In Acts 6:9-10, Luke records that some who were of the synagogue called The Libertines, and the Cyrenians, the Alexandrians, and those of Cilicia and Asia, argued with Stephen, but they could not stand up to his wisdom and the Holy Spirit working inside him. The word in the Greek translated "argue" means to seek or examine together, to discuss or question. It does not carry the idea of quarreling. Stephen was answering their questions, clearing up their misunderstandings, and discussing the differences between his beliefs and theirs. Within this discussion would have been correction.

The same word is used to describe Paul's interaction with the Jews in Jerusalem in Acts 9:29. After he fled for his life from Damascus, he landed in Jerusalem. Immediately, Paul began preaching the gospel of Jesus Christ courageously to every person who wanted to listen. Luke portrays Paul as talking and arguing with the Hellenistic Jews. The desire of these Jews was to put Paul to death for the gospel. Yet, Paul tried to answer all their questions, clear up misunderstandings, and discuss the many differences between his beliefs and theirs. Within this verbal interaction was correction.

In Acts 14:24-48, when Paul returned to Antioch after his first missionary journey, he reported to the church how God had brought the gospel to the Gentiles. Everyone was elated! In Acts 15:1-2, some Jews came from Judea and claimed that the Gentiles had to be circumcised according to the custom of Moses. To Paul, these Judeans were obviously confused. They might have misunderstood how Gentiles were saved. Paul and Barnabas began a discussion with them.

Luke recounts the incident using the words "discord and discussion." In this context, the first word in the Greek has the meaning of taking a stand on an issue. The second word means a seeking, an inquiry, questioning back and forth, or a debate about a controversy. Both sides took their stand and there was a debate. Since Paul was ultimately right, from his perspective he was simply correcting them. Remember, the Jewish believers were adamant that new Gentile Christians should be circumcised for salvation. Though these were not his enemies, they did oppose Paul's position.

In Acts 17:18, Luke details Paul's close encounter with the Epicurean and Stoic philosophers of Athens as "conversing." In this context, the Greek word means to bring together in the mind. These pompous pundits were attempting to piece together Paul's teachings with theirs. The apostle was trying to correct their false worldly wisdom and set them straight on God's divine wisdom.

These intellectuals displayed much hostility toward Paul and his message, and one of them ventured to wonder what this "babbler" wanted to say. The Greek word for "babbler" meant seed picker. Paul was picking up seeds from many different religions and philosophies. This implies he wasn't really smart enough to possess a logical, coherent, organized philosophy or religion. So, Paul attempted to correct these mistaken notions of the antagonistic group of sages.

In Acts 18, Luke records the meeting of both Aquila and Priscilla with Apollos, a powerful preacher of Jesus. He was an Alexandrian Jew who had come to Ephesus to share the gospel. Since Apollos was only acquainted with the baptism of John, he was corrected theologically by this husband-and-wife team.

In verses 27-28, Apollos traveled to the region of Achaia and powerfully refuted the Jews in public. These would not be Jews who supported his beliefs but opposed them. The term translated "refuted" comes from a Greek root word that means to convict, call to account, or correct. It has the feeling of almost a competition as one is mutually exchanging ideas. It does not mean to quarrel or be contentious. When people respond negatively to the gospel, even bent on persecution, Christians might have to engage in a powerful discussion. It could still entail a gentle correction.

Timothy encountered this very issue in his congregation. As a young Pastor, Timothy had involved himself in arguing and quarreling.

> The Lord's servant must not quarrel, but be gentle towards all, [be] able to teach, patient, in gentleness correcting those who oppose him: perhaps God may give them repentance leading to a full knowledge of the truth.
> 2 Timothy 2:24

In 2 Timothy 2:24, Paul explains that gentle correction is a better alternative to the arguing and quarreling. The pastor's congregation had a cluster of contentious people who loved to speculate and discuss peripheral issues within the church. This could only lead to ungodliness and ultimate ruin for the hearers of these controversies. Instead, the Lord's servant must not quarrel but patiently and gently correct those who oppose him. Their hope should be that God may give them repentance and full knowledge of His truth. Through gentle correction, the Lord would retrieve them from this snare of the Devil since they have been taken captive by him to do his will.

Christians who attempt to fight, argue, and quarrel with their enemies or persecutors will not lead them to salvation. The gentle correction of their false beliefs compared to the truth may clear up their doctrinal confusion. As the Spirit leads, this may direct them to the narrow path of salvation.

> *Key Concept: When unbelievers react negatively to the gospel, Christians should share the gospel and gently correct any misunderstandings as the Spirit leads.*

A Rebuke with a Strong Exhortation

In the New Testament, sometimes the believers provided careful admonitions. Yet, at other times, believers gave very strong exhortations. In 2 Timothy 3:16, Paul indicates that one of the important ways in which the Scriptures should be utilized is for the purpose of rebuke. This discussion which includes a rebuke with a strong exhortation is a part of that crucial utilization. This is more than a careful admonition.

This is not just a warning of judgment but an indictment for the hardness of their hearts, sinful stubbornness, or other extreme sinful attitudes. Why? These are blocking them or others from the gospel. The Greek word translated "rebuke" comes from the root word which means to convict. It has the sense of shaming, reprimanding severely, or chastening. It suggests the simple rebuke for error or a powerful reproof for opposition to the truth.

In Titus 1, Paul describes certain empty talking, rebellious men from the circumcision who were continually deceiving believers and had disrupted whole households for shameful gain. In verse 13, Paul commanded Titus, his companion, to rebuke or chastise these liars severely. His purpose was so they help them become sound in their faith and doctrine.

In Acts 7, Stephen preached the gospel and defended the faith to a hard-hearted Jewish Sanhedrin then he concluded his sermon with a strong exhortation. In verses 51-53, he termed them stiff-necked and uncircumcised in the heart and ears. He designated them as resisters of the Holy Spirit. He condemned them as acting just like their fathers who persecuted the prophets and became betrayers and killers of the righteous. This was foretold by the prophets. Stephen then accused them of receiving the law as if ordained by angels, and then disregarding it. These were fiery words for this group of persecutors and enemies of the gospel.

In Acts 8, Philip traveled into the region of Samaria and baptized a magician named Simon. Peter and John arrived to lay hands on these new converts, in order to baptize them in the Spirit. When Simon saw the power they possessed, he attempted to purchase it from them. In verses 18-23, Peter rebuked Simon. He exclaimed that Simon would perish with the silver he wanted to use to buy the Spirit's power. He condemned him for having a heart that was not right before God full of the gall of bitterness and the bondage of iniquity. As Peter told Simon to repent, Simon was so shaken up by Peter's strong exhortation, he begged for prayer asking them to pray that the harsh things they said would not happen.

A similar strong exhortation can be seen by Paul, when he encountered opposition from Elymas.

> But Saul, who is also called Paul, filled with the Holy Spirit, fastened his eyes on him, and said, "Full of all deceit and all cunning, you son of the Devil, you enemy of all righteousness, will you not cease to pervert the right ways of the Lord?
>
> Acts 13:9

In Acts 13:9-11, Paul strongly exhorted and rebuked Elymas, who was keeping him from preaching to Sergius Paulus. In addition to his rebuke, he struck him with blindness.

On several occasions, Jesus rebuked the Pharisees with a strong exhortation (Matthew 23). Over and over, He warned them that judgment and condemnation would come due to their hypocrisy. In verses 13-37, he calls them blind guides, fools, whitewashed tombs with dead men's bones, clean cups on the outside full of robbery and self-indulgence, and sons of those who murdered the prophets. Jesus warned these Pharisees and Scribes who rejected Him that they would be sentenced to a hell of fire. Then He laments aloud over their coming judgment! The Lord expresses His desire to gather them under His wings as the hen does her chicks. Now, their house will be left desolate, and condemnation will come. Often, the Lord Jesus had stern warnings for these hypocrites who were laying heavy burdens upon the people of the Lord God (verses 1-12).

If the Spirit leads Christians to make strong exhortations, it should not be presented in sinful anger but in righteous rebuke. Jesus cleansed the temple out of zeal, not righteous anger (John 2:17). It should be done to turn them to the Lord. When all else has failed a rebuke may be necessary.

SHARING THE GOSPEL: THE DOCTRINE OF EVANGELISM

Key Concept: When unbelievers react negatively to the gospel, Christians should share the gospel and rebuke with a strong exhortation as the Spirit leads.

A Termination with an Obvious Avoidance

There will be times when Christians share the gospel, and people will not listen. They might be so spiritually dead, so controlled by their lusts and sin, so prideful, so ignorant and blind, so hardened and calloused that believers simply end up going around and around in their preaching or sharing of the gospel with no result but more opposition. Eventually, the presentation must end. All that can be said has already been said.

In Acts 13, Paul and Barnabas entered Pisidian Antioch and preached to the Jews and God-fearing Gentiles in the synagogue. The preaching was so powerful that they asked them to come back the next Sabbath. This time almost the whole town turned out. But when the Jews saw the crowds, they went into a jealous rage and began interrupting and contradicting the apostle as he was speaking. As a result, he rebuked them with the strong exhortation by declaring that they were unworthy of God's eternal life. Then the apostle Paul terminated his presentation with an obvious avoidance by exclaiming he was now going to the Gentiles.

A similar incident occurred in Acts 18. In Corinth, Paul preached the gospel, and they kept resisting his gospel and blaspheming. In Acts 18:4-6, as a result, he rebuked them with a strong exhortation by declaring their blood was now on their own heads. They would receive the judgment they deserved. Then the apostle terminated his presentation with an obvious avoidance by exclaiming that he was now going to the Gentiles. He would turn his attention to the non-Jews.

As has been examined, in the church Timothy pastored, He had a group of contentious people who argued, debated, quarreled, and bickered about theological issues. Yet, these were not legitimate theological problems causing them to be legitimately confused and perplexed, which required gentle correction. These were speculative and controversial subjects that were not directly addressed in the Bible. According to Paul, these inquiries were made up myths, strange doctrines, vain discussions, endless genealogies, useless speculations, and with no spiritual gain (1 Timothy 1:3-7).

In each letter, his mentor cautions Timothy to avoid this empty chatter (1 Timothy 6:20; 2 Timothy 2:16).

> Holding a form of [true] godliness, but having denied its power. Turn away from these, also.
> 2 Timothy 3:5

In 2 Timothy 3:5, he warns this minister to also avoid the contentious people propagating this false knowledge. Paul continues by describing these religious antagonists as having a form of godliness without power. Though they appeared, sounded, and acted godly, it was all outward. Why? It had no real spiritual power to change lives, only destroy them.

This principle is perfectly applicable to the persecutors of Christians. They may also want to debate and debate about minor issues without any end in sight and no real progress toward their salvation. So, Christians should terminate the discussion and avoid these persecutors.

Is this not how Christ behaved when they finally arrested Him? He had preached, and they had heard over and over. There was nothing else He could say. All had been said and done. Jesus had answered all of the questions, performed all the miracles, and fulfilled all the prophecies needed. Once He was arrested, He was questioned by many officials but did not give an answer. Many charges were brought against Him; yet he did not answer (Matthew 27:12-14; Mark 14:60-61).

Christians may have to refuse to get involved in endless discussions with believers who oppose them or unbelievers who persecute them. There comes a time when everything has been said that needs to be said. Christians must rely on the Holy Spirit to guide them in this important area.

> *Key Concept: When unbelievers react negatively to the gospel with endless discussions, the saints may terminate with an obvious avoidance, as the Spirit leads.*

Chapter 14

The Proper Utilization of Rights

Most Christians are ignorant of their rights both legally and biblically. They are confused about their utilization in the midst of persecution as they proclaim the good news. The Bible gives direction and examples concerning the times for the use of one's biblical rights, legal rights, or both. This use will be once again governed by the leading of the Spirit.

> *Key Concept: When unbelievers react negatively to the gospel, Christians may use their biblical rights, legal rights, or both under certain conditions as the Spirit leads.*

The Obedience to the Law in Human Affairs

Christians should obey the law in human affairs. This is a principle that is clearly taught in Scripture. In Romans 13:1, Paul commanded that every person be in subjection to the governing authorities. This means that all Christians are to subordinate themselves to the government, its leaders, and its laws. Peter gave a similar command in 1 Peter 2:13-14. The apostle stated that Christians were to submit themselves to every human institution, to kings and governors, and its ordinances as sent by the Lord.

In Titus 3:1, Paul commanded Titus to remind the church to subject itself to rulers and authorities and to be obedient to them. Why? First, government is established by God (Romans 13:1). Second, any opposition to the government is opposition to God (Romans 13:2). Third, to disobey the law is to bring the

SHARING THE GOSPEL: THE DOCTRINE OF EVANGELISM

Almighty's immediate condemnation from the law (Romans 13:2-4). Fourth, breaking the law violates the God-given conscience (Romans 13:5). Fifth, governments are really servants of God (Romans 13:6-7). Sixth, obedience to the law is God's will (Romans 13:15). Seventh, following the law is a good testimony (Romans 13:15).

Obedience to the law was a pattern set by the Lord Jesus when He was questioned about His allegiances.

> They said to him, "Caesar's." Then he said to them, "Give therefore to Caesar the things that are Caesar's, and to God the things that are God's."
>
> Matthew 22:21

In Matthew 22:15-22, the Lord was asked if He believed in paying the poll tax to Caesar. Jesus explained that they were to render to Caesar the things that were his and to God the things that were God's. In Matthew 17:24-27, when Peter asked Jesus if they should pay the temple tax, Jesus ordered him to go to the sea. Next, Peter was to drop a fishing hook, catch a fish, take the coin out of its mouth, and then pay the tax. Afterwards, the Lord Jesus explained that though He was exempt, He would not offend them.

Christians are to obey all governing authorities and their laws. This is the most basic and fundamental principle when attempting to discern whether believers should exercise their biblical rights, legal rights, or both. The standard for every saint in every land under every government is to obey all the laws of the land.

> *Key Concept: When unbelievers react negatively to the gospel, Christians should normally obey the law in human affairs.*

The Defiance of the Law to Obey A Divine Command

One deviation from this important standard would be the next principle. The saints must defy the law to obey a divine command. Christians should subjugate themselves to every ordinance and law until the government violates God's law. When the government demands Christians to do or not to do something that violates God's clear, direct command in His Scriptures, they may defy it. Notice, it must be the violation of a clear, direct command, otherwise, they should obey.

This is the distinct exception in the Scriptures. When any command of a governmental authority is at odds with the commands of God, then without any reservation in the full knowledge of what they are doing Christians may defy the law. This is never done in anger or pride or self-righteous indignation. This is simply done to obey a command of God in His Word. It should reflect a humble and gentle spirit.

In Daniel 3:1-7, Shadrach, Meshach, and Abed-Nego were Jewish high officials in the Babylonian Empire. The emperor, Nebuchadnezzar, created a golden image of himself. Then he asked the entire kingdom to bow down to it in worship. Anyone who refused would be thrown into a fiery furnace. In verses 13-18, the three refused. They told the Emperor that they would not serve his gods, nor would they bow down to his image in worship. This would be a violation of God's first commandment (Exodus 20:3-6). As a result, they were thrown into the fiery furnace and delivered by God.

In Daniel 6, Daniel defied Darius, Emperor of the Medes and Persians. His evil Satraps, who were in the court of the emperor with Daniel, were jealous of him. As a result, they tried to trap him by convincing Darius to make an edict. The edict stated that no man in the land could make a petition to

SHARING THE GOSPEL: THE DOCTRINE OF EVANGELISM

a god or man for 30 days, except to the emperor himself. The penalty would be death by being cast alive into the lion's den. These wicked officials knew Daniel would defy this, and Daniel did. He went to his house and began praying three times a day in front of his window in full view of the city. He did not do it out of pride or anger. As a result, Daniel was thrown into a lion's den to be devoured by wild animals, but God rescued him.

In the New Testament, the apostles also were compelled to take similar actions of defiance of the law to obey a divine command. In Acts 4:1-3, after Peter and John healed the lame man, they preached Christ and won saved many souls. This upset the Jewish leaders, so the apostles were arrested and brought before the Jewish council, the Sanhedrin. In Luke's account of Acts 4:4-18, the Sanhedrin ordered the apostles to stop preaching Jesus.

Their response was immediate. They would obey God in defiance of man.

> But Peter and John answered them, "Whether it is right in the sight of God to listen to you rather than to God, judge for yourselves, for we can't help telling…things which we saw and heard."
> Acts 4:19-20

In Acts 4:19-20, they declared to the council that they would not obey them and stop. Since it was not right in the sight of God, they would continue preaching the gospel. No one had the authority to stop the spread of the good news.

When the Sanhedrin dragged all the apostles before their council in Acts 5, this body of men asked the apostles again for a reason for their disobedience. In verse 29, they repeated themselves. God's divine commands are a higher authority than man's laws. When man's ordinances oppose God's clear precepts, obedience to God prevails.

In every example, there was no disrespect, anger, harsh language, or violence. There was simply a straightforward defiance of the law. When asked, they gave a simple, clear answer. These apostles defied the authorities because they had a much higher authority (Acts 5:29), purpose (Acts 5:30-31), and calling (Acts 5:32).

One day, Christians might find themselves being asked to do something or not do something that is clearly contrary to the Scriptures by the government. Believers must obey their God, rather than man. The only caution that should be taken by Christians is that they must be certain they are obeying a clear, direct principle of Scripture.

> *Key Concept: When unbelievers react negatively to the gospel, Christians should defy the law to obey a divine command as the Spirit leads.*

The Acceptance of the Punishment The Law Provides

When Christians decide to defy the law in order to obey a divine command, they must be willing to accept any kind of punishment the law provides. They may not defy governing authorities to follow God, and then hide, lie, or assault the police of that government. As will be seen, they may use the laws to protect themselves as citizens. The saints do not have to wave their legal rights or surrender their day in court. This is still acceptance. No one would argue that following the law was not accepting the law. This would simply not make sense. If the government allows citizens to challenge its laws in specific ways, Christians may do so, as the Spirit leads them.

Meshach, Shadrach, and Abed-Nego faced a fiery furnace (Daniel 3:16-18). Daniel faced a lion's den (Daniel 6:16-18). Peter, John, and the rest of the apostles faced imprisonment, beatings, and death (Acts 5:40-42). They never pulled back; instead, they continued to preach. They knew God had the power to protect them from physical death or deliver them into heaven. In either case, they would be delivered. Paul explained to the Philippians that to remain would produce fruitful ministry, but to depart would send him to Christ. Both were good; the second was better (Philippians 1:21-24).

If Christians defy the law to obey a divine command, they must be willing to accept the consequences. This may also mean using the law to protect themselves. God will give all the grace needed to endure (2 Corinthians 1:3-4, 12:9-10).

> *Key Concept: When unbelievers react negatively to the gospel, if Christians defy the law in order to obey a divine command, they should accept all of the consequences, as the Spirit leads.*

The Utilization of the Law To Advance and Protect

Though Christians are the citizens of heaven, they are also the citizens of the state, region, or municipality within which they reside; they are subjects of both kingdoms. The saints must follow the rules and dictates of heaven and Earth. In a sense, believers bear a dual citizenship. When people have dual citizenships on Earth, they must follow both sets of laws. It is the same with believers who desire to live for their Savior and Lord. In Philippians 3:20, the apostle Paul states the saints are all citizens of heaven. Yet, in Romans 13:1-4 and 1 Peter 2:13-15, Paul and Peter state that we are to obey all the governing authorities.

In Luke 20, the Pharisees and Herodians had attempted to trick Jesus by asking Him whether it was lawful to pay the poll tax to Caesar or not. They figured, since Jesus claimed to be in the kingdom of God, He would deny the obligation. Then, they would catch Him in an act of sedition against Rome. Instead, something truly amazing occurred.

> He said to them, "Then give to Caesar the things that are Caesar's, and to God the things that are God's."
>
> Luke 20:25

In Luke 20:25, Jesus obtained a coin and asked them whose image was on it. When they replied that it was Caesar's, He told them to render to Caesar that which is Caesar's and to God that which is God's. He was stating that there are two kingdoms in a believer's life, the heavenly and the Earthly, and each should be given their due.

First, in many places, the words and actions unbelievers might take in the persecution of Christians are illegal. This can occur with any citizen, regardless of their religion. Just because people are believers, does not mean they cease being citizens. They are still protected by their government which was created by God and is His protection from persecution.

Second, one of the essential responsibilities of believers is advancing the gospel. There is no reason why they cannot utilize every opportunity afforded by the law to share their opinions about spiritual things. Jesus and Paul, both being Rabbis, used the normal forums afforded Jewish Rabbis (the synagogue) and Gentiles (the marketplace) to advance the gospel. So, this is where they went to preach.

In Acts 17, when Paul went into Athens, he found himself sharing his opinion about spiritual things (the gospel) before the Areopagus, which was the official council in the city. Anyone who came into the city with a new teaching was brought to this council of leaders. As a result, Paul did not hesitate to preach the gospel.

Utilizing the law to protect oneself from persecution or to advance the gospel is illustrated in the ministry of Paul, the apostle, in the book of Acts. On several occasions, Paul used his rights as a Roman citizen to terminate different kinds of illegal persecution or to preach the gospel. These powerful examples of Paul's use of the law will be examined in their order of appearance in Luke's account in the book of Acts.

In Acts 16, Paul encountered persecution because he had removed a demon from a fortune telling slave girl. After losing their profit from her demonic skills, her legal masters dragged Paul before the city magistrates. Paul and Silas, his companion, were publicly accused of agitating the people and advocating customs that were illegal for Roman citizens to practice. In a great display of pomp and circumstance, the rulers tore their robes, ordered them to be beaten with rods, and secured in prison. The jailer threw them into the inner prison and locked them up in the stocks.

In Acts 16:35-40, Luke records that the day finally arrived for the two of them to be released. Then, the jailer declared that the rulers of the city had sent word that they could now go in peace. Rather than quietly leaving, Paul challenged the magistrates legally. He simply revealed what these rulers had forgotten to ask them. They were Roman citizens. They could not be beaten or imprisoned without a trial.

As a result, they would not leave secretly to hide what had been done. Instead, he demanded that the leaders escort them out of the city safely for all to see. After they saw the brethren, then he would leave. When the magistrates found out the two were Romans, they literally begged the two to leave quietly. They greatly feared the exposure of Paul's illegal imprisonment. Paul may also have been securing the safety of the little church in Philippi so it would be left alone.

Upon his arrival in Philippi, Paul did not disclose his true citizenship. Why? By faith, Paul knew God was at work. The Philippian jailer and all in his household would never have received Christ without his illegal imprisonment. Here, Paul chooses not to utilize the law to win the jailer to Christ. Yet later, Paul employs the same law for his own protection and the protection of all the saints in Philippi. This would allow all of them to freely share the gospel. The law was used to protect believers and advance the gospel as the Spirit led.

In Acts 21, Paul entered the Jewish temple area in the city of Jerusalem. Some irate Jews from Asia recognized Paul. Since they had seen him with a Gentile in the city, they supposed Paul had brought him into the temple. They stirred up the crowds because of this defilement. The mob grabbed Paul, dragged him out, and began beating him. When the Roman cohort discovered that a mob murder was about to occur, they stormed into the crowd and rescued Paul. Here the government is protecting its citizens against harm even if it is of a religious nature. The point is that God protects his persecuted people through the government He creates.

In Acts 22, the commanding officer ordered his soldiers to question Paul through scourging. They would torture him to discover why he had incited such an uproar. Paul allowed himself to be tied up in chains in preparation for the beating. Then, he casually inquired of the centurion near him as to whether any Roman citizen could be scourged without the ruling of a court. When the soldier answered in the negative, Paul identified himself as a Roman citizen.

SHARING THE GOSPEL: THE DOCTRINE OF EVANGELISM

The commander was frightened because he had illegally bound Paul with chains. Consequently, Paul was released and now was a free man. Here again, Paul utilizes the law to protect himself from persecution. It is interesting to note that Paul manipulates the situation to place the commander in a difficult dilemma. This provided Paul with an upper hand in this drama. He did not lie. They should have asked him if he was a Roman; instead, they made a foolish assumption. From then on, the commander would be more vigilant and careful as he handled Paul.

After this, the commander brought Paul safely before the Jewish council. What did Paul do? He preached the gospel. The apostle Paul utilized the law to provide safe travel to the Jewish council so he could preach the good news to them. It is obvious that the crowds were still milling around to catch Paul if he was released.

In Acts 23, Paul proclaimed the gospel to the Sanhedrin. These leaders become so enraged that the commander sent his soldiers to seize Paul and bring him to their barracks. Notice, this time he was not imprisoned without a trial. A group of forty Jews bound themselves to not eat or drink until they had assassinated Paul. They convinced the council to ask for Paul's return so they could murder the apostle on the road. Paul's sister found out and informed the apostle.

Paul informed the commander who decided to send him to the governor in Caesarea. Due to Paul's earlier disclosure of his citizenship and the commander's illegal actions, it is not surprising that the commander sent Paul with a small army to protect the apostle from the persecution of these Jews. What else could the commander do?

In Acts 24, when Paul stood before Felix, the governor, he complemented him for his many years of service as a judge.

Before making his gospel defense against the inflammatory accusations of Tertullus, the Jewish lawyer, Paul indicated how joyful he was to be able to make his presentation before such a capable man as he. Here again, Paul acknowledges the power of the government's authority to protect him from persecution. Unfortunately, though Felix protected him from persecution from the Jews, Paul was still in his custody for two years to appease these rebellious people. Two years Paul sat waiting. His advance of the gospel may have slowed, but Paul shared the Christ with all who visited him.

In Acts 25, after two years had passed, Festus succeeded Felix as governor. The Jews were right there to make their accusations about him again even after two years. When the apostle was finally called before the governor's seat, Festus had a ridiculous request for him. Would Paul be willing to go to Jerusalem to be tried by his countrymen? In his feeble attempt to appease the Jews, Festus was about to send his prisoner to his death.

Knowing this, the apostle Paul chose to invoke a Roman citizen's ultimate protection from the law and appealed to the emperor. This appeal to Caesar was irrevocable. Once declared by a Roman citizen, it could not be stopped. Every Roman citizen who felt he was not receiving justice could travel to Rome and stand trial before the emperor himself and present his case. The charges could now be answered face to face with the ruler of the entire Roman Empire. It had been continually revealed to the apostle by the Lord that he would preach the gospel to the emperor himself. How was a simple Rabbi from Tarsus ever going to stand before the most powerful man in the world and proclaim the plan of redemption? It was done as a citizen utilizing the law!

If Christians truly desire to advance the gospel or protect themselves from persecution, they should utilize the law to

Christ's advantage. This should be done as the Spirit leads. The Earthly citizenship of believers should not be left at the door of God's kingdom; instead, it should be used wisely.

I have purposely left out a discussion on the concept of self-defense in the midst of persecution. This would entail the persecution by those who are not governing authorities. This is a subject for another book. Suffice it to say that the principles that have discussed in this chapter indicate that the kind of self-defense that the government would allow in its laws would be applicable to those who attempt to harm the saints for their Christian faith.

> *Key Concept: When unbelievers react negatively to the gospel, Christians should utilize the law for the advancement of the good news and protection from persecution as the Spirit leads.*

Chapter 15

The Personal Attitudes

After considering how Christians should react or respond to persecutors, a final key question arises. How should the saints respond or react to the persecution itself? Fortunately, the New Testament is filled with exhortations and examples concerning the handling of persecution. One might think that persecution would bring fear and trembling to those who share the gospel. The pain and suffering for Christ would cause the saved to go into hiding and never be heard from again. Instead, the torment and antagonism for Jesus actually furthered the gospel. The more the enemies of the good news attempted to stamp out their fire for Christ, the more it ignited them. Until the good news of the risen Jesus had spread all throughout the Roman Empire.

In Acts 8, after Stephen was martyred, Saul began his own persecution. The saints, who were scattered, shared the good news everywhere they went (Acts 8:4). Though they were running for their lives with Saul in hot pursuit, these bold believers preached the gospel. They proclaimed the good news, even though their fellow Christians were imprisoned and murdered for the blessed Savior.

Then the mantel of martyrdom was now passed down to the most unlikely character in this drama of redemption: the protagonist of this persecution - Saul. He was miraculously converted by the resurrected and ascended Jesus Christ on the road to Damascus (Acts 9). Once converted, the newly named Paul became the recipient of the afflictions that he himself had afflicted upon others. In Acts 9:16, a prophet came to declare how much he would now suffer for Christ.

SHARING THE GOSPEL: THE DOCTRINE OF EVANGELISM

Paul describes his attitude toward suffering for the Lord's sake to the church at Corinth. Martyrdom was continually stalking him and knocking at his door.

> For we who live are always delivered to death for Jesus' sake, that the life also of Jesus may be revealed in our mortal flesh.
>
> 2 Corinthians 4:11

Paul's supernatural response was recorded in 2 Corinthians 4:11. The persecution of Paul and his companions felt like they were constantly being delivered over to death. In the larger passage, he asserts that they were constantly pressed on every side, perplexed, pursued, and even struck down but were never crushed, despairing, forsaken, or destroyed. They were always willing to carry in their physical bodies the constant putting to death of Jesus, so His life would be revealed in their bodies.

In these very words is the key that opens the treasure of the understanding of persecution. It will help believers cope with the suffering that comes with sharing the gospel. Paul was demonstrating over and over that Jesus was still alive. Jesus was active in his life and in the world still proclaiming the kingdom of God through him. These enemies of the Lord were attempting to crucify Jesus Christ in Paul's body and in the bodies of his companions again and again. They hated Christ and kept encountering Him through His disciples.

In Galatians 6:17, Paul observed that he had branded on his body the marks of Christ. In the Hebrew world, a slave would bear the mark of his master, if he willingly wanted to remain a slave (Deuteronomy 15:17). Paul willingly bore the marks of persecution from the many floggings, stonings, and beatings he received (2 Corinthians 6:4-6; 11:23-27). These identified Christ as his owner.

In Colossians 1:24, Paul explains the reason for the great joy he experienced in his suffering for Christ. It came from the knowledge that Paul was filling up what was lacking in Christ's afflictions. The apostle was bearing in his own body the persecution that was truly for His Savior and Lord. They could no longer persecute Jesus, but they could take it out on Paul. In 2 Corinthians 1:5, he wrote that he experienced the sufferings of the Lord in abundance. They had been given all of the terrible persecution and evil retribution bountifully which was intended for their Lord Jesus. What the Lord had suffered, Paul was now experiencing. He felt the Lord's pain and anguish to the point of overflowing because he shared His gospel and spoke of Him.

In Philippians 3:7-11, Paul argues that he had counted all things of his former life as loss compared to the surpassing value of knowing Christ. Then He affirms his life goals. The apostle explained that he desired to fully know Jesus Christ, the power of His resurrection as He worked in and through Him, and the fellowship of His sufferings as Paul partnered with Christ in suffering for Him.

If Christians share the gospel and it leads to persecution, they must seek to possess the following attitudes toward their suffering. The apostle experienced more persecution than most but possessed all of the following attitudes which allowed him to handle them in a divine way. Through these supernatural considerations, all Christians will find a deep fellowship with their Savior in their suffering for Him. The Spirit will provide the grace needed when the time arrives.

> *Key Concept: When unbelievers react negatively to the gospel through persecution, Christians should know they are filling up Christ's afflictions and bearing the marks of His ownership through the partnership of their suffering.*

A Greater Boldness in Preaching

The Christian's response to persecution is even greater boldness in preaching the gospel. In Acts 4:13-20, Peter and John appeared before the Sanhedrin, the most powerful men in Judaism. These religious leaders had just crucified Christ a short time ago. They commanded Peter and John to stop all preaching and teaching in the name of Jesus Christ or suffer the consequences from their wrath. These two apostles boldly told these men that they could not stop proclaiming Christ. These judges of God's people would have to decide for themselves whether it was right for Peter and John to give heed to them or to God. They would continue testifying to the people what they had seen and heard.

In Acts 4:21-32, when the two disciples were released, the two apostles went immediately to their own brethren. These Christian followers praised God together for His sovereignty over their persecution. Then they prayed for the boldness, courage, and confidence they needed to continue preaching His good news. After the prayer, they proceeded back to the streets of Jerusalem to proclaim His Word again.

Consequently, in Acts 5, all the apostles were imprisoned and brought before the Sanhedrin. Peter was asked why they did not obey the previous command not to preach. In verses 29-31, Peter reiterated boldly what he had told them before. They must obey God rather than mere men. Once he said this, Peter proceeded to preach the gospel to the Sanhedrin. Afterward, the council threatened them with the loss of their lives. To make sure the apostles understood the seriousness of their message to stop, they beat them and warned them again. Luke recorded the strong response of the apostles in verse 42. These men went out every day and continued their preaching and teaching of Jesus in the temple and also from house to house. The threat of death did not deter them from the evangelism they were involved in. It only made them bolder. His courage grew to greater heights.

While Paul waited for his trial before Caesar, he wrote to the Philippians and explained his conviction as he prepared himself for his court appearance. Due to their prayers and the provision of the Holy Spirit, he was confident that he would not be put to shame. Instead, with great courage he would exalt Jesus Christ in his own body whether by life or death (Philippians 1:19-20). Paul would demonstrate bravery in his sharing of the gospel. If required, he would also be brave in his resultant death for his Lord. Paul's fearlessness had even stirred up the Roman church to find the fortitude in the Holy Spirit to share the gospel (Philippians 1:14).

Paul told the Thessalonians he boldly preached the gospel to them in the midst of great opposition.

> But having suffered before…been shamefully treated, as you know, at Philippi, we grew bold in our God to tell you the Good News of God in much conflict.
> 1 Thessalonians 2:2

In 1 Thessalonians 2:2, Paul described the courage that he experienced in proclaiming the gospel to them amid great conflict. Then in verses 13-16, he explained the thanksgiving he was constantly offering to God for them. They were now sharing the gospel in boldness amid the same persecution.

Where can a Christian find this kind of boldness? As has been presented, this supernatural courage comes through prayer, the Word, and the Holy Spirit. It also proceeds from the support of other Christians and the believer's confidence in the sovereignty of God (Acts 4:13-20). God is in control of all persecution. As was seen earlier, the knowledge that His persecuted followers are filling up what is lacking in Christ's afflictions and bearing the marks of His ownership through the partnership of their suffering for Him can greatly add to their boldness. They can walk into strife boldly proclaiming the gospel.

> *Key Concept: When unbelievers react negatively to the gospel through persecution, Christians should face affliction and share the gospel with even greater boldness.*

A Greater Persistence in Preaching

Persecution should only make Christians more persistent in proclaiming the gospel. It should make them work that much harder at announcing the plan. Throughout the first century, the more effort the world exercised in squashing the gospel, the more energy Christians exercised in spreading it. When real persecution began with Saul (who later became Paul), the good news rapidly spread through Judea (Acts 8:1), Samaria (Acts 8:5), into Phoenicia, Cyprus, and Antioch (Acts 11:19-20).

Then Saul was converted, and the gospel of Jesus literally exploded throughout the world (1 Thessalonians 1:4). Why? Paul was persistent in his preaching.

> Not that I have already obtained, or...already made perfect; but I press on, if it is so that I may take hold of that for which also I was taken hold of by Christ Jesus.
> Philippians 3:12

He described this diligent effort in Philippians 3:12. He was taken hold of by the Lord for his own salvation but also to spread the gospel. Paul was pressing on to take hold of this and spread it everywhere. This required immense tenacity.

The Sanhedrin did everything they could to stop Christ and eventually crucified him. This evil group of men, along with the Jewish people, did everything they could to destroy Paul, including stoning him (Acts 14:19-20) and attempting to kill him by ambushing him (Acts 23:12), but they were unsuccessful. Even imprisoning him did not help because he simply shared Christ with those who visited him (Acts 28: 23) and the guards with whom he was chained (Philippians 1:13). The good news even reached into Caesar's very own household (Philippians 4:22). This was before the Emperor would hear the gospel for himself at Paul's trial.

Christians should have the exact same kind of persistence in suffering. As was previously discussed, the knowledge that their persecuted followers are filling up what is lacking in Christ's afflictions, and bearing the marks of ownership by Him through the partnership of their suffering for Him will increase their persistence. Regardless of the strife, they will proclaim Him.

> *Key Concept: When unbelievers react negatively to the gospel through persecution, Christians should face affliction and share the gospel with even more persistence.*

A Greater Reliance on Judgment

Persecution might make Christians so angry they might want to become their own judge and jury in order to bring punishment upon their adversaries. As has been seen earlier, believers must always love their enemies and rely on God to avenge their suffering from the gospel. The believers from the tribulation under the altar cried out for God to avenge their martyrdom (Revelation 6:9-11). These saints relied on His power and His justice. When Christians are persecuted, they should do the same. God is the sole authority to judge the sins of unbelievers. Some of the judgment may occur upon the Earth, but a day will come when all deeds will be judged, and everything will be made right before God.

The best example of this is seen in the behavior of Jesus. As He journeyed to the cross, He was punched in the face before Annas (John 18:22). Caiaphas and the Sanhedrin blindfolded, mocked, and beat Him (Matthew 26:67-68). He was treated like some kind of cheap magician, when he was asked to perform a miracle before Herod. The king then dressed Christ up in a royal robe in mockery and returned the Lord to Pilate (Luke 23:6-12). Pilate had Him scourged, crowned with thrones, and led away to His crucifixion (John 19:1-2). Jesus was scorned, blasphemed, criticized, laughed at, and humiliated before men on the cross until he breathed his last breath. Throughout all this persecution, He did not retaliate in like manner.

Peter discusses this very point in his first letter, when he discusses the importance of suffering for living righteously.

> Who did not sin, "neither was deceit found in his mouth." Who, when he was cursed, didn't curse back. When he suffered, didn't threaten, but committed himself to him who judges righteously.
>
> 1 Peter 2:22

In 1 Peter 2:22, the apostle describes how Jesus never reviled or uttered threats in retaliation, but He entrusted Himself to God who judges. Jesus left all judgment up to God, and Peter exhorted Christians to do the same.

In Romans 12:19-20, Paul encouraged Christians in Rome to provide a place for God's wrath, rather than seek revenge. Christians must always remember that vengeance belongs to God and He will repay. This is difficult when suffering is afflicted on this Earth. All will be made right in the next life.

As was discussed, the knowledge that their persecuted followers are filling up what is lacking in Christ's afflictions, and bearing the marks of ownership by their Lord through the partnership of their suffering for Him will increase their reliance on God's judgment. They can walk into strife with confidence in His future condemnation. This does not negate self-defense.

> *Key Concept: When unbelievers react negatively to the gospel through persecution, Christians should face affliction and share the gospel as they rely on God's future judgment.*

A Greater Confidence in Suffering

Christians should meet persecution with the confidence that the Holy Spirit will provide the patient endurance they will need to glorify God. God will give them whatever they need to handle the situation. Often, believers will begin to anticipate some kind of persecution. They will begin to think that how they feel at the moment will be how they will react when the persecution is encountered. This simply is not true.

All suffering is fearful upon reflection, but as the moment comes, God always provides His strength. Paul affirmed this when he suffered from his thorn in the flesh. He begged the Lord three times to remove it, but the Lord refused to do it. He desired that Paul learn that in his weakness he would find God's strength (2 Corinthians 12:7-10).

SHARING THE GOSPEL: THE DOCTRINE OF EVANGELISM

When Stephen faced his own death by stoning, there was no pleading for his life. He did not beg for mercy or cry out in terror and fear. The Lord gave him a confidence in the suffering through a vision of Jesus Christ welcoming him to heaven. This vision was a message to all believers. Jesus will be there to welcome His saints home. In 2 Corinthians 5:8, Paul explains that to be absent from the human body means that Christians are at supernaturally at home with the Lord. What an assurance a believer has!

In Acts 20, Paul met with his longtime friends, the elders of Ephesus, on his way to the city of Jerusalem. In verses 22-24, he explained to them that the Spirit had testified of the terrible suffering that awaited him. There was no real fear or concern. He did not hold his life as dear to him. He desired to fulfill his ministry. In Acts 21, Paul arrived in Caesarea and was about fifty or so miles from the city of Jerusalem. Again, a prophet warned him of the impending danger. The saints begged the apostle to turn back from his journey to Jerusalem. Paul refused explaining that he was ready to not only be bond but even die for the gospel (Acts 21:11-14).

In Acts 13:50, when Paul was physically thrown out of city of Pisidian Antioch, he confidently went into the city of Iconium. He had no fear and no terror. In Acts 14:19-20, he was dragged out of Lystra, stoned, and left for dead. He got up and entered the city of Derbe to continue his ministry. This man, who is an example for all Christians, had a quiet, yet determined and fearless resolution to share the gospel no matter what came his way.

Christians should have the exact same kind of confidence in suffering. As was previously discussed, the knowledge that their persecuted followers are filling up what is lacking in Christ's afflictions and bearing the marks of ownership by Him through the partnership of their suffering for Him, will increase their confidence. They knew they would be able to handle the persecution, if it came. They can walk into the strife from proclaiming the gospel with greater confidence. These will know that the Lord will provide the strength to handle the suffering.

> *Key Concept: When unbelievers react negatively to the gospel through persecution, Christians should face affliction and share the good news with even greater confidence in the Lord Jesus to provide His strength in their suffering.*

A Greater Joy in Suffering

In spite of the difficulty of persecution, Christians are to experience real joy in suffering. This appears to be exactly the opposite of what most people think would happen, if one suffers for the gospel. Who has joy in suffering of any kind? With physical suffering one would expect to feel sad, angry, or depressed. This is not the case of suffering from general trials for believers, nor is it the case when suffering persecution for Christ's sake.

In 1 Thessalonians 1:6, Paul praised the church because these saints became imitators of Paul and the Lord in their tribulation. Why? In their affliction for the gospel, they not only received the Word and believed it, but they found the joy in the Holy Spirit. For the believer, when sharing the gospel, tribulation and joy will go hand in hand.

First, it's a function of the power of the Holy Spirit. One of the fruits of the Spirit listed in Galatians 5:22 is joy. The fruit of the Spirit is produced in a Christian's life as a response to being filled with the Holy Spirit, not because of any kind of positive circumstances (Ephesians 5:18-19). The Christian's response to any of life's woes should be a reaction from the filling of the Spirit, not the deeds of the flesh (Galatians 5:16-24. The flesh will desire to be angry, grieved, and depressed at suffering for Christ, but the Spirit will provide joy.

Second, joy is a characteristic of the walk of Christians no matter what the Lord will allow life to bring their way. Paul, who had experienced much persecution, told the church at Philippi, who also had experienced much persecution, to be rejoicing in the Lord always. Then he repeats himself, just so he can make sure they fully understood its importance. He declared that they should be joyful in the Lord (Philippians 4:4). This is not a human joy or persecution would destroy it. It is supernatural.

Third, Christians rejoice in the fact that standing firm in suffering is a clear proof of their faith in Christ. In 1 Peter 1:7-9, Peter told his readers that their faith was tested by fire in suffering. This produced proof of their faith, which was more precious than gold. It would result in praise, glory, and honor at the appearing of the Lord. He then praised them because though they have not seen Christ, they believed in Him. Also, they loved Him and greatly rejoiced in a joy that was inexpressible and full of glory.

Fourth, Christians are to find real joy in suffering because suffering is honorable.

> They therefore departed from the presence of the council, rejoicing that they were counted worthy to suffer dishonor for Jesus' name.
> Acts 5:41

In Acts 5:41, the apostles were flogged viciously and ordered not to preach publicly by the Sanhedrin. Then they went away rejoicing that they were worthy of suffering shame for Him.

Fifth, Christians rejoice because suffering tests their faith. This produces endurance leading to maturity in Christ. Paul explained to the Galatians that the goal of his ministry was for Christ to be formed in them (Galatians 4:19). He desired to present the church holy and blameless at the appearance of Jesus Christ (Colossians 1:22).

One of the ways in which the Father accomplishes this is through suffering. James told his many readers to consider it all joy when they encountered a wide variety of suffering. Why? It produced patient endurance which would result in making believers perfect and complete, lacking in nothing (James 1:2-4). So, suffering aids in producing full maturity.

Sixth, believers should rejoice in persecution because it results from sharing the gospel which brings people into His kingdom. In Philippians 2:17, Paul told the Philippians that he rejoiced as he was being poured out as a drink offering upon the sacrifice and service of their faith. He was willing to be a sacrifice for their souls. He used the Old Testament concept of a drink offering which was to be poured out on the altar (Leviticus 23:37). Paul was being poured out in service to them as a sacrifice in suffering for them.

If Christians are to suffer, they should count it a privilege and joy to suffer for the sake of Christ. As was seen earlier, the knowledge that their persecuted followers are filling up what is lacking in Christ's afflictions, and bearing the marks of ownership by their Lord through the partnership of their suffering for Christ will increase their joy. These believers can walk into strife proclaiming the good news with joy.

> *Key Concept: When unbelievers react negatively to the gospel through persecution, Christians should face affliction and share the gospel with joy amid their suffering.*

Conclusion

I received Jesus Christ as Savior and Lord in 1972 on the campus of USC in my second year of college. I immediately became involved in an evangelistic organization on campus. I was seven weeks old in the Lord and was off evangelizing. My three years with these saints included a wide variety of evangelistic activities including sharing Christ with students on campus, taking surveys in the neighborhood, passing out brochures at football games, and even sharing Christ with audience members at the Rose Parade in Pasadena.

As I grew in Christ, I became a youth director, associate pastor, then a senior pastor and once again participated in a variety of evangelistic activities. These included Christmas caroling, neighborhood barbecues and concerts, evangelism crusades, and sharing evangelistic messages at youth and family camps. As an individual, there was a host of sharing God's good news with those who walked in off the street, on their deathbed, and those considering suicide. I have shared the gospel with many people in my years of counseling as a Christian Pastoral Counselor.

While participating in all of these evangelistic activities, I have read many books on evangelism, participated in many evangelistic training seminars and classes, and have become acquainted with many evangelistic strategies. In most of the evangelistic materials I have read and encountered, I have found a lack of a biblical evangelism framework, an absence of key evangelistic concepts, and the priority of method over doctrine.

In recent years, something new in mainline Christianity has developed. The gospel has changed. Some elements of it have been removed and other elements have been added or reinterpreted. This puts many souls at risk. This has resulted in a large group of so-called Christians who cannot articulate how they actually received Christ or what it means to be saved. In the past, baptism services involved new believers sharing how they became Christians and what their new life in Jesus Christ really meant to them. Today, baptism focuses on interesting facts about the new believers and how much impact the church has had on them rather than Jesus Christ. The good news has become so foggy that people who even mention something positive about Jesus or attend church services is presumed to be saved. No one is allowed to ask about their salvation because it would be judging them.

Another dangerous trend in the church today is the false notion that if you believe Jesus is the Son of God, then you can believe anything else and you will be saved. Also, if you have Jesus in your heart, you can live any way you like, and heaven is yours. This is terribly imaginative thinking which is not true. It is from the liar of liars, the Devil.

This book is my solution to the great need for this biblical evangelism framework, these critical evangelistic concepts, appropriate applications, and a clear articulation of the true gospel of Jesus Christ. Therefore, all who have had "an encounter with Jesus" or "accepted Jesus as their personal Savior" should set aside everything they have heard, seen, felt, and experienced and peer solely into God's Word. This book clearly explains what the Bible says one must believe and do to be saved for all eternity.

This book concerns the Lord God's design and plan for how He will allow humans into His heaven. The heaven He created. It also discloses what happens to those who reject Him and their eternity in judgment and the fire of hell, the place God originally created for the Devil and his demons. This book explains what the Scriptures say concerning His kingdom of priests that was planned in eternity past and has been given as a gift to His Son.

I present to the church of Jesus Christ this simple, clear, and pure teaching of God's Word on evangelism. God, the Father, has given every Christian the amazing privilege and responsibility to share this incredibly good news. May this book excite and incite everyone who reads it to offer eternal life through the gospel to everyone they know and all they encounter. May this book help all who claim to know Christ determine that they are truly His and not a member of some fabrication of the true church with a man-made conception of a false, sentimental Jesus that cannot save them.

As my readers walk among the broken, the disturbed, the afflicted, and the weak, and offer them a glass of water may they also offer them a cup of living water. This will not only quench the thirst of their physical bodies but the eternal thirst of their spiritual souls. For those Christians who walk among the prominent, the famous, the strong, the beautiful, and the capable of this temporal world may they never be fooled by their outward prosperity. It is my hope that my readers will see the true darkness these prosperous ones are in. May they be reminded of the many deaths from overdose and suicides that have resulted when they have achieved all that man can offer and it is simply not enough.

May they offer them a lighted path to eternal life leading away from the dark road to eternal destruction. May every Christian see the unsaved, not as simply wicked but terribly lost and in need of some really good news! May this book about the Book be used even in a small way to be a part of another's journey to our only Savior and Lord Jesus Christ, who is forever and ever our mediator and intercessor before the great and all powerful, ever glorious God, my Father. Amen and Amen.

ABOUT THE AUTHOR

Dr. Donald Jones is currently a Christian Pastoral Counselor with thirty-eight years of experience in the fields of pastoral ministry, public education, and Christian counseling. He carries degrees and certificates from four major universities and from a variety of educational institutions. He has been a professor of Languages and Bible, a television commentator, and a featured speaker at a variety of events and seminars at churches, schools, and other organizations across the United States. He is a member in good standing of several secular and Christian professional organizations. Dr. Jones has been a published author since 1976. For further information view his website at www.donjonesphd.com.

www.ingramcontent.com/pod-product-compliance
Lightning Source LLC
Chambersburg PA
CBHW032033150426
43194CB00006B/260